TO BE A JEW

TO BE A JEW

A Guide to Jewish Observance
in Contemporary Life

SELECTED AND COMPILED
FROM THE *SHULHAN ARUKH*
AND *RESPONSA* LITERATURE
AND PROVIDING A RATIONALE
FOR THE LAWS AND
THE TRADITIONS

RABBI HAYIM HALEVY DONIN

Basic Books, Inc., Publishers
NEW YORK

The Author wishes to acknowledge his indebtedness to DAILY
PRAYER BOOK, HA-SIDDUR HA-SHALEM by Philip Birnbaum, Copyright 1949 by Hebrew Publishing Company which
the Author consulted in preparing the Hebrew versions of the
prayers and some of the English language translations thereof
which are printed in this book.

20 19 18 17 16 15

To Our Children
Haviva, David, Rena, and Miriam
whose lives, we pray, will always
be guided by Torah and Halakha

and to my revered teacher
Rabbi Dr. Samuel Belkin,
President of Yeshiva University
without whose understanding, kindness, and warmth
during the days of my youth
this book would never have come to be

PREFACE

D‍ESPITE the availability of an abundance of books on Judaism that range from the most elementary to the most sophisticated, including excellent translations of the great Hebrew classics, I do not know of a single compact volume that combines (1) a review of basic Jewish belief in terms that an educated layman can understand, (2) a handbook covering the basic laws and observances needed for daily Jewish living under contemporary living conditions, and (3) a rationale for these observances. This book is intended to fill that gap in the contemporary literature dealing with Judaism.

While there are many excellent and useful volumes about Judaism, they do not give a reader who has not previously been exposed to Jewish religious life any precise directions on *how* to go about observing the teachings of the faith. This book is intended to provide just that sort of guidance. My aim is to set forth in condensed form the laws that govern Jewish living under contemporary conditions in the United States, Canada, Great Britain, Western Europe, Israel, and other modernized societies.

This is a practical handbook on *how to live a Jewish life*, while trying to answer the constant query, "Why?" The *why* is partially dealt with in the part on "The Underlying Creed," in the introductory essays to each of the chapters, and in the sections on the Law.

In writing this book, I had in mind the great numbers of Jewish people who have had a minimal Jewish education and/or have not been brought up in an intensive religious environment. I hope that it will be useful for (1) college study groups, (2) adult education, (3) the guidance of proselytes, (4) young couples about to be married, (5) Jewish families interested in enriching their lives through the study of their ancient heritage—a heritage which speaks to modern man and relates to contemporary issues.

Yet this book cannot be termed complete. There is no substitute for a thorough study of the Five Books of Moses, the Prophets, and the Writings, with their many commentaries; nor for laboring over the Talmud, the various Codes of Jewish Law, and the various compilations of Responsa on continuing halakhik questions. There is no substitute for studying the philosophy of Judaism as expounded and expressed in the brilliant classical works of Judah Halevi and Maimonides, Saadia Gaon and Bachya Ibn Pakuda, of Hasdai Crescas, Joseph Albo and Samson Raphael Hirsch, nor for delving into the writings of many contemporary scholars who have been seeking to translate the eternal truths of the Jewish faith into the contemporary idiom and to grapple with problems, old and new, on the basis of the knowledge and the insights that we have access to in the second half of the twentieth century. There is no substitute for studying in depth the history of the Jewish people—the challenges it has faced from without and from within, its defeats and victories, its suffering and redemption. There is no end to the depths of meaning to be found in studying the Torah; there is no limit to the new facets of understanding to be discovered as one carefully examines this extraordinary gem. "Turn it and turn it over again for everything is in it" (Ethics of the Fathers 5:25).

The Talmud tells the story of a proselyte who came to the great sage, Hillel, in the first century B.C.E. and asked to be taught the whole Torah quickly, in the time that he could remain standing on one foot. Instead of losing his temper at this impossibly presumptuous request, Hillel showed great patience and understanding. He answered by saying: "What is hateful to you, do not do to others. This is the whole Torah, the rest is its commentary. Go and study it" (Shabbat 31a).

Hillel's statement, his way of expounding upon the Biblical commandment, "and thou shalt love thy neighbor as thyself" (Lev. 19:18), may still stand as the capsule summary of Judaism. It *is*, however, still essential to "go and study the rest." This book has been prepared to help the interested questioner take the first steps in going on to "study the rest" and apply what he learns to his daily life.

A rough draft of this book was prepared and substantially completed in Jerusalem from October, 1968, through July, 1969, while I was on leave from my congregation. It was a year that left its everlasting impact upon me and my entire family, an opportunity and an experience for which we shall be ever grateful.

I wish to express my sincere thanks to Rabbi Joshua Hutner, Director of the Rabbi Herzog World Academy in Jerusalem, to Rabbi

Shlomo Joseph Zevin, its venerable President, and to Rabbi Shear-Yashuv Cohen, Deputy Mayor of Jerusalem and Vice-Chairman of the Academy's Board of Directors for graciously providing me with the physical space and congenial surroundings at the Academy where I could concentrate on my work, for putting at my disposal the library and facilities of the Academy where major work is being done on the publication of the Encyclopedia Talmudica, and for helping me to make the acquaintance of the group of great scholars who labor there in rabbinic research, whose friendship, kindness, and accommodation I shall always cherish.

I am most thankful to and appreciative of my editor Erwin Glikes whose wise counsel and professional guidance contributed immensely to this book.

I am also deeply grateful to Rabbis Max Kapustin, David Silver, and Pinhas Stolper for their many suggestions and helpful observations, and particularly to Rabbi Yehudah Parnes, Rosh Yeshiva at the Rabbi Isaac Elchanan Theological Seminary of Yeshiva University for the meticulous care with which he critically reviewed the entire manuscript. While I shoulder all responsibility for whatever errors may be found in this text, I am deeply indebted to all the above for contributing to whatever excellence or merit this work can claim.

1972   HAYIM HALEVY DONIN

CONTENTS

Part One

THE UNDERLYING CREED

Part Two

THE DAILY WAY OF LIFE

CONTENTS

Part Three

THE SPECIAL OCCASIONS OF THE YEAR

CONTENTS

Part Four

THE SPECIAL OCCASIONS OF LIFE

xiv

CONTENTS

~~~~~~

TO BE A JEW

Introduction

PERHAPS more than any generation in memory, ours is one consciously searching for meaning. Pressed by questions from the younger among us, our concerns turn increasingly to a search for human values, away from the race for yet greater affluence and toward finding greater purpose for our lives.

In a sense, many in this generation have come to the same conclusion as did King Solomon in the remarkably exciting Biblical book of Kohelet (Ecclesiastes) which concerns itself most directly with a search for a meaning to life. Many today have also come to the conclusion that so many of the things to which they have been exposed, the material values they have hitherto confronted, the pleasure principle that has in effect determined their values in life —"this too is a vanity . . . an empty wind . . . ." Like Kohelet, the contemporary generation has been discovering for itself that happiness is not secured solely by physical comfort or economic well-being. The latter surely enables one to be more comfortable in his misery; it provides one with more ways by which to salve a spiritual emptiness or to anesthetize an emotional pain. But it is of little value in curing. In the long run, it is the discovery of meaning that is the key to personal fulfillment; it is the discovery of purpose that gives a man or woman a reason to want to live. In feeling useful and needed, man finds his happiness.

The modern Jew who has come to view with justified disdain the vain pursuits of a superficial, materialistic culture should realize that the purpose and meaning to life he is seeking can be found in his very own heritage. A Jewish life, reflecting the authentic values and life style of the Jewish heritage, is beautiful and good in a particular sense, and possesses meaning and significance also in a universal sense. But it may lie there as a buried treasure, perhaps totally unknown to him. If he has heard about it, he may be skeptical of its worth because his own experience with that heritage has been only superficial, his knowledge of it at the very best only elementary, and his understanding of it either incomplete or distorted. So he proceeds to reject it even before he has ever possessed it, often making no effort seriously to dig out that treasure, to experience it, and to appraise it. The Hebrew Prophets early noted that Israel often plants the seeds and cultivates the vineyards of everyone else while neglecting its own. The quirk in the character of the Jewish people which permits such self-neglect is surely not even in the long range interest of the world.

The Jew is today desperately needed *as a Jew* by the Jewish people. And I daresay that it is only *as a Jew*, consciously reflecting the values and ways of authentic Jewish life, that he is also desperately needed by the world. Since the dangers confronting the Jewish people in their struggle to assure physical and spiritual survival must not be underestimated, it is essential that more of Jewish intellect, energy, skill, and sacrificial idealism be redirected toward the strengthening of what is authentically Jewish.

Part One

THE UNDERLYING CREED

CHAPTER

1

~~~~~~

The Cornerstones of Judaism

ISRAEL—THE PEOPLE

The terms Hebrew, Israelite, and Jew have historically been used synonymously and interchangeably. The Bible refers to Abraham as Ibri (Hebrew), probably because he migrated from the other side (east) of the Euphrates River and Ibri means "from the other side." Israel was the alternate name of Jacob, the grandson of Abraham. Hence his twelve sons and their descendants became known as the children of Israel, or the Israelite Nation or People. Jew is derived from Judah, the son of Israel, the most prominent of the Twelve Tribes. This became the prevalent name for the entire people when the Judeans from the Kingdom of Judea survived the downfall of the Northern Kingdom of Israel in 722 B.C.E. when Ten Tribes were led into captivity. Thus today, the people are called Jewish, their faith Judaism, their language Hebrew,* and their land Israel.

---

* European Jews in the Middle Ages developed a dialect based mostly on German and some Hebrew; it has since absorbed words from many other languages as well. This language, so familiar to a great number of American Jews, is called Yiddish. Written in Hebrew characters it is not the same language as Hebrew. Jews stemming from Spain developed a dialect based upon Spanish and some Hebrew. This language is called Ladino.

7

This people, Israel, started life as one family tracing its antecedents back to Abraham, the Hebrew who lived approximately 3800 years ago. The monotheistic faith firmly held by Abraham, and the "Covenant with God" entered into by him and reaffirmed by his descendants, identified this family as the adherents of a special faith. The family did not claim exclusive rights to this faith, but on the contrary, were eager to attract others to it. As this God-intoxicated family and those who joined them in faith grew in number, accepting the Torah as their Divine Constitution, taking possession of the land promised to them by the Master of the universe, they assumed the characteristics of a nation, a people speaking a common language, living within a specified geographic area, sharing common memories and a common destiny, and exercising the attributes of national sovereignty.

On the basis of their origin, Jews everywhere have regarded themselves as members of a family, an expanded family to be sure, and oftimes a far-flung family, but a family nevertheless. Membership in this family derives from the mother. The child of any Jewish woman is thus considered to be a member of the family. But membership in the family has never been limited by birth. It has always been open to all, and those who share the faith of this family may be "adopted" into it. Thus, the convert to Judaism not only becomes a partner in faith with the children of Israel, but through faith, the proselyte himself becomes one of the children of Israel, sharing fully in its heritage and its privileges and assuming its burdens and tribulations. In accepting the Jewish faith, the proselyte thus joins the Jewish people or nation. In accepting the religious duties of the present, and in assuming the spiritual mission of the future, he also ties himself to the collective past.

Although the natural tendency for any family is to be exclusive and to look inward, this particular family was never exclusive. In times of persecution it was sometimes forced to withdraw in self-defense, but generally it looked outward and reached out to the world at large. When the central sanctuary in Jerusalem was built, Jews saw it as a "House of Prayer for all peoples" (Isaiah 56:7, see also Kings I 8:41–43).

In the very emphasis upon the particular, this singular family reflected the noblest form of universalism. The universalism that permeates the faith of Israel is reflected not only in its theological formulations and in its visions of the future, but in the very composition of its people. This seemingly "exclusive" people includes those whose skins range from the lightest to the darkest in colors, and within it a broad range of cultural diversity is represented. Yet despite the diversity that exists among them and the multitude of languages they speak, Jews regard themselves as related, as true brethren stemming from a common Semitic family. Although it is religion which unites them and it is only on the basis of religion that newcomers are admitted into fellowship, this feeling of kinship is very strong—and the mystery deepens when we realize that even Jews who rebel against the faith and discard its religious beliefs and practices are still regarded as Jews, and generally themselves still feel the bonds of kinship.

This sense of kinship felt by the Jewish people may be more of a "mystical" experience than a rationally definable one. Perhaps that is one of the reasons why Jews have never quite been able to fit into the convenient categories used by historians or sociologists to define nations, races, religions, and other social groupings. Except for the fact that the Jews obviously do not constitute a race (for race is a biological designation), the Jews are *not just* a religious faith, even though they are that; and they are *not just* a nation, even though they are that too, according to definitions of the term "nation." The problem is usually resolved by using the term "people" instead of either "faith" or "nation."

This difficulty in categorizing the Jewish people may well be part of their uniqueness. It is a uniqueness which according to the believer was given its permanent stamp by the Divine command, "You shall be to Me a kingdom of priests and a holy nation" (Exodus 19:6).

The Jewish people were once described in these poetic terms:

There is a river in the ocean. In the severest droughts it never fails, in the mightiest floods it never overflows. The Gulf of Mexico is its fountain and its mouth is in the Arctic seas. It is the Gulf Stream. There is in the world no other such majestic flow of waters. Its current is more rapid than the Mississippi or the Amazon, and its volume more than a thousand times greater. Its waters as far out from the Gulf as the Carolina coasts, are of an indigo blue; they are so distinctly marked that their line of junction with the common sea-water may be traced by the eye. Often one-half of a vessel may be perceived floating in the Gulf Stream water, while the other half is in the common water of the sea—so sharp is the line and such the want of affinity between those waters, and such too the reluctance, so to speak, on the part of those of the Gulf Stream to mingle with the common waters of the sea. This curious phenomenon in the physical world has its counterpart in the moral. There is a lonely river in the midst of the ocean of mankind. The mightiest floods of human temptation have never caused it to overflow, and the fiercest fires of human cruelty, though seven times heated in the furnace of religious bigotry, have never caused it to dry up, although its waves for two thousand years have rolled crimson with the blood of its martyrs. Its fountain is in the gray dawn of world's history, and its mouth is somewhere in the shadows of eternity. It too refuses to mingle with the surrounding waves, and the lines which divide its restless billows from the common waters of humanity are also plainly visible to the eye. It is the Jewish people.

Although a small people, separate and distinct, Israel has nevertheless not been a withdrawn people. Though standing alone, it has not stood aside. Jewish history is interlaced with that of every other nation and empire. "Jews . . . have witnessed and taken part in more of the human career, they have recorded more of it, shaped more of it, originated and developed more of it, above all, suffered more of it, than any other people," wrote Ernest van den Haag. The history of the Jews has been a history of interaction with the rest of the world—although Western scholars reared in a Christian-dominated society have tended to perceive only myopically the role of the Jew and of Judaism in that history, and to treat condescendingly anything that related to Jews or to Judaism. Textbooks of history, sociology or philosophy rarely have anything significant to say about the Jewish people or Jewish thought after the beginning of the Christian era. The bias against Judaism and the Jews that was reflected for so long in the texts and the curricula of the Christian universities was bequeathed to the secular academic world even after theological influence waned and the institutions became secular. Even Jews who entered this academic milieu were subtly influenced by the existing bias and unquestioningly accepted it themselves. Generally ignorant of their own history and philosophy, they fell sway to the notion that serious Jewish thought beyond the Biblical period either did not exist or did not merit the concern of serious scholarship.

Though denied, despised, rejected, persecuted, confined, and restricted through history, Jews and Judaism, the people itself and its sacred books, have nonetheless often set in motion forces that marked major revolutionary changes and advances in Western religions, in the natural and medical sciences, and in social philosophies. The contributions by individual Jews in every field of creative endeavor, in the advancement of human knowledge, in the elimination of suffering, in the development of commerce, have filled volumes. Judaism's traditional emphasis on social justice through social action has had a noticeable effect in contemporary times.

For a people who have always been numerically insignificant, "the fewest of all the nations," *ha-m'at mikol ha-amim* to use the words of the Torah, to have compiled such a record of achievements, and to have been on the scene of world history for so long while surviving all attempts to assimilate it and even to annihilate it, *something more* must be involved than the capacities of the people themselves.

The devout Jew looks upon that "something more" as a fulfillment of Divine prophecy that "through you and your descendants will all the families of the earth be blessed" (Genesis 28:14), and as a vindication of Israel's Covenant with God: "For you are a holy people unto the Lord your God, and you did God choose to be unto Him a treasured people from among all the peoples upon the face of the earth" (Deut. 14:2). The devout Jew accepts the status with humility and thanksgiving, seeing it as a yoke and a burden as well as a distinction. He sees himself as a servant of the Lord, ready to do His bidding at all times. Serving the Lord takes many forms: spending one's life studying Torah, faithfully observing the ritual and ethical commandments, struggling for justice and righteousness in society. The learned and observant Jew ignores none of the ways.

Whatever the believing Jew may find himself doing in fulfillment of that role, and whatever apparent "smallness" or "insignificance" his existence may appear to have, for him there is cosmic significance and purpose in doing the bidding of the Lord.

The skeptical Jew, on the other hand, who does not at all see himself as a servant of the Lord, is embarrassed by any reference to Israel's enjoyment of Divine favor or any notion of a special national mission. Such talk even on the part of non-Jews tends to embarrass him, and he is eager to repudiate all such notions. But his attempts at repudiating the meaning of Jewish history are invariably contradicted by history itself, which does not permit Jews to become "like all the other nations," to become merely another national entity among nations.

We believe that the nations and peoples of the world have their Divine purposes and their assigned roles to fulfill, too, for God is the God of all the world, not just of Jewry. And we see our divinely ordained assignment as involving a unique role, one to which history itself bears witness. It implies a special purpose in life, a reason for our existence. That purpose is not to make Jews of all the world, but to bring the peoples of the world, whatever their distinctive beliefs may be, to an acknowledgment of the sovereignty of God and to an acceptance of the basic values revealed to us by that God. It is to serve as a means by which blessing will be brought to "all the families of the earth" (Genesis 12:3).

It is this mission which underlies for Jews the coming of the day "when the world shall be perfected under the reign of the Almighty, and all mankind will call upon Thy name." It is only in these terms, supernatural though they be, that any plausible explanation can be offered for Israel's ability to survive against the many obstacles and threats to its very existence, and its success in penetrating the thought of most nations. It is in these terms that we discover meaning even in Israel's historical suffering and dispersion, as in its achievements, its strengths, and its restoration to Zion.

ISRAEL—ITS LAND

The bond between the Jewish people and the land which came to be known as Eretz Yisrael, the land of Israel, began at the time of Abraham.

> I will maintain My covenant between Me and you and your offspring to come as an everlasting covenant throughout the ages, to be God to you and to your offspring to come. I give the land you sojourn in to you and your offspring to come, all the land of Canaan, as an everlasting possession.
>
> (Genesis 17:7-8)

Thus began Israel's bond to what was then—3800 years ago—the land of Canaan and was to become the land of Israel. The long sojourn by the children of Israel in Egypt, where they were enslaved and oppressed, was followed by their mass exodus and their return to the land that had been *promised* them. In the final prophecy to Moses just before his death, we read again "And the Lord said to him; this is the land of which I swore to Abraham, Isaac, and Jacob, 'I will give it to your offspring'" (Deut. 34:4). Hence the name: The Promised Land; it was promised to Israel.

The exodus from Egypt and the possession of the land of Israel, serve as the historical fulcrum of Israel's Covenant with God. It was only on the soil of Israel that all the commandments of the Lord could be implemented; it was only on the soil of Israel, "at the place that He will choose" (Mt. Moriah in Jerusalem) that the permanent central sanctuary of the Jewish people could be built; it was only on the soil of Israel that the children of Israel would realize their fullest potential as a people; it was only on the soil of Israel that God's promises to Israel and His blessings would take on reality—if Israel proved itself worthy by its adherence to the commandments and by its loyalty to the Covenant. As the people were called upon to become a "holy people," their land was to be a "holy land." It was not to be defiled by the pagan practices that were then prevalent in the land and in the world at large. These pagan rites, the abominations, the idolatries, the Israelites were bidden to purge from the soil.

According to Nachmanides (Rabbi Moses ben Nachman, the great scholar and sage who lived in the thirteenth century), to take possession of the Holy Land and to live in it must be counted among the Biblical commandments incumbent upon Jews to fulfill. It is written "You shall take possession of the land and dwell therein, since I have given you this land to inherit it" (Numbers 33:53). He sees Israel's possession of the Holy Land as tied in fact to the destiny of the world. "So long as Israel occupies it, the earth is regarded as subject to Him," said Nachmanides. A contemporary American folk philosopher may have inadvertently made the same point: "I have a premonition that will not leave me; as it goes with Israel, so will it go with all of us."[1]

Ever since the Israelites first settled the land of Canaan about 3200 years ago (approximately 1200 B.C.E.), the land was never again devoid of Jews. Though they were conquered by foreign armies and ruled by foreign rulers, sometimes becoming a minority in their own country when the majority fled or was expelled, they never entirely left it. Many Jews stayed even after the destruction of the First Temple and the downfall of the First Commonwealth in the year 586 B.C.E., when large numbers of other Jews were exiled to Babylonia. The Babylonians had conquered the land and exiled most of its people, but by 515 B.C.E., after the Babylonians themselves were conquered by the Persians, the Jews were ready to return to rebuild what had been destroyed and to reestablish the Second Commonwealth, symbolized by the rebuilding of the Second Temple.

About five and a half centuries later, in 70 C.E., the destruction of the Second Temple and the downfall of the Second Commonwealth at the hands of the Romans dealt another severe blow to the Jewish people. Several attempts to reestablish independence and to throw off the yoke of foreign rule took place during the next sixty-five years, but all these attempts failed. While small settlements of Jews remained on the soil, the bulk of the people scattered to countries far and wide, almost literally to the ends of the earth.

Wherever they were, Jews dreamed of some day returning and reestablishing their independence, of restoring their national existence. They dreamed of it and prayed for it; never for a day was the Holy Land out of their thoughts. During the centuries, the land was overrun by a series of invading and conquering armies—Romans, Byzantines, Arabs, European Crusaders, Turks, and finally by British forces during World War I. And while individual Jews throughout the centuries sometimes returned to the Holy Land, if only to finish out their years and be buried there, an organized effort for a mass return and resettlement of the land aiming toward the reestablishment of an independent sovereign Jewish State did not begin to materialize until the latter part of the nineteenth century. Zionism, the name given to this organized effort, was and is a struggle for national liberation and for the crystallization of a national identity on the part of a nation that had been forced to wander from country to country over the centuries.

The early settlers found a land that had been neglected through the centuries, abounding in malarial swamps and diseases. It was a barren land—of rock, sand, and desert. The few remaining Jewish communities were concentrated in the cities of Jerusalem, Hebron, Tiberias, and Safed.

While not all Jews were involved in the organized struggle to achieve these aims, every devout, believing Jew was *in faith* a Zionist, since the aspiration to return to Zion is built into the very fabric of traditional Jewish faith.

Wherever we find any mention of God's blessings upon Israel in the religious literature or any vision of "the end of days" which speaks of the coming of the Messiah* and the Messianic period for all the

---

* The word *Messiah* is derived from the Hebrew word *mashiach* which means *anointed* (with oil). The Messiah in Jewish thought was never conceived of as a Divine Being. As God's anointed representative, the Messiah would be a person who would bring about the political and spiritual redemption of the people Israel through the ingathering of the Jews to their ancestral home of Eretz Yisrael and the restoration of Jerusalem to its spiritual glory. He would bring about an era marked by the moral

world, it also refers to Israel's return to the land of Israel and to its dwelling safely and securely therein. The Jew living in any other land was regarded in every religious source as being in a "state of exile," regardless of how comfortable, how secure the Jew may have been in the land of his dispersion and how satisfying his personal life.

The return to the land of Israel was not only a nationalistic sentiment harbored by the Jewish people, but a deeply religious sentiment providing the opportunity for a fuller relationship to God than was possible anywhere else and paving the way for the Messianic era which would bring peace not only to Israel but to all mankind. Such religious sentiments were incorporated into the prayers of the daily, Sabbath, and festival services. There is hardly a religious ritual where Zion is not recalled, where the return to Zion and the restoration and rebuilding of Jerusalem is not mentioned.

The *Amidah*, the central prayer recited thrice daily, includes prayers for the realization of these dreams. Major portions of the grace after meals are devoted to remembering that "Thou didst give as a heritage to our fathers a desirable, good and ample land," and to prayers pleading for the rebuilding of Jerusalem, the Holy City.

The fast of Tisha b'Av as well as the minor fast days of the year mourn the destruction of the Temple and of Jerusalem, as do the prayers of Supplication which follow the daily morning and afternoon service. At weddings, a glass is broken to symbolize the same tragedy, and in times of bereavement similar symbolic reminders take place. The very formula used to comfort a bereaved family never lets us forget that all of Jewry was in constant mourning for the loss of Jerusalem. "May the Lord comfort you," goes the prayer, "together with all who mourn for Zion and Jerusalem."

The seder on the night of Passover, as well as the service of the Day of Atonement, concludes with the cry "Next year in Jerusalem," *L'shanah habaa b'Yerushalayim.*

The Sabbath and holiday prayers are all constant reminders of

---

perfection of all mankind and the harmonious coexistence of all peoples free of war, fear, hatred, and intolerance (see Isaiah 2 and 11, Micah 4).

Claimants to the Messianic title arose at various times throughout Jewish history. The criterion by which each was judged was: Did he succeed in accomplishing what the Messiah was supposed to accomplish? By this criterion, clearly none qualified. The Messianic era is still ahead of us. The reestablishment of a Jewish State in our times and the restoration of a united Jerusalem as the capital of that State has led many devout Jews to hope that these times may be the beginning of that process of redemption that will ultimately lead to the realization of all the other ideals inherent in the Messianic belief.

Zion and Jerusalem. The prayers for rain and for dew, the observance of Tu b'Shevat, the New Year for Trees, are all tied to the climatic conditions of Israel. The agricultural aspects of each of the major festivals are constant reminders of the way the land of Israel is interwoven in the very fabric of the Jewish people's religious observances.

The historic Jewish Messianic vision was expressed by Isaiah in his prophecy in terms of Zion and Jerusalem, namely that "out of Zion shall go forth the Torah and the word of God from Jerusalem." To eliminate such aspirations would be tantamount to emasculating the religious faith of Israel. The passage from the Book of Psalms sums up the religious and historic attitude toward Jerusalem,* the historical capital of Eretz Yisrael, and all it symbolized: "If I forget thee, O Jerusalem, let my right hand forget her cunning. Let my tongue cleave to the roof of my mouth, if I remember thee not; If I set not Jerusalem above my chiefest joy" (Psalms 137:5–6).

Under such circumstances, it is no wonder that even the non-devout, non-praying Jew who is at all familiar with the literature of his people, who is at all knowledgeable about the teachings of the Hebrew Prophets and the books of the Hebrew Bible, and who is at all familiar with the history of Israel should be emotionally overwhelmed both by the restoration of a Jewish State and by the return of Jerusalem to its central position within that State.

Is it any wonder that the totally unexpected, unplanned recovery during the Six Day War in 1967 of the older eastern portion of Jerusalem containing the site of the Temple Mount, and the sacred Western (Wailing) Wall, and the old Jewish Quarter with its historic remnants, all of which had been captured and held by Jordan since 1948, should have brought forth the emotional outpouring that it did on the part of young and old, believer and skeptic alike!

Many maintain that the spectacular victories of June 1967, culminating with the recapture of East Jerusalem, represent an extraordinary manifestation of Divine purpose in history. It certainly revealed an unsuspected reservoir of religious faith and fervor. Even for the Jew who is completely integrated into the life of his native or adopted country in the Diaspora, and is totally loyal to it, the awesome events

---

* The Prophets of Israel in speaking of a return to the land of Israel and of the restoration of Jewish sovereignty speak in terms of Jerusalem or Zion, another name by which Jerusalem is called. Whatever role the entire land of Israel played in Jewish thought and faith was often expressed in terms of Jerusalem, the Holy City of the Holy Land. Jerusalem was the symbol for all of Eretz Yisrael and was synonymous with it. It was as a head is to a body.

of 1967 could not help but bring out a renewed enthusiasm and identification with the cause of Israel.

Israel is today a country in the finest tradition of democracy. But though Moslems and Christians and peoples of other faiths dwell there in full freedom and equality, the country bears the unmistakable stamp of Jewish values and Jewish culture, just as other countries in the world bear the unmistakable stamp and influences of their respective majorities, regardless of other minority groups who dwell in their midst.

From many parts of the world, Jews have been streaming back to Israel; some to find the fulfillment of their religious or national aspirations, some to avoid assimilation and the loss of their Jewish identity; others because they have escaped from countries of oppression where Jews continue to be deprived of their basic rights, or where they constantly live in dread of anti-Jewish outbreaks. Israel is their only refuge, the only country in the world that welcomes them with open arms, that helps them settle, and that is concerned with whether they live or die. Almost a million Jewish refugees, survivors of the concentration camps, came to Israel from Europe following the European holocaust. More than a half-million Jewish refugees have come from the Arab countries where their communities date back as far as the twelfth century and earlier because life was made increasingly intolerable for them: Egypt, Syria, Iraq, Algeria, Morocco, and Tunisia. Jews have also come from the Western, more affluent countries, not as refugees, but as immigrants in pursuit of a more meaningful life. There are still a number of countries where Jewish minorities are in fact denied equal rights and forbidden to leave. Hopefully the time for their freedom will come, too. But never again should the situation be permitted to arise in which it is necessary to save the lives of Jews and yet appeals to do so fall on deaf ears and all doors remain closed to them.

The fate of the refugee ship *Struma* remains a symbol of such a frightful occurrence. A broken-down, overcrowded ship filled with over 750 Jewish refugees—men, women, and children—was refused admission to Palestine early in 1942 when it was under British rule, and denied entry into the ports of other countries as well. The Turkish authorities actually had the unseaworthy ship towed out to sea from the port of Istanbul, where the *Struma* finally sank. Only two passengers managed to survive. Four hundred twenty-eight men, 269 women, and 70 children drowned.

When a deal to secure the release of 100,000 Jews from Nazi concentration camps was offered to the British during the Second World War, the British Foreign Secretary allegedly said in rejecting the offer: "What are we going to do with 100,000 Jews?" The American Government likewise remained deaf to all plans that might have saved the lives of untold numbers of Jews, denied the pleas of Jewish leaders to bomb the German railways taking Jews to concentration camps and to destroy the crematoriums. Even after the Second World War, other ships laden with concentration camp refugees were turned away from the ports of many countries. Each country had its own political considerations which outweighed its concern for Jewish lives. The Christian religious establishment also maintained its silence throughout that period as the callousness of a world to the fate of the Jewish people reached its terrible conclusion. On the ashes of these dead, the State of Israel rose as a living memorial.

Of how many nations of the world today can it be said that they speak the same language, profess the same faith, and inhabit the same area that they did over 3000 years ago? It may therefore be understood why the Jewish people are so emotionally attached to the land of Israel. It is a land possessed not only by right of conquest and settlement, but also as a fulfillment of history, faith, and law.

ISRAEL—ITS GOD

"Hear O Israel, the Lord is our God, the Lord is One" (Deut. 6:4). These words express the underlying faith of Israel that there exists a one, indivisible God by whose will the universe and all that is in it was created. In what was a radical departure from polytheism and idolatry, Abraham the Hebrew was the first to give effective expression to this monotheistic faith, becoming the founding Patriarch of the Hebrews or as they were also to become known in later generations, the Israelites, or the Jews.

It is not that Abraham was the first human being to become aware of this spiritual truth. Even the Torah mentions that Hanoch and Noah, who preceded Abraham, were righteous men who "walked with God." They too believed in the existence of a one, supreme Spiritual Being, worshipped Him and lived in accordance with His wishes. There may have been others. Maimonides believed that at one time early men did know the one, true God, but that this knowledge and faith was lost to them. Historical researchers may unearth records of other men who may have voiced similar beliefs earlier and given expression to similar insights. But Abraham is credited with being the founder of the world's first monotheistic faith because unlike others whose monotheism was like an oasis in a spiritual wilderness which dried up and disappeared with their death, Abraham devoted himself to the propagation of the faith. He succeeded in passing this faith on to his son, Isaac, and Isaac in turn passed it on to his son, Jacob (Israel), the latter to his twelve sons, the heads of the Tribes of Israel, and thence into the stream of Israel's history and the history of all mankind. "For I have known him, that he may instruct his children and his posterity to keep the way of the Lord by doing what is just and right . . ." (Genesis 18:19).

This ability of Abraham to transmit his faith may be what most qualified him in the sight of God as the person with whom to establish a "Covenant" that involved eternal responsibilities in bringing the name of the Lord to all the peoples of the world. The physical and spiritual seed of Abraham has ever since borne the burden and the yoke of that Covenant, as well as enjoying its spiritual joys and blessings, for it set the seed of Abraham apart from other nations and other peoples. There were those who felt the burden too difficult, the disciplines too restraining, and sought various ways out. But the world often set its own barriers to such escape. The Covenant with the Lord brought not only Divine punishment when Israel weakened spiritually and reneged from time to time on its part of the agreement, but it also brought trials of faith of the noblest magnitude when Israel, precisely because of its loyalty to the Divine Covenant, had to endure the causeless animosity, the senseless hatred, and perverted antagonisms of countless oppressors throughout the ages. The declaration recited during the Passover seder is unfortunately far from being purely theoretical: "In every generation, there are those who rise up against us, to destroy and annihilate us." The moments of respite from the struggle to resist such annihilation have been few and far between. Yet the latter part of the same declaration gives expression to the eternal optimism of the Jew and his faith in somehow being delivered, "but the Holy One, Blessed be He, delivers us from their hands." That eternal faith has not been unjustified.

Of course, one cannot offer scientific proof that God exists, or that it was through His will that the world was created, or that He is concerned with the perfection of that which He created. But neither can it be proven that He does not exist. The use of rational methods to "prove" or "disprove" God's existence, after the fashion of the medieval scholastics, may appeal to some. Since the dawn of modern philosophy, however, these proofs have been seriously questioned. Contemporary arguments pro and con are equally futile. That is why the acceptance of God's existence is a matter of faith (*emunah*). The one, indivisible, spiritual Supreme Being in whom Abraham and all his descendants expressed their *faith* and saw fit to worship defies proof. He is infinite and man is finite. Not only is man finite physically, but his perceptual and intellectual abilities are also finite. If God were part of the framework of man's five physical senses, such a "God" would have to be someone or something more restricted than the omnipotent, the omnipresent Spiritual Being in whom we express our faith. Such a "God" would be reduced to the finite, thus capable of being altered and transformed by man, even killed and destroyed. Such a "God" would indeed not be the one, universal God at all, but yet another of many deities to whom men over the centuries ascribed supernatural powers and to whom they paid allegiance. If proof of God's existence is then beyond our capacity, why should rational man proclaim such faith with the same fervor and intensity that comes with truly *"knowing the Lord"*?

To first answer this question from the negative, let it be said that the rejection of God's existence ought to strain man's rational credibility even more. We must then assume that the functioning of the world under the sort of mathematical precision that we can only today fully begin to appreciate is a result of coincidence, and that the intricate coordinate functioning of life, from the very lowest forms to man himself is a matter of chance. Certainly, this requires a blind faith of its own. To ascribe the precise functioning of the universe and all the amazing wonders of life to "Nature" is only to resort to a synonym for natural laws that beg for explanation. The mystery remains. I do not hesitate to call atheism a form of faith too, not very different from the many idolatries that men have worshipped. In our time, atheism seems "sophisticated" and timely. So did the worship of Baal in its time. All one can ask himself, especially in view of the amazing scientific knowledge now at our disposal and also in view of Israel's history is whether it is more reasonable to say that God exists or to say that He doesn't. The greatest rationalists among

20

Jewish philosophers had no doubts about the great reasonableness of the basic Jewish principles of faith.

Jewish scholarship and religious leadership have from the very beginning shown sensitivity to the demands of reason, and have always emphasized that Judaism is a reasonable faith. While miracles and wondrous events play a role in the faith, Judaism clearly draws a distinction between such views or occurrences that are clearly *against reason* and such views or events that are only *above reason.* The two are very different. There are many matters in human experience *above* reason—outside man's scope of knowledge and beyond his comprehension—that are accepted on faith. We are not confronted by a theology which is clearly against reason. The basic theological premises of the Jewish faith, namely that God exists, that He created the world by His will, that He revealed His will to Israel and mankind at Sinai and at other moments in history—though these are all in the realm of the spiritual unknown and their processes unknown to us, none of them can be categorized as against reason. *Reason and faith* in the Judaic framework are not antagonists but complement one another. One fills in for the limitations of the other.

Even on the subject of miracles, which abound in the religious sources, it is important to remember that the teachings of Judaism are not based on them. Miracles were vehicles in achieving certain historical ends, even to inspire faith, but the truth or validity of the faith does not hinge on them. Had none of them occurred, the basic truths taught by Judaism would not be compromised. There are valid religious views which in fact maintain that even God works his miracles and wonders only through the orderly natural laws which He Himself set into motion, and that while certain events may be highly unusual, even awesome and incredible, genuine wonders in which the Divine role cannot be doubted—they are not *super*natural in the sense that they are contra-nature.

The concept of God to which the Jewish people stubbornly clung is one which admits of no compromise with the universality of God, with the spirituality of God, and with the unity of God.

"In the beginning God created the heavens and the earth," are the opening words of the Torah. He is the God of the universe. "I am the Lord your God who took you out of the land of Egypt" are the opening words of the Ten Commandments in that historic revelation to Israel. The universal God is the same God who brought freedom to Israel and to whom Israel declared its allegiance.

The Jewish conception of God is of a moral God who demands moral, ethical living and justice of all mankind. He is a universal God, whose sovereignty is over all the world. If Jewish prayer uses the expression, "the God of Abraham, Isaac and Jacob," or "the God of Israel," it is not to imply that God belongs to Jews alone or that He is a special God. This would imply either a limitation of God's sovereignty or an admission that there are other gods who look after other nations. The child who says "my father" does not thereby deny that the man he is talking about is also father to his brothers and sisters. The phrase "God of Israel" implies only an affirmation of the special relationship that Israel believes it has with the universal God by virtue of the Covenant entered into with Abraham, and reaffirmed on subsequent occasions in the spiritual odyssey of the people. To say, "the God of Israel," is only to remind ourselves of our Covenant with the universal God to whom all mankind owes allegiance.

The Jewish conception of God has not admitted any physical qualities to Him. The expressions in the Torah "the face of God," "the hand of God," "the feet of the Lord," or "the throne of God" are terms used symbolically because there exists no other language by which certain qualities or characteristics of God can be described. Only the poverty of man's language to describe what belongs to a spiritual world is responsible for such usages. The Sages of the Talmud said: "The Torah speaks in the language of men." It is "in the language of men" that the spiritual attributes of God are summarized in the following passage: "The Lord! the Lord! a compassionate and gracious God, slow to anger, rich in steadfast kindness extending kindness to the thousandth generation, forgiving iniquity, transgression and sin; acquitting (the penitent—but not acquitting the unpenitent guilty)" (Exodus 34:6-7). This passage, known as the Thirteen Attributes (*midot*), refers "exclusively to the inexhaustible Love and eternal Justice of God. It has stamped itself upon the Jewish consciousness as the sublimest expression in human language of the essential nature of God."[2]

The Jewish conception of God also rejected any compromise with the spirituality of God. The notion of man becoming God or God assuming the form of man was equally repugnant to the Jewish religious spirit. The Jewish mind and faith cannot accept the notion of the infinite Divine reducing Himself to a finite mortal.

Furthermore, the very representation of God by an image was forbidden to the Jew. The second of the Ten Commandments that "You shall not make for yourself a sculptured image . . . you shall not bow down to them nor serve them" was understood as applying even when the worshipper did not actually believe that the image was God but was only a symbol representing God. The sin of the Golden Calf was not that the Israelites suddenly denied their belief in God and thought the calf to be God, but that they insisted on a visual image to represent Him.

Where we talk of God as "our Father," and refer to men as the "children of God," we refer to all men who follow in His ways and who are thus in a spiritual sense children of the Lord.

As for utilizing man's technical achievements and his increasing ability to control the physical world as a basis for casting doubt on the Divine role, are not these very achievements among the blessings that the Infinite Being bestowed upon man? "God blessed them and said to them, 'Be fertile and increase, fill the earth and master it; and rule the fish of the sea, the birds of the sky, and all the living things that creep on earth' " (Genesis 1:28).

The man of faith humbly sees in these wondrous achievements not the absence but the very presence of God:

> When I behold Thy heavens, the work of Thy fingers,
> The moon and the stars, which Thou hast established;
> What is man, that Thou art mindful of him?
> And the son of man, that Thou thinkest of him? . . .
> Yet, Thou hast made him to have dominion over the works
> of Thy hands . . . .
> O Lord, our Lord
> How glorious is Thy name in all the earth.
>
> (Psalms 8:4-10)

The man who views God in disbelief is tempted to set *Man* up as the object of his belief, to view *Man* as the all-knowing creature who is subject to no laws or rules other than those which he himself sees fit to promulgate. To worship man in general, or to worship some special man in particular, is the height of idolatry. If man, with his endowed intelligence and spiritual capacities is the most sophisticated of all God's creatures, he is also the object of the most sophisticated forms of idolatry.

To accept the yoke of the Kingdom of Heaven is to throw off the yoke of human domination and dictatorship. "You shall be servants unto Me," said the Lord, "and not servants unto My servants." Man

23

is given a choice. Some think they can pursue a middle road between these two forms of servitude, free of both. Such hopes have invariably proved illusory. If it is not the one, it will invariably be the other. The Jewish people has declared its choice.

ISRAEL—ITS TORAH

The Jewish faith does not stop with "And God created the heavens and the earth." It starts there. It continues to acknowledge that "I am the Lord your God who took you out of the land of Egypt." He is a living God, who continues to play a role in the universe He created. He is a sovereign God, who is concerned about the behavior of the people He created, and to that end has found ways to make His will known to mankind. In His own inscrutable ways, He continues to judge the behavior of all men, rewarding and punishing either in this world or in the spiritual world to come.

Judaism insists that there is no practical distinction between one who entirely denies the existence of God and the one who admits to the existence of God and even to His role in Creation but denies that God has anything more to do with this world. The distinction between such views is purely academic, for there are no differentiating implications for human life. In either case, there are no compelling reasons to worship Him or to follow in His ways.

Central to the belief in a living God is the Jewish belief that in some spiritual fashion He communicated His will and His commandments to the creature whom He endowed with free will, but whom He called to be His obedient servant. The very essence of Judaism rests upon the acceptance of a spiritual-historical event in which our ancestors participated as a group, as well as upon acceptance of subsequent spiritual revelations to the Prophets of Israel. The extraordinary historical event I refer to is the promulgation of the Ten Commandments at Mount Sinai seven weeks following the exodus of the children of Israel from Egypt. God's will was also made manifest in the Written Torah, written down by Moses under Divine prophecy during the forty-year period after the exodus. Side by side with the Five Books of Moses (Pentateuch), we believe that God's will was also made manifest in the Oral Tradition or Oral Torah which also had its source at Sinai, revealed to Moses and then orally taught by him to the religious heads of Israel. The Written Torah itself alludes to such oral instructions. This Oral Torah—which clarifies and provides the details for many of the commandments contained in the Written Torah—was transmitted from generation to generation until finally recorded in the second century to become the cornerstone upon which the Talmud was built.

Non-traditionalists regard the Torah as the inspired writing of great men, as a record of man's attempt to reach out to God. According to this view, there is nothing eternal about the Torah and nothing Divine about it. It is subject to the errors that men, even great men, are capable of making. If this is the case, why indeed should it be treated as any more authoritative a guide to behavior or as any more the embodiment of Truth, than say, the ethics of Aristotle, or Kant, or Spinoza? If it is only a set of man-made tribal laws, anyone is indeed justified in eliminating what no longer suits him, changing or amending it as it strikes the fancy of each generation or religious leader. This is precisely the rationale used by non-traditionalists to justify the far-reaching changes in Jewish practices that they have introduced.

However one chooses to visualize or understand or comprehend the specific nature of God's revelation to Israel and the Prophets, what stands out is that if the Torah means anything at all, it is a record of God reaching out to man, and not vice versa. If it possesses any enduring value and truth, the Torah must be seen as a record not of man's spiritual genius, but of God's will communicated to mortal and finite man. No interpretation of Judaism is Jewishly valid if it does not posit God as the *source* of Torah.

What is Torah? Technically it refers to the Five Books of Moses. This is the Written Torah (*Torah SheBiktav*). The scroll upon which it is written and which is kept in the Holy Ark of the synagogue is called a scroll of the Torah (*Sefer Torah*). In a sense, this is the constitution of the Jewish people. But this constitution was promulgated not by men, but revealed by God. By Torah is also meant the Oral Torah (*Torah She-B'al Peh*) "which Moses received at Sinai, and transmitted to Joshua, and Joshua to the Elders, and the Elders to the Prophets, and the Prophets to the Men of the Great Assembly . . ." (Ethics of the Fathers 1:1).

The Oral Torah included the finer points of the commandments, the details of the general principles contained in the Scriptures and the ways by which the commandments were to be applied. For example, the Torah forbids "work" on the Sabbath. What constitutes "work"? How shall "work" be defined for purposes of the Sabbath? Except for several references to such tasks as gathering wood, kindling fire, cooking and baking, the Written Torah does not say. The Oral Torah does.

The Written Torah commands that animals needed for food be killed "as I have commanded thee." How shall this slaughtering take place? What regulations govern such slaughtering? The Written Torah does not say. The Oral Torah does.

The Written Torah commands us to "bind them as a sign upon your hands and as frontlets between your eyes." This reference to *tefillin* leaves us in the dark as to how they were to be made up, what they were to consist of, how they were to be donned. The Written Torah does not say. The Oral Torah does.

The Written Torah prescribes capital punishment for various crimes. What legal rules and procedures had to be followed before such a verdict could be handed down? What were the limitations? The Written Torah does not say. The Oral Torah does.

Ultimately, this Oral Torah was reduced to writing. During the second century C.E., it was incorporated into the Mishna, which in turn became the cornerstone for the Gemara which consists of the monumental records and minutes of the case discussions and legal debates conducted by the Sages. Mishna and Gemara together make up the Talmud.

The Torah, whether Written or Oral, is the teaching that directs man how to live. Although it speaks primarily to Israel, it also has directives for all men. It is concerned with every aspect of human life. Ritual laws, generally thought of as "religious observances," are only part of the total complex of commandments. The commandments of the Torah, its statutes and regulations, cover the entire range of human and social behavior. It asserts its jurisdiction in areas of behavior which in other religions are generally thought of as belonging to the ethical or moral domains or to the jurisdiction of secular civil and criminal codes of law. Even its non-legal and non-statutory sections stress spiritual truths and convey insight into the still finer extra-legal ethical and moral norms of behavior.

The rest of the books of the Hebrew Bible, written over a period of many centuries, consists of the Prophets (*Neviim*) and the Sacred Writings (*Ketuvim*). These books convey the teachings of the Prophets in the context of Israel's history over a period of about seven hundred years. They tell of the Prophets' visions of God and of their ongoing struggles to promote greater allegiance among the people to the teachings of the Torah; of their struggles against the many false prophets and priests who so often misled the people and turned them away from God and the Torah. Among these books is the inspirational Psalms that reflects man's deepest religious sentiments.

The Torah, with the Neviim and the Ketuvim are together referred to as *Ta Nakh*. (This is what non-Jews call the "Old Testament" but which to the Jew has always been the *only* Testament.) In the broadest sense, however, the study of Torah refers not only to the Scriptures and the Oral Torah, but also to the entire body of rabbinic legislation and interpretation based upon the Torah that developed over the centuries. For the Torah was always a living law, constantly applied by a living people to real conditions that were often changing. Though these are obviously the result of human efforts, they are an integral part of the entire body of religious jurisprudence to which the Torah itself grants authoritative status: "And you shall observe and do according to all that they shall teach you. According to the law which they shall teach you and according to the judgment which they shall tell you, you shall do" (Deut. 17:10–11).

Torah is the embodiment of the Jewish faith. It contains the terms of his Covenant with God. It is what makes a Jew a Jew.

CHAPTER
2

~~~~~~

Halakha: The Jewish Way

ALTHOUGH an effort has been made to summarize some of the ideas which Jews have always believed deeply and which constitute the basic principles of faith that have characterized Judaism through the ages, I have made no effort to delve deeper into Jewish theology or to explicate the philosophical-religious insights into the nature of man, of life, of good and of evil, that emanate from Jewish teachings and permeate its entire view of the world. To have done so would have been to go beyond the scope and the purpose of this book. But the chief reason I will restrain myself from delving deeply into theology here is perhaps best summed up in the words of Samuel Belkin, President of Yeshiva University:

Many attempts have been made to formulate a coherent and systematic approach to Jewish theology. All such attempts, however, have proved unsuccessful, for Judaism was never overly concerned with logical doctrines. It desired rather to evolve a corpus of practices, a code of religious acts, which would establish a mode of religious living. True, these acts and practices stem from basic theological and moral concepts, but most significantly, these theological theories of Judaism always remain invisible, apprehensible only through the religious practices to which they gave birth. Great rabbinic scholars—philosophers, therefore, found a greater measure of agreement among themselves in their *minyan hamitzvot*, the classification of the 613 religious duties which the Torah places upon the Jew, than in their attempts to present basic Jewish dogma in the forms of articles of faith. . . . In Judaism, articles of faith and religious theories cannot be divorced from particular practices . . . the theology of Judaism is contained largely in the Halakha—in the Jewish judicial system—which concerns itself not with theory but primarily with practice. . . . (If Judaism can be said to rest) upon the twin principles, the sovereignty of God and the sacredness of the individual . . . this philosophy (as all its philosophic foundations) is clearly reflected in the Halakha.[1]

Halakha is the overall term for Jewish law; it refers also to the final authoritative decision on any specific question. It rests first and foremost upon the Biblical statutes and commandments in the Written and the Oral Torah, then upon all the rabbinic legislation and enactments, including the religious-judicial decisions that were handed down through the ages in the form of Responsa and Commentaries by great rabbinic scholars. All of this serves as the authoritative basis and provides legal precedents for the ever-continuing process of religious-legal decision making in our own day. The word halakha itself means "the way on which one goes." Halakha is practical, not theoretical. Halakha is legal, not philosophical. Although faith is the basis out of which the halakha develops, its major emphasis is on deed. Halakha is concerned with the proper application of the commandments (*mitzvot*) to every situation and circumstance. (The *mitzvot* which are of Biblical origin are in essence unchangeable. Those of rabbinic origin may be under certain circumstances and conditions modified by authoritative and ordained scholars.) Halakha asks for a commitment in behavior. It deals with ethical *obligations* and religious *duties*.

As the Jewish judicial system, halakha covers every aspect and relationship of life, whether it be between man and man or between man and God. Thus the halakha concerns itself not only with those areas that are generally regarded as being in the realm of ritual and religion, but also with those areas that are generally assigned by non-Jewish scholars to the spheres of morality and ethics, or to civil and criminal law.

As the halakha is all-encompassing, so might it be said that the Jewish religion is all-encompassing. There are no areas in the realm of human behavior with which it does not deal or offer guidance. To the extent that every aspect of life is regarded as subject to the guidelines established by the halakha, one cannot regard the Jewish religion—when properly observed—as filling up but one of life's many compartments, or that it is separate and distinct from other areas of one's life and concern. A person's eating habits, his sex life, his business ethics, his social activities, his entertainment, his artistic expression are all under the umbrella of religious law, of the religious values and the spiritual guidelines of Judaism. Jewish religion does not disassociate itself from any aspect of life, and does not confine its concern only to ritual acts that have a mystical significance within a supernatural world. Fully and properly observed, the Jewish religion is life itself, and provides values to guide all of life.

This is the nature of the religious tradition handed down to the Jew. That is why the Prophets of Israel spoke and fought with as much fervor for social justice and for the elimination of poverty as they did for the sanctity of the Sabbath and the abolition of idolatrous worship. Indeed, all books about Judaism emphasize the fact that Judaism is *a way of life*, that it is deed, not just faith. While there is no minimizing the central role that doctrine plays, the emphasis is assuredly on the deed. The essence of the Jewish faith was cultivated not in doctrinal assumptions or dogmatic declarations, but in the practical implementation of Torah, *mitzvot maasiyot*.

The conceptual truths of Judaism and its values mean little unless they are translated into a way of life. The halakha is the means by which the concepts and values are applied to everyday living. Halakha prescribes the ways for the *concretization* of theory, of principles, of creed.

The halakha, with its focus on the implementation and fulfillment of the commandments (mitzvot), serves *to make concrete that which is otherwise in the realm of the abstract, while serving to sanctify that which is otherwise in the realm of the mundane.*

Ernst Simon of the Hebrew University in Jerusalem offers a balanced rationale for the observance of the halakha by the modern Jew. He explains that:

there is a relative identity between the faith and the people, and this relative identity can be established and maintained only by a sanctified way of life. *Halakha* is our only means to establish and maintain this sanctified way of life.

Above all, says Simon:

. . . *halakha* can have profound relevance for the modern Jew because it embodies and represents an attitude towards life which emphasizes the need for the restitution of the intellect in a partly anti-intellectual society, for discipline in a partly libertarian world, for orientation and a sense of direction in a chaos of over-information, and for a rational religion in the face of inroads of mysticism and obscurantisms.[2]

As Louis Ginzberg put it: "It is only in the *halakha* that we find the mind and the character of the Jewish people exactly and adequately expressed."[3]

Seymour Siegel said it well:

We remain Jews not because we are members of a philosophical society with superior principles (although it is a source of pride and a challenge to perpetuate and to deepen the heritage of ideas and concepts we have inherited). We remain Jews because we are part of the community of Israel, which has agreed to live its life as a separate community, for all time, in obedience to God. To be sure, certain ideas flow from this premise. But our existence is defined by the fact of the covenant (with its necessary implication of Torah and *halakha*, or Law); it is not defined merely by ideas.[4]

The fear is expressed in some circles that strict adherence to the halakha, unaccompanied by deep spiritual faith and feeling, becomes reduced to a form of behaviorism lacking all spiritual quality and dimension. Yet such fears do not justify the elimination of the halakhik obligation; on the contrary, it emphasizes the need to keep stressing the spiritual quality of all acts. The rabbis long ago recognized the problem and sought to deal with it when they taught, for example: "Do not make your prayers routine . . ." (Ethics of the Fathers 2:18). Because an act may be carried to an undesirable extreme does not justify its abrogation. The abuse should be checked without eliminating the essence of the act.

Even Abraham Joshua Heschel, a foremost exponent of the view which stresses man's inner spirit (he calls this the realm of the *agada*), who objects strenuously to any view which confines Judaism exclusively to its halakha, insists that:

Indeed the surest way to forfeit *agada* (faith, inwardness) is to abolish *halakha*. Without *halakha*, *agada* loses its substance, its character, its source of inspiration, its security against becoming secularized. By inwardness alone we do not come close to God. The purest intentions, the finest of devotion, the noblest spiritual aspirations are fatuous when not realized in action.[5]

Like all legal systems based upon a "constitution" or some other body of law, it is true that the halakha itself often allows for differences of opinion and for differences in behavior, particularly in areas where Divine Torah Law is not affected. But all different religious decisions by authoritative, ordained scholars must be capable of justification and defense under the halakhik rules of interpretation. It must be based on sound religious scholarship. It is of such differences of opinion that our religious sources say "These and these are the words of the living God," because they both emerge out of faith in that God and out of a sincere desire to perform the will of that God. There is a great difference between disagreeing over what it is that the Torah and the traditions require of us where questions must be resolved, and renouncing outright the authority and the jurisdiction of the Torah and its halakha. The latter attitude removes one from within the legitimate boundaries of Judaism.

The halakha is the Jewish way for securing and perpetuating the Jewish way of life. Disregard the halakha or reject it, and slowly the way of life also disappears; and with its disappearance, the distinctive and cherished values of Judaism fade away. It doesn't happen all at once; it may take a generation or two, but it happens. This is the process known as assimilation. It begins when Jews discard the binding character of the halakha and it ends with the disappearance of Judaism. This is not speculation or polemic, but historical fact which, sadly, has repeated itself over and over again under many different conditions and circumstances. For where all the distinctive observances of Judaism have disappeared, the only thing that has retarded the total physical assimilation of the Jewish people has been some threatening crisis of anti-Semitism.

CHAPTER

3

The Reasons for the Commandments

THE reasons for the mitzvot (*taamei hamitzvot*) occupied the attention of all the great scholars and rabbis of Israel. A great body of literature was built up whose purpose was to explain the reasons for all the laws of the Torah, as well as for the many regulations and customs that have grown up in the course of Jewish history. The Torah itself does not offer specific reasons for most of the commandments. While reasons were often suggested by the Earlier and Later Authorities, their views were not regarded as necessarily correct or valid. The greater the rabbi and scholar, the more his explanations and reasoning carried weight, but in no instance did they assume the level of imposed doctrine. Sages who lived in different ages and under different conditions would often see different purposes, different reasons for the observance of this or that particular law. Rather than detracting from the validity of that law, such variety of explanation only provided added testimony that the Torah was indeed a law for all times, "throughout your generations, a statute forever." Despite changing conditions and circumstances, it was ever meaningful and relevant to those who delved into it and sought to understand it.

The only reason that a devout Jew needs for the observance of any

33

of the commandments—however they may be classified—is that they reflect the will of God. As an obedient servant of the Lord, it is his duty to carry them out. However, this has never stopped the Jew from *trying to understand the reasons* for the various laws and commandments. By searching for the reasons, he felt he was drawing himself closer to the Mind of the Divine, that he was thereby raising himself spiritually. Only when confronted by a statute whose reason totally escaped him (such statutes are called *hukim* in the Torah), did he resort to that ultimate reason: this is what God wants of us. The inability to grasp a sensible purpose or to find a reason was never used by a man of faith as the pretext for discarding the observance or even for asserting that no reason and no purpose existed. One either gave up and admitted his limitations, or continued trying even harder to discover the meaning and purpose.

There were periods in Jewish life, particularly when Jews lived in ghettos, removed from contact with competing influences, when the mass of Jews did not find it necessary to understand *why* and were satisfied with knowing *how*. That time is gone. Today, as during other times in the history of our people when Jews were in contact with other cultures and confronted with competing ideologies and movements, it is vital for Jews to develop an understanding and an appreciation of the reasons, some grasp of the *why*. This is important not only to strengthen the convictions of the observant Jew himself, but also to provide him with the wherewithal to rebut those who may mock or question his practices. It is also necessary to be able to present Judaism to the Jew and non-Jew alike as a dynamic creed, as a living faith, as a relevant philosophy and way of life capable of challenging the various "isms" and spiritual fads that from time to time sweep across our society.

To arrive at an understanding of the reasons for many Jewish laws, it is important to recognize the importance of mastering not only the particular but also the general. Whereas some laws, such as those which deal with acts of kindness and justice, do not require elaborate explanations and may be understood quite independently of all other laws, others are not as easily grasped in isolation. While the notion of a day of rest is easily understood, the underlying principles which determine the halakha and the rituals associated with the Sabbath require an understanding of some of the basic ideas in Jewish religious philosophy. In still other laws, such as those of *kashrut*, the entire panorama of interlocking halakhic principles and spiritual purposes must be understood in order to assign any meaning to the details. Try to explain kashrut without reference to the rest of Judaism and one is bound to go astray. This is where superficial students of Judaism are usually misled.

We might compare the total panorama of Judaism to a giant jigsaw puzzle, which when put together shows a beautiful and inspiring picture. Remove any of the pieces from the middle, and not only is there a gaping hole which mars the beauty of the entire picture, but if you ask someone to identify the individual pieces he may find it quite hard to do. A single piece of the jigsaw puzzle may make no sense at all; it may just appear as a mass of confusing, meaningless lines and colors. But put it back where it belongs in the picture, and not only is the beauty of the whole picture restored but the meaningless confusing piece when fitted to all the other pieces suddenly makes sense; its lines and colors assume a very clear-cut design. So it is with kashrut and some other laws that in isolation may not appear to have any rational reason. But considered against the background of which they are a part, as a continuation of a whole series of religious disciplines that touch every aspect of life and that are intended to teach men to control their passions and their appetites, the specific details of each law begin to be seen in sharper focus.

Before getting into the specific laws dealt with in this book, I wish to elaborate on the overall reason given by the Torah for demanding of the Jew that he follow all its laws and regulations: it is so that Israel will become holy or sanctified. "Speak to the whole Israelite community and say to them: you shall be holy, for I the Lord your God am holy" (Lev. 19:2). Again: "You shall be to Me a kingdom of priests and a holy nation" (Exodus 19:6). This call for the sanctification of Israel as *the* reason for the observance of the commandments is repeated over and over again throughout the Torah, sometimes in introducing, sometimes in concluding entire sections of laws, sometimes in relation to individual statutes.

The purpose of holiness permeates all of Jewish religious law, and encompasses every aspect of human concern and experience. We find that Judaism is concerned with (1) the sanctity of the person, (2) the sanctity of time, and (3) the sanctity of place. All of Jewish law can be defined in terms of one or another of these categories.

Concern for the *sanctity of the person* is reflected by laws dealing with social and business ethics, sexual relationships, eating habits, patterns of dress and of speech, family relationships, personal hygiene and health care, the supreme importance of life, even the honor due a corpse.

Concern for the *sanctity of time* is emphasized by the laws relating to the Sabbath and the festivals. The *sanctity of place* is reflected in the commandments relating to the Temple in Jerusalem. (In Hebrew, it is known as the *Beit Hamikdash,* which literally means "The House of Holiness.") It is also reflected in laws relating to the *Beit Knesset,* the synagogue, and the *Beit Midrash,* the study hall.

Just as the observance of the laws relating to the sacred places contributes to the holiness of such places and their violation contributes to their desecration, so the observance of the laws of the Sabbath and the festivals contribute to the sanctity of the day and establishes their sacredness; and the keeping of the laws concerned with the sanctity of the person and of the other sancta contributes to the making of a holy person.

It might be appropriate at this point to define just what is meant by "a holy person" in the Jewish conceptual framework. In the tradition of other faiths and peoples, the image of a holy person is generally one who is removed from life, who disdains earthly pleasures and desires, and who retreats from the ordinary problems of life and society. This image of the ascetic is not the Jewish idea of a holy person. On the contrary, there is reason to argue that although such asceticism is not forbidden, such a disassociation from life and the assumption of additional prohibitions is actually frowned upon in Judaism.

A Jewish definition of holiness may be put in these terms: Holiness does not lie in the ascetic, saintly withdrawal from life, or in excessive denial to oneself of all human pleasures, or in the repression of all human drives. It consists, rather, of full participation in the stream of human community life, sharing the joyous as well as the sorrowful experiences which life has to offer, denying to oneself no legitimate pleasures; but at the same time so developing one's sense of discernment as to be able to distinguish and choose the right from the wrong, the true from the false, the good from the bad, the sacred from the profane, the pure from the impure, and the clean from the unclean. The greater the sense of ethical-moral-religious discrimination, the greater the holiness of the individual.

The common denominator between the Jewish concept of *holiness* and that of other faiths is indeed expressed in the crucial concept of being removed. The great Bible commentator Rashi explains the phrase *kedoshim tiheyu—you shall be holy* as meaning *perushim tiheyu—you shall separate yourselves*. Views differ, however, when one proceeds to consider the question—separated from what, removed from what? To others it has meant *being removed from life*. To the Jew, it has meant *being removed from idolatry; being removed from secularism; being removed from the vulgar and the profane*.

Just as a sacred place is set apart from secular, ordinary places, just as a sacred time is set apart from the ordinary, secular times, so a sacred person is set apart by his behavior and his actions from those whose lives are secular, or whose behavior is vulgar and profane.

The Torah calls upon the Jews to become the sacred people by living a life of sanctity at all times. This then is the purpose for the observance of the laws of the Torah—to contribute to personal sanctity and help create a more sanctified society.

This is not an easy task. And people being people, not all Jews have even looked upon it as a desirable goal. All too often, they have sought to "escape" from the "burden" imposed upon them. "Let us be as all the other nations," was a cry that was heard throughout the centuries from the earliest periods of Israel's history. Occasionally the cry was a legitimate demand for normalization, for Jews grew tired of serving as the eternal scapegoat for the ills and the frustrations of other societies. They desired an end to discrimination and the rights and privileges of a nation among nations. But all too often it was a cry of rebelliousness against the requirements of the Torah, against its disciplines and restraints, against the duties it imposed.

Moses anticipated such a reaction 3200 years ago when in his final parting message to the people, he pleaded with them:

> Surely this Instruction, which I enjoin upon you this day; it is not too hard for you, neither is it beyond reach. It is not in the heavens, that you should say: "Who among us can go up to the heavens and bring it to us, and impart it to us, that we may observe it?" Neither is it beyond the sea, that you should say, "Who among us can cross to the other side of the sea, and bring it to us, and impart it to us that we may observe it?" No, the thing is very close to you in your mouth and in your heart, to observe it.
>
> (Deut. 30:11-14)

In other words, Moses was telling his people: *It is up to you!* Given the will and the conviction, given the desire and the faith to do it

—it can be done. The parting words of Moses have never lost their freshness, their relevance, their impact, throughout thousands of years. They are equally in place today, for nothing much has changed in the human character except perhaps the kind of rationalizations being used. Today, the blanket term "needs" is used as the all-purpose, all-useful pretext for justifying and legitimizing every conceivable kind of immoral, amoral, anti-social, or non-religious behavior.

A real problem confronting even well-intentioned people who live in a non-religious environment was recognized by Maimonides in the twelfth century as "man's natural tendency to think and act like his friends and colleagues, and to follow the custom of his fellow countrymen." His advice, as useful today as it was then, was that it is therefore particularly important "to associate with good and wise men . . . and shun wrongdoers that one may not be influenced by their ways" (Hil. Deot. 6:1).

In approaching the practical observances, we call to mind the admonition of Moses to those who might think that the effort to observe them is not worthwhile, that the goal of sanctity imposed upon Israel by God is of no merit: "See I have imparted to you laws and ordinances, as the Lord my God has commanded me . . . . Observe them faithfully for that will be proof of your wisdom and understanding in the sight of other peoples, who on hearing of all these laws, will say; 'Surely this is a great nation of wise and understanding people . . . .' For what great nation is there, that has laws and ordinances as perfect as all this Teaching that I set before you this day?" (Deut. 4:5–8).

Part Two

THE DAILY WAY
OF LIFE

CHAPTER

4

Kindness: A Means and an End

THE first words of any introduction to the Jewish daily way of life must speak of kindness (*hesed*), because we believe that Jewish religious faith and ritual observance aim, above all, to achieve a perfection of the human relationship and to create a better society. While we cannot possibly cover all the laws, teachings, or guidelines dealt with by Jewish law and faith in this area, we can draw upon a short selection that will reflect the broad spectrum of the ethical concerns with which Jewish law deals.

We must remember that the great sage Hillel summed up the essence of Judaism by saying: "What is hateful to you, do not do to others." (A reformulation of this dictum later came to be known as the Golden Rule in Christendom.) Rabbi Akiva, at the beginning of the second century c.e., cited Leviticus 19:17: "Love your neighbor as yourself" as summarizing the essence of the whole Torah. When Rabbi Yochanan ben Zakkai asked his disciples to investigate "Which is the good way to which a man should cleave," all the answers were phrased in ethical terms. And the answer which appealed to him the most was that of Rabbi Elazar ben Aroch who said "a good heart," for this quality, said the Master, was inclusive of all the others. When the Talmud speaks of the characteristics of Israel, it does not do so

41

in terms of the unique ritual observances and disciplines. Rather, it adopts humane criteria: "Three characteristics does this (Jewish) people possess: they are merciful, modest and perform deeds of kindness" (Yevamot 79a). All who possessed these three characteristics were considered "worthy of becoming part of this people." On the other hand, Jews who lacked these qualities were considered unworthy members of the people. Maimonides went so far as to declare that "there is reason to be suspicious of the Jewish credentials of one who is cruel" (Isurai Biah 19:17). When the ancient rabbis wished to indicate the characteristics which distinguished the Jews from the ancient heathens, they did not do it on the theological grounds that Jews worshipped one God, the heathens pagan idols or no god at all; that Jews rested one day a week, heathens did not; or that Jews performed certain ritual disciplines and heathens did not. Though all these were important and were certainly distinguishing characteristics of the Jew and his way of life, they emphasized that "the Jew was merciful, he was modest, he was charitable."

The "good heart" is actually the Talmud's prerequisite for a truly pious and observant individual. The absence of a "good heart," as it might be reflected in untold ways, is a blemish upon the religious "wholeness" of the individual. An ethical act, an act of kindness or of charity performed not for any ulterior motives but in the belief that this too is God's will, is very much in the category of a religious act and constitutes the fulfillment of religious law. To the extent that it provides spiritual satisfaction, it is a legitimate religious experience. The Talmud says that "whoever aspires to piety and saintliness, let him fulfill all the laws of *nezikin*" (Baba Kamma 30). These laws deal with monetary, civil, and criminal matters. By the same token acts of injustice, of brutality, of dishonesty, of deception, of slander, of unkindness, are all *religious transgressions against* God no less than they are crimes against man. They are regarded as grave religious sins, perhaps even more than ritual violations. Consider the *Al Het* confessional which occupies a central place in the Yom Kippur service. It consists primarily of ethical-moral transgressions rather than ritual ones. The laws of Yom Kippur emphasize that God will forgive transgressions against Himself, but will not forgive transgressions against our fellow men unless amends are made and forgiveness is first obtained from the wronged party.

The Sages did not hesitate to dismiss the value of a ritual observance if it came about through a transgression. A mitzvah observed by committing a transgression had no validity nor merit. "One who stole a *seah* of wheat and scrupulously took from the dough the required amount as an offering, in accordance with Divine Law, what blessing does he recite? Whatever such a one says is not a blessing, but constitutes a curse" (Sanhedrin 6).

According to the Talmud, the very Sanctification of God's Name and the credibility of the religious life hinges, in fact, on the quality of the ethical-moral life.

"If someone studies Scripture and Mishna, and attends on the scholars, is honest in business, and speaks pleasantly to persons, what do people then say concerning him? 'Happy is the father (and teacher) who taught him Torah, . . . for this man has studied the Torah—look how fine his ways are, how righteous his deeds!' But if someone studies Scripture and Mishna, attends on the scholars, but is dishonest in business and discourteous in his relations with people, what do people say about him? 'Woe unto him who studied the Torah, woe unto his father (and teacher) who taught him Torah! This man studied the Torah; Look how corrupt are his deeds, how ugly his ways' " (Yoma 86a). For a religiously learned or ritually observant person to act in a way that would invite such remarks was regarded as a Desecration of the Divine Name (*Hilul Hashem*), a transgression of the severest spiritual magnitude.

In emphasizing the Divine priority of values, one Talmudic Sage taught that "the very *first* question that a person is asked when he is brought to his final judgment is 'Have you dealt with integrity and faith . . .' " (Shabbat 31a).

Samuel David Luzzatto, a rabbinic scholar who lived about a century ago in Italy, expressed the view in his *Yesodai Hatorah* (Foundations of the Torah), that Torah is based upon three foundations, the first being that of compassion. The quality of compassion, he writes, "is the root of love and kindness and righteousness; and it alone brings us to the doing of good deeds without ulterior motives." In a footnote, Luzzatto adds that "Compassion which is the root of love and kindness, is also the source of love, *justice* and hatred of violence," and that from compassion, "there will also be drawn forth the love for righteousness and justice." He thus sees righteousness and even justice not as independent virtues but as extensions of the virtues of kindness and compassion.

Luzzatto marshals impressive evidence both in the aforementioned volume, and especially in his *Tzedakah Umishpat* (Righteousness and Justice), to support his contention that compassion and mercy are not only important features of the Jewish moral system and of the entire religious framework, but are in fact at the very heart of Jewish faith and Jewish living. Although Luzzatto emphasizes emotion as a more important behavioral determinant and ethical factor than reason (in contrast to Maimonides who emphasized the rational influence) it is compelling to note that one of the world's greatest contemporary rabbinic scholars, Joseph B. Soloveitchik takes note of three traditions (*masoret*), three threads that have historically run through Judaism, all three being intrinsic to the basic fiber of the faith. The first is the tradition of *Torah*, which he relates to intellect, reason, and knowledge. The second is that of *mitzvot*, of doing and observing. The third, he says, is that of *regesh*, of feeling, of emotion, of sentiment. Although stress is sometimes laid upon one or the other by different rabbinic scholars, there is no denying that all three are vital and indispensable ingredients in Judaism.

While some Jewish thinkers saw the unique greatness of Jewish ethics as the "endeavor to imbue all of social life with the feeling of sympathy," others based it on "its unsentimental and thoroughly objective viewpoint." Undoubtedly the truth lies in a delicate balance and controlled tension between the two.

The Biblical call to walk in the ways of God has been regarded from earliest times as a call to man to imitate the Divine qualities of compassion and kindness. "And now Israel, what does God require of you, but to revere Him . . . and to walk in His ways" (Deut. 10:12). As to what constitutes *the way of God*, ancient sources teach us: "Just as He is gracious, so be you gracious; just as He is merciful, be you too merciful . . . just as He is full of kindness and truth . . . , so you too . . ." (Shabbat 133b). The Biblical book of Micah also says it clearly, "He has told you what is good and what God requires of you, but to act justly, to love kindness, and to walk humbly with your God" (Micah 6:8). In his book *Ahavath Chesed*, The Chafetz Chaim emphasizes that the "entire Torah is permeated by this (kindness) concept."

The Prophets of Israel also condemned the callousness of the people to human suffering, to inequities, and to social injustices when they reprimanded Israel for backsliding from the Laws of Moses and the Divine commandments. It was not the Temple sacrificial system itself which Isaiah, Jeremiah, and Micah condemned, for they included prayers and singing, i.e., present day type of worship, in their criticism. What they condemned was religion that was reduced to nothing more than worship (whether that worship be in the form of sacrifices or prayers, in the form of solemn assemblies in the ancient Temple courtyard or in contemporary-type Sanctuaries) and which lacks the essentials of justice and mercy, of kindness and righteousness. Such a disregard for the Divine commandments between man and his fellow man, they insisted, makes a mockery of the commandments between man and his God, and is regarded by Him as an abomination. With kindness and justice (*hesed u'mishpat*), all else in the religious life is sweet. Without it, all else is despised.

"If a man shows no mercy," says an ancient source, "what difference is there between him and a beast which can callously stand by and not feel the anguish of its fellow creature?"

Simon the Just used to say: "On three foundations does the world stand: On the Torah, on Divine worship and on acts of kindness" (Avot 1:2). Acts of kindness are included in the Mishna among those things "that have no limits" (Mishna Peah 1).

This continual emphasis upon justice, upon compassion and kindness over long periods of time was not without its results. For compassion and social justice became the distinguishing hallmark of Jewish communal life even in the centuries before the common era, and has remained so through the centuries.

"Classical philosophy extolled the four cardinal virtues: courage, justice, wisdom, and temperance. But it did not rank high or even urge the qualities of generosity, compassion, sympathy, and mercy, which figure so prominently in the ethics of the Talmud."[1] If there have been differences of view between the Jew and the gentile even in what constitutes justice and righteousness, it may well have been because the Jewish views of justice and righteousness have invariably involved qualities which the world sometimes despised as a mark of weakness and cowardice.

It is only where compassion would serve to pervert justice and perpetuate wickedness that Israel was cautioned against allowing that noble sentiment to prevail. "You shall not respect (show favor to) the poor, nor honor the person of the mighty, but in righteousness shall you judge your neighbor" (Lev. 19:15). Just as it is wrong to pervert justice in favor of the rich or the privileged, so it is equally wrong to do so out of a sense of compassion, in favor of the poor or the underprivileged. While the tradition required justice to be tempered by mercy, the delicate balance between the two must not be so upset as to cause injustice to others.

The emphasis upon the sacredness of life to the point where Jewish law sanctions, in fact *insists* upon the temporary suspension of all its laws (except for the laws against murder, idolatry, incest, and adultery) to save a life, brings into clear focus the ethical considerations inherent in the functioning and implementation of the halakha itself. Even the exceptions are noteworthy, for these transgressions involve destroying the intrinsic holiness of man, and compromising the sacredness of the human life. The very exceptions constitute a judgment on which is the lesser of two evils when confronted by this moral dilemma.

While the whole range of Jewish law may be classified on the basis of commandments which have to do with man's relationship to his Maker, or *mitzvot shebain adam lamakom*, and those which have to do with man's relationship to his fellow men, or *mitzvot shebain adam lehavero*, there is often an overlapping. For even the ritual law appears to have ethical implications in that the purpose for many of them is the perfection of the ethical-moral qualities of the individual who is observing the ritual. Many Biblical commentators saw an ethical basis in such prohibitions as the eating of blood or the mixture of meat and milk. And where the ritual observance itself did not contribute to such ends, the Sages often endowed the ritual with meaningful interpretations that emphasized moral norms and ethical values (e.g., the removal of the leaven *hametz* for Passover was utilized as an opportunity to identify the leavened bread with haughtiness and arrogance and to urge their removal as well).

It is a psychological truth that behavioral ideals assert themselves more firmly when tied to concrete everyday actions than when derived solely from symbolic or philosophic abstractions, however lofty they be. The ethical imperatives and values of Judaism may have received their very strength and historical permanence from the ritual foundations. We ought never to lose sight of the fundamental role of the ritual in the development of the ethics, in the building of character and in perfecting the human relationship.

The enduring theme of Judaism is the quest of the good life, "to do that which is right in the sight of man, and good in the sight of God" (Sifre Deut. 12:29). One cannot understand Judaism and one cannot live Judaism without its goal of holiness. If one separates its ethics of righteousness and justice from its disciplines of kashrut and Shabbat, if one separates compassion and mercy for humanity from the disciplines of religious family life, one does not understand nor live Judaism. The love of God cannot be separated from the love of man. The observance of those commandments which implement the love of man are no less imperative than those commandments which symbolize the love of God, and vice versa. He who thinks he can do with one and not the other will discover too late that he ends up with neither.

The laws and teachings that follow constitute a sampling of the broad spectrum of the religious duties between man and his fellow men, or *mitzvot shebain adam lehavero*. The following is intended only to provide the reader with an insight into the wide range of areas covered and with the general guidelines of the ethical law. It is far from a detailed code, which would require an entire separate volume.

ACTS OF KINDNESS

&ﬤ The concept of kindness (hesed) includes all forms of kindness shown by a person whenever he exerts himself on behalf of another.[2] To refuse "all such services as one may render a neighbor without himself suffering detriment is worthy of Sodom. But even when to serve other people may result to our inconvenience or to the injury of our interests, we are commanded in every page of the Scriptures and in Talmudical works to exercise humanity and show love for our fellow mortals."[3]

&ﬤ The Torah teaches us, "And you shall love your neighbor as yourself" (Lev. 19:18). Therefore, a person is bidden to praise the virtues of another just as he would like himself to be praised and to be as protective about his friend's assets as he is about his own. In commenting upon the practical implementation of the above Biblical verse Hillel said: "What is hateful to you, do not do to others."

&ﬤ It is a religious duty (mitzvah) to extend the hospitality of one's home for food and lodging as the need arises.

&ﬤ It is a religious duty (mitzvah) to visit a person who is taken ill. Friends or family who regularly see the sick person should visit him

47

as soon as possible upon hearing of the illness. Others should wait a period of at least three days.

&ague; It is a religious duty (mitzvah) to visit a person in mourning and to comfort him in his sorrow.

&ague; It is also a great mitzvah to provide funds to enable orphaned girls or very poor girls to marry.

&ague; It is a mitzvah to personally provide for the return of a lost object to its rightful owners, for it is written ". . . *you must surely return it*" (Deut. 22:1).

&ague; One is required to protect the money or property of another from being lost, destroyed, or damaged. This falls within the observance of the Biblical precept of returning a lost item.

&ague; If one sees a neighbor whose life is in danger and he is in a position to help or can engage the help of someone else, he is obligated to go to every trouble and expense to do so (though he may later seek to be reimbursed for the expense). If he refrains from taking any action, he transgresses the Biblical precept "You shall not stand idly by the blood of your neighbor" (Lev. 19:16).

Similarly, if one becomes aware of a conspiracy against another and continues to mind his own affairs doing nothing to reveal the danger to his fellow man, he also transgresses the Biblical precept "You shall not stand idly by the blood of your neighbor."

&ague; Rabbi Joshua said: "The evil eye (jealousy), the evil inclination (lust), and hatred of mankind put a man out of this world. What is hatred of mankind? Whenever one says: 'Love the Sages, but hate the disciples; love the disciples (students) but hate the common people.' "

LAWS OF CHARITY

&ague; *Tzedakah* (literally meaning righteousness but commonly used to signify charity) is a trait of the seed of our father, Abraham, for it is written "For I have known him, that he may instruct his children, and his posterity . . . to do righteousness (tzedakah) and justice" (Genesis 18:19). The giving of charity is greater than all the offerings for it is written "The doing of righteousness and justice is preferable to the Lord than the sacrificial offering" (Proverbs 21:3).

Israel will not be redeemed except through the practice of tzedakah, for it is written "Zion will be redeemed in justice, and her returnees with tzedakah" (Isaiah 1:27).

ᢓᜆ It is a Biblical precept to give charity to the poor, for it is written "If there be among you a needy person, one of your brethren . . . you must surely open your hand to him . . ." (Deut. 15:7–8); and "you shall maintain him; whether stranger or sojourner, he shall live beside you" (Lev. 25:35).

ᢓᜆ If one sees a poor man seeking charity and turns his eyes away so as to avoid giving charity, such a person transgresses the Biblical commandment "Do not harden your heart, nor shut your hand from your needy brother" (Deut. 15:7).

ᢓᜆ One must feed and clothe the poor of the gentiles together with the poor of Israel.

ᢓᜆ Every person is required to give tzedakah according to his means. Even a poor man who is himself a recipient of tzedakah (or who is himself sustained only on social welfare) is required to give tzedakah even if he can only give a little. His little is as worthy as the greater sums given by the rich. But if the poor man has barely enough to sustain himself, he is exempt from giving since sustaining himself takes precedence over sustaining anyone else.

ᢓᜆ How much tzedakah must a person give? A medium measure would be a tenth of what one has earned during the year. In our day when taxes must be paid to the government and these taxes are often withheld from one's wages, it must be surmised that one's "income" is the amount that a person is left with after taxes.

ᢓᜆ All who show mercy, mercy will be shown to them, for it is written "The Lord will be kind and compassionate to you and will multiply you . . ." (Deut. 13:18).

ᢓᜆ Giving gifts to one's mother and father, if *they are needy of such help*, is also regarded as an observance of the mitzvah of tzedakah. The poor of one's own household take precedence over the poor of one's city; the poor of one's own city take precedence over the poor of another city; and the poor inhabitants of the Holy Land take precedence over the poor inhabitants of the Diaspora.

49

&❧ It is forbidden to turn a poor person away empty-handed, even if he is given but a small amount. If one truly has nothing to give, the poor person's feelings should at least be assuaged with some comforting words.

&❧ Tzedakah should be given cheerfully and sympathetically. If one gives it in a surly manner and with a gloomy expression, even if he gives a magnificent amount, he loses the merit of his own deed and violates a commandment of the Torah: "And your heart shall not be grieved when you give him . . ." (Deut. 15:10).

It is forbidden to rebuke a poor man in anger or to raise one's voice to him for his heart is already broken and his spirit crushed. "Woe to him who puts a poor man to shame!"

&❧ There are eight degrees or levels of charity, each one higher than the other. On an ascending level, they are as follows:

· The eighth and lowest level of charity is when one gives charity grudgingly.

· The seventh level is when one gives less than he should, but does so cheerfully.

· The sixth level is when one gives directly to the poor upon being asked.

· The fifth level is when one gives the alms directly to the poor without being asked.

· The fourth level is when the giving is indirect. The recipient knows who the giver is, but the giver does not know the identity of the recipient.

· The third level is when the giver knows the identity of the recipient, but the recipient does not know the identity of the giver.

· The second highest level is when the one who gives is unaware of the recipient, who in turn is unaware of the giver. In contributing to a charity fund, one gives in this way. Communal funds, administered by responsible people, are also in this category.

· The highest form of charity is to help sustain a person *before* he becomes impoverished, by offering a substantial gift in a dignified manner or by extending a suitable loan, or by helping him find employment or establish himself in some business so as to make it unnecessary for him to become dependent upon others.

৶ To make it possible for a sage or scholar to do his work while secure in his livelihood merits inheritance of the world to come. This also refers to handling the assets of a scholar in a way that will provide him with an income and free his mind to engage in the study of Torah.

৶ To inspire and bring others to give tzedakah is a great virtue and merits an even greater reward than that of the donor. Of those who do this it is written "Those who turn the many to righteousness shall be like the stars" (Daniel 12:3).

৶ A pledge to tzedakah must be paid immediately. To be tardy, although one is capable of immediately redeeming a pledge, is a violation of a Biblical precept "When you make a vow to the Lord your God, do not put off fulfilling it . . ." (Deut. 23:22). However, if it is understood at the time of the pledge that it is to be redeemed at specified times, one may wait until those times.

All of the foregoing rules about tzedakah concern themselves with the obligations and the duties of the donor. There are also rules that devolve upon the potential recipient:

৶ One should strive not to become a public charge and not to become dependent upon others. Even a distinguished scholar and an honored person who becomes impoverished should find manual labor even of the most menial type rather than become dependent upon the charity of others. The Sages taught us to act in this way and set the example.

৶ But if one cannot subsist unless he does receive tzedakah he should not hesitate to accept it. If he be proud and refuses tzedakah, he is compared to one who takes his own life, and who to his sorrow adds a transgression.

৶ It is a religious duty (mitzvah) to lend money to the poor, for it is written "If you lend money to any of My people, to the poor with you . . ." (Exodus 22:24). Even though Scripture says "if," our Sages regarded this "if" as implying "when," i.e., not as a permissive act but as an obligatory one.

৶ The mitzvah of lending money to the poor is greater than the mitzvah of giving tzedakah to those who ask for it. For the latter were already compelled to ask, and the former were not yet reduced to that level.

Even if a rich man has to borrow, it is a mitzvah to lend to him. It is also meritorious to offer beneficial advice and guidance.

ಶಾ It is forbidden to press for the return of a loan when one knows that the borrower does not yet possess the means to repay it. The Torah says; "They shall not be to him as a creditor" (Exodus 22:33).

It is similarly forbidden for the borrower to procrastinate with repayment when he has the funds with which to repay his debt, for it is written "Do not tell your neighbor go and come back again" (Proverbs 2:28).

ಶಾ He who has the funds of another in his possession, either as a loan due or as wages that are due, and does not pay it but procrastinates and says "go and come back again tomorrow," violates the commandment, "You shall not oppress your neighbor" (Lev. 19:13).

LAWS RELATING TO SLANDER, REVENGE, AND DECEIT

ಶಾ The Torah states: "You shall not go about as a tale bearer among your people" (Lev. 19:16). A tale bearer is one who goes about saying, "I heard this and this about so and so." Even if what he says is true, he still transgresses the commandment. Tale bearing is a great sin and can cause great bloodshed (literally or figuratively) and that is why this precept is immediately followed by the one, ". . . And you shall not stand idly by the blood of your neighbor."

There is an even greater sin that is included in the prohibition and this is an evil tongue, *lashon hara*. This refers to one who goes about discrediting another, telling uncomplimentary things about him *even if they are true*. One who speaks outright falsehoods is called a spreader of evil, malicious, and false reports, or a *motzi shem ra*. He is the lowest of the low and is regarded as a "moral leper."

A Hasidic tale tells of a man who went about the community slandering the rabbi and spreading malicious falsehoods about him. One day he felt remorse at what he was doing and so visited the rabbi to beg his forgiveness. He indicated that he was willing to do anything to make amends. The rabbi told him to take several feather pillows from his home, cut them open and scatter the feathers to the wind. While it was a rather strange request for the rabbi to make, it was a relatively simple matter to execute.

Having done as he was told, he came back to so inform the rabbi. "Now," said the rabbi, "go gather up all the feathers. For despite your obviously sincere remorse and willingness to correct the evil that was done, it is about as possible to repair the damage done by your words as it will be to recover all the feathers."

ಶ್ One who unprotestingly listens to an evil tongue is morally of lower caliber than the one who possesses one. Were it not for those willing to listen, no damage could be caused.

ಶ್ To make snide remarks or pass on nasty gossip, not in any hateful way but in levity, in the style of "I'm only kidding" borders on the category of an evil tongue.

ಶ್ He who insists upon praising a person before that person's enemies, encouraging them to respond with criticism and fault-finding, causes no good but only harm.

ಶ್ Four types of persons are not worthy of the Divine Presence (i.e., God does not enter their midst): idlers, insincere flatterers, liars, and those who talk with an evil tongue.

ಶ್ It is forbidden to take revenge. It constitutes a violation of a Torah commandment, "You shall not take revenge" (Lev. 19:18). Our religious teachers advised that "if one is possessed by a strong desire for revenge one should instead try adding to his own good qualities. Let this be your revenge" they said, "for surely your enemy will be upset upon hearing your virtues extolled and your good name spread. On the other hand, if you resort to ugly deeds, your enemy will rejoice at the shame and discredit you are causing yourself thereby revenging himself."

ಶ್ It is forbidden to carry a grudge. This too is a transgression of the Torah, "You shalt not harbor a grudge" (Lev. 19:18).

ಶ್ It is forbidden to curse another person in any language.

ಶ್ It is forbidden to wrong another with words (to insult, to cause anguish or pain). To wrong with words is a greater sin than to wrong one in money matters, for the latter is subject to compensation (it

53

can be made good) and the former is not; the latter is against a man's possessions, the former is directed against the person himself. The Torah states: "You shall not wrong one another but you shall fear your God . . ." (Lev. 25:17).

ৰ৶ "Wronging with words" includes any statement that will cause another pain or distress; any remark that will hurt another by bringing up unpleasant reminders of the past, or that will be insulting or embarrassing to a person when he hears it.

ৰ৶ It is forbidden to call someone by a derogatory nickname even if the person to whom it is directed is already accustomed to hearing it and is no longer embarrassed by it, as long as he who uses it intends thereby to embarrass the other and to deliberately emphasize its derogatory meaning.

ৰ৶ It is forbidden to put another to shame, be he child or adult, whether by words or by deed. This is so in private and especially so in front of others. One may not call another by a name that is embarrassing to him, or say things that might embarrass him before others. Of such actions, it is said that "He who puts another to shame in public is as though he has spilt blood," and that "One who puts another to public shame or ridicule has no share in the world to come."

ৰ৶ It is forbidden to "steal another's thoughts," i.e., to deceive another person even in non-monetary matters. Some examples of stealing another's thoughts are:

    · A man should not insist that his friend eat with him (thus intending to "prove" his friendship) when he knows that the friend cannot or will not accept the invitation.
    · A man should not offer a gift knowing in advance that it will not be accepted.
    · A man is prohibited from selling even to a non-Jew non-kosher meat, if the non-Jew is under the impression that he is buying kosher meat.

ৰ৶ A man's heart and mouth should be the same. One must not speak one way and think another; that is hypocrisy.

ৰ৶ From the words "you shall have an honest *hin*" (Lev. 19:36), the Sages derived the lesson that a man's "aye" should be "aye" and his "no" should be "no," i.e., he must be a man of his word. One must abide by his word even when it is not given in the form of an oath or a promise. He who does not, lacks integrity, and the spirit of the Sages is grieved by such behavior.

Thus a man who says to a friend that he intends to give him a gift and then doesn't give it to him lacks integrity. This is so whenever the potential recipient took the promise at its face value and believed that he would receive it.

If the promise of a gift was made to a poor man, whether it be a small or large gift, whether it be of the sort which the poor man believed he would receive and took the statement at its face value or not, the benefactor may not go back on his promise. A statement to a poor man assumes the status of a vow, concerning which the Torah teaches us "what proceedeth out of your lips, you shall keep."

&❧ The verse, "he who speaks the truth in his heart" (Psalms 15:2), teaches us an even higher level of ethical virtue. In all matters arising between a man and his fellow man, one should fulfill even that which he has only mentally decided upon. If one decides in his own heart to make a particular charitable contribution, one is duty bound to pay it in accordance with the decision one made to oneself, even if one did not actually utter any words of promise.

LAWS PERTAINING TO WORK AND WAGES

&❧ It is a Torah commandment to pay the wages of a hired person at the agreed time. Delay constitutes a violation of a Biblical precept "You must pay him his wages on the same day, before the sun sets" (Deut. 24:15). The reference is to a night laborer. In the case of a day laborer who collects his salary during the night, it says: "The wages of a laborer shall not remain with you all night until morning" (Lev. 19:13).

&❧ If a person is hired by the week, the month, or the year, one has only a night or a day after the work is finished to complete payment (or as per prior agreement).

&❧ If a person is hired to perform some job and in the course of his work causes a loss to the employer, even if it be through negligence, in such a way that he is legally responsible for the damage incurred, it is a mitzvah (in this case, a moral duty) for the employer to act beyond the literal application of the law (*lifnim mishurat hadin*) and to refrain from collecting damages for it is written ". . . so that you may go in the way of goodness" (Proverbs 2:20).

If the employee is a poor person, it is a mitzvah even to pay him his wages for that job (on which the loss or damage was sustained). This is the way of the righteous, to keep the way of the Lord, to perform deeds of righteousness and justice, *lifnim mishurat hadin*.

&❧ Just as an employer is cautioned not to steal or cheat on the wages of his employee, so is the employee cautioned not to idle or waste time on his job but to do his work conscientiously.

An employee is therefore not permitted to work at night and then hire himself out for the day (i.e., he is not permitted to do anything that would weaken him or cause him to be unable to do his work properly for his main employer).

KINDNESS TO ANIMALS

&❧ The Torah prohibits the torture or causing of pain to any living creature. One is duty bound to save every living creature from pain or distress, even if it has no owner (*hefker*).

&❧ If an animal is inflicting pain or causing grief to human beings, or the creature has utilitarian value (i.e., medical research), one is permitted to kill it. After all, the Torah does permit the slaughtering of animals for food.

&❧ Hunting as a sport has historically been looked upon with disdain as a violation of the spiritual norms of Judaism, particularly if there is no utilitarian purpose, for it invariably involves an element of cruelty to animals.

&❧ One who is responsible for feeding animals is forbidden to sit down to eat until he has fed the animals. This lesson is derived from the verse in the Torah where the feeding of animals is given precedence over the eating of man. It is written "And I will provide grass in the fields for your cattle, and you shall eat and be satisfied"

(Deut. 11:15). When it comes to drinking, man takes precedence, because man is less capable of enduring thirst than hunger. Here too Scripture provides the basis. It is written "Drink, and I will give your camels drink also" (Genesis 24:14).

ࣷ The duty to show kindness to animals and to avoid actions that would cause them anguish or suffering is found in many Torah passages: "You shall not muzzle an ox while it is threshing" (Deut. 25:4); "You shall not plow with an ox and an ass together" (Deut. 22:10). To spare the feelings of a mother bird, "do not take the mother together with her young. Let the mother go . . ." (Deut. 22:6–7). The laws of the Sabbath demand rest also for the beast. The laws of kosher slaughtering provide for the most painless and swiftest killing to avoid the slightest suffering to the animal. The Biblical book of Proverbs sums it up: "A righteous man considers the life of his beast" (Proverbs 12:10).

ACTS OF JUSTICE

ࣷ "You shall not oppress a stranger for you know the feelings of the stranger, having yourselves been strangers in the land of Egypt" (Exodus 23:9). Anyone who mistreats or deceives a stranger—either monetarily or through words—is guilty of three separate transgressions.

ࣷ The responsibility that the Torah places upon us in the treatment of proselytes is great. We have twice been commanded to love anyone who enters under the wings of the Divine Presence, once because he is in the category of a neighbor, "*And you shall love your neighbor as yourself*" (Lev. 19:34), and once because he is a stranger, "*And you shall love the stranger*" (Deut. 10:19).

ࣷ It is forbidden to assault another. One who physically assaults another violates a Torah commandment. It is written, "If the wicked man shall deserve to be beaten, then the judge shall . . . (but) he shall not exceed . . . to beat him . . ." (Deut. 25:2). The implication is that, beyond the punishment inflicted by a court of law, which may not be excessive, it is wrong to strike another. He who lifts a hand to strike another even though he does not strike is called wicked.

But if one is a victim of attack or sees another so victimized and he cannot save either himself or his friend from the attacker unless he strikes the attacker, it is permissible to strike him.

⳿ At a time when laws regarding fair weights and measures, fraudulent selling practices, and usury were still unknown in Western countries, Jewish communities had such laws and engaged the officials to enforce them. The basis for these regulations is the Torah, "You shall not have in your pouch alternate weights larger and smaller. You must have completely honest weights and completely honest measures. . ." (Deut. 13, 15). Thus the Talmud (Baba Batra 88a) rules that "a shopkeeper must clean his measures twice a week, wipe his weights once a week, and cleanse the scales after every weighing" to remove accumulated residue affecting true weights. Whatever contributed to fraudulent selling practices was similarly forbidden by the Talmud.

⳿ "You must take no bribe, for a bribe blinds the clear-sighted, and perverts the words of the righteous" (Exodus 23:8).

⳿ "In righteousness shall you judge your neighbor" (Lev. 19:15). This precept makes it incumbent upon each person to judge his fellow men in all interpersonal relations on the scales of merit and to give others the benefit of the doubt, especially where a person's record had previously been beyond reproach. Even if his guilt be proven beyond a doubt, one should look for mitigating circumstances.

⳿ If one sees another committing a sin or going astray, it is a religious duty to inform him of the error of his way and return him to the right path. The Torah states, "Reprove your neighbor" (Lev. 19:17). One should not claim that "it's none of my business."

When one does reprove another in matters that are between them or in ritual matters between man and God, it must be done privately and gently, with kind words. It should be made clear that the rebuke is intended only for the benefit and the good of the person.

Whoever can erase the traces of improper deeds and does not do so, violates this commandment. This is so only when one has the slightest reason to believe that he will be listened to. But if one knows that his words will fall on deaf ears, then it is forbidden to reprove.

⳿ If one is certain that no attention will be paid to his reproof, just as it is a religious requirement (mitzvah) for a person to say that which will be listened to, it is as incumbent upon him (a mitzvah too) not to say that which will surely not be listened to. "Do not reprove the fool lest he hate you, reprove the wise man and he will love you" (Proverbs 9:8).

THE MIDDLE ROAD

&> Maimonides writes, "Lest a person says: Since jealousy, lust, and desire for honor are evil ways . . . I will separate myself completely from them and go to the other extreme, to the point where he refuses to enjoy the pleasure of food by abstaining from eating meat and drinking wine, where he refuses to marry a wife, or to live in a pleasant house or to wear nice clothing but instead chooses to dress in rags . . . *this too is an evil way, and it is forbidden to go that way.* One who goes in such a path is called a sinner . . . therefore did our Sages ordain that a person must deny himself only that which the Torah has forbidden unto us, but he must not forbid upon himself things which according to the Torah are permitted. . . . And concerning all such matters, King Solomon said, 'Do not be overly-righteous, and do not be too wise, lest you be led to iniquity' (Ecclesiastes 7:16)."

&> The best and straightest road that a person should train himself to go on is the middle road (where he develops the moderate quality in each and every personality trait). And he who goes along this middle road is called a wise man.

&> A man must not feel shame before his fellow men if they mock him for worshipping the Holy One, Blessed Be He, and for abiding by His commandments. In any case, one should not respond to such taunting with insolence or impudence, so that he himself does not acquire the habit of being impudent.

&> "Do not side with the multitude (a majority) to do wrong; neither shall you bear witness to pervert justice in a dispute by leaning towards the multitude" (Exodus 23:2). Although the Biblical law is in the context of judicial practices, its moral significance was more broadly applied.

The rabbis also derived a lesson from the literal meaning of the last three words in the Hebrew text—*ahre rabim l'hatot*—and took them to imply that, except when it is "to do wrong," one should follow the majority.

෫๑ A person must keep away from things that cause illness and train himself to do only things that are healthy. It is written "For your own sake, therefore, be most careful" (Deut. 4:15) and "Take utmost care and watch yourselves scrupulously" (Deut. 4:9). Thus, excessive drinking, smoking, the abuse of drugs, or the eating of foods that may prove harmful to health are forbidden from the halakhic view.

෫๑ Yom Kippur does not atone for transgressions between man and his fellow men until the grieved party is pacified and forgives. The person whose forgiveness is sought is, however, duty bound to forgive wholeheartedly. He must not react cruelly, for this is not the Jewish way.

෫๑ To hate evil is as much a virtue as to love justice; to hate cruelty is as much a virtue as to love mercy. But it is not enough only to refrain from evil or to disdain cruelty. One must also actively pursue justice and mercy for it is written *Turn away from evil* (step one) *and do good* (step two). (Psalms 34:15, 37:27.)

CHAPTER

5

The Sabbath: An Island in Time

"Six days shall you labor, and do all your work; but the seventh day is a sabbath unto the Lord your God, in it you shall not do any manner of work . . . for the Lord blessed the Sabbath day and sanctified it" (Exodus 20:9–11). This passage from the Ten Commandments does not in itself reveal the absolutely profound role that the Sabbath has played in Jewish life throughout history and the role that it continues to play in the lives of those who lead Jewish lives. But the fact that it is the only commandment among the Ten Commandments which deals with a purely ritual observance ought to indicate the priority assigned to it by the Almighty Himself in the broad context of all the commandments that concern man's relationship to God.

That Divine priority has in fact been paralleled by the emphasis given to it by the Jews themselves. Although the observant Jew subjects himself to many commandments, he harbors a special love for the Sabbath. There is no other commandment or ritual observance in all of Judaism for which you can find such expressions of affection and devotion as for the Sabbath. It is the only observance which has become personified in the religious poetry of the prayers. It is affectionately referred to as the Sabbath Bride. Just

61

as a bride is traditionally radiant and beautiful, a poetic symbol of charm and purity, an object of love and affection, so is the Sabbath to the Jew. It is also called the Sabbath Queen, *Shabbat Hamalkah*, for queens, too, in the imagination of poets and mystics, are symbols of majesty, beauty, and grace, and so is the Sabbath to Jews. These poetic descriptions of the Sabbath have always retained their full flavor for the Sabbath-observing Jew.

To persons looking in from the outside—Jew or gentile—the Sabbath might appear to be restrictive. A cursory acquaintance with its restrictions might lead one to assume that it is an austere day for those who observe it, a day lacking joy and spirit. Yet experienced from within, it is just the reverse. It serves as a glorious release from weekday concerns, routine pressures, and even secular recreation. It is a day of peaceful tranquillity, inner joy and spiritual uplift, accompanied by song and cheer.

To describe the feeling that overcomes one on the Sabbath is like trying to describe a beautiful sunset to a blind man. However rich in words one may be, the sense of rapture that even a simple person with sight senses at the sight of such beauty can never be totally conveyed even by a master poet. Looking in from outside at those who observe the Sabbath might be compared to a deaf man coming upon a scene where people are dancing to music being played by an orchestra hidden from sight. Not hearing the music, the deaf man might well mistake the dancers for a group of people who have gone mad. Of course, *he* does not hear the music, and so the movement of the body which the music inspires is unappreciated and leaves him cold. And so might the Sabbath with its restrictions leave an observer—unless he has had an opportunity to become part of the experience. Only then may it dawn upon him that what he may have thought of as burdensome and inconvenient is really deliciously desirable and eagerly awaited. It is not without reason that the Midrashic description of the eternal Paradise, of the world to come, is that of one long extended, unending, eternal Sabbath day *"yom shekulo shabbat,"* or that the Biblically-derived expression the Delight of the Sabbath, "Oneg Shabbat" (Isaiah 58:13), has become so commonplace a phrase, used—and sometimes misused today—by Jews everywhere.

Another Midrash portrays God as saying: "A precious jewel have I in my possession, which I wish to give to Israel, and Sabbath is its name." No Jew who has ever truly observed the Sabbath will argue with that description. If anything, he will tell you that it is an understatement.

It is a pity then that so many Jews in the twentieth century forfeited this most precious possession. Some did so deliberately and consciously under the impact of a general ideological rebellion against Judaism in which they turned to atheistic and secular ideologies for their salvation and for that of mankind. Others did so unwillingly and regretfully under the impact of economic pressures and aspirations in the non-Jewish environments of the Diaspora in which they lived, where Sunday was the national day of rest. While a minority of Jews continued to resist the economic temptations if it meant forfeiting their Sabbath, most were not so spiritually strong.

And while the first generation among these groups who gave up the Sabbath still harbored precious memories of the Sabbath, their children and grandchildren, the second and third generations, were raised without any but the most superficial knowledge of the Sabbath and its spirit. To revert to our metaphor, these generations were permitted to become deaf and blind to the music and beauty of the Sabbath.

Nor was it just the Sabbath that was affected by this neglect. Knowledge of Judaism began to deteriorate . . . and then all of Jewish life. For the Sabbath is truly the pivotal point for all of Judaism. When the Sabbath is discarded, attendance at synagogue becomes reduced to the vanishing point. And when that happens, the best form of Jewish education disappears. It is no secret that the level of Jewish education reached by most Western Jews today rarely exceeds the second or third grade. This is true even of those who receive some Jewish education, even of those who complete five or six years of a Sunday or afternoon Hebrew School. One who has achieved the equivalent of what ought to be objectively regarded as an eighth-grade level is already reckoned as a scholar in the community.

When the Sabbath is neglected, the Torah and the Prophets are no longer reviewed on a regular or weekly basis. Eventually its contents are forgotten. The sermons of the rabbi, however excellent or poor, do serve to provide some additional awareness, some extra bits of knowledge of rabbinic and Talmudic sources. The Talmud expresses the view that "the Sabbaths were given to Israel in order that they might study Torah." Furthermore, without the Sabbath and the regular attendance at a synagogue which it generates, the motivation for religious and Hebrew study by the children is reduced to the minimal, reducing the effectiveness of whatever education is received. Within a generation of two, the discarding of the Sabbath causes a knowledge of Judaism to deteriorate, which leads to the discarding of still other religious observances, and eventually to the dissipation even of the moral values of Judaism.

Herman Wouk has observed, with much insight into the problem, "The Sabbath is the usual breaking off point from tradition, and also the point at which many Jews rejoin Judaism."[1]

Far from being behind the times, the spirit of the Jewish Sabbath is still far ahead of the times. Far from being impractical for advanced Western societies, it is what is needed most by contemporary man. It is what is needed most in the competitive, tension-packed, hurried, frenzied life of this society. The brilliant Greek civilization which bequeathed us Plato and Aristotle, which served as the bedrock for Western civilization and provided the impetus for scientific inquiry, mocked the Jews in its time for not working one day a week. Jews were then called shiftless and lazy, not by barbarians, but by people whose writings are still studied in the universities of the world. It took the civilized world all these centuries even to begin to realize the value of a day of rest, and make the six day work week the basis of its social order.

It may take many more centuries before the world at large even begins to catch a glimpse of that spirit which the Jewish Sabbath possesses. Even the early American Puritans, who, in their Sunday observance came closest to the Sabbath in the strictness with which they enforced their day of rest, did not come close to capturing the Jewish Sabbath in spirit. Their Sabbath day, according to their own testimony, was a day of somberness, of gloom. To us it is a day of joy, of delight.

Most people think of the Sabbath as just a day of rest, when work is prohibited. This is only partially true: it was intended to be a *holy* day, a *yom kadosh*, different and set aside from the other days. It is not just a day of leisure. It is the high point of the week, around which all the other days revolve. If on the one hand it is a day in which we withdraw totally and completely from the demands of the world about us, on the other hand it is a day that we try to imbue with spiritual significance and meaning. It is a day filled, not with vain pursuits, but with edifying ones. If it is a day that is intended to refresh the body, it is also a day intended to refresh the soul.

"Resting" on the Sabbath has a totally different meaning to the Sabbath observer than that which is conveyed by the word "relaxing."

The Torah gives two *motifs* for the Sabbath, which we will examine. The first is as "a memorial to the creation of the world."

> In six days the Lord made heaven and earth and sea, and all that is in them . . . and rested on the seventh day . . . therefore God blessed the Sabbath day, and hallowed it.
>
> (Exodus 20:11)

> It shall be a sign for all time between Me and the people of Israel; for in six days the Lord made heaven and earth, and on the seventh day He ceased from work and rested.
>
> (Exodus 31:17)

The second motif is as "a memorial to the exodus from Egypt."

> . . . remember that you were a slave in the land of Egypt and the Lord your God brought you out from there with a mighty hand and an outstretched arm.
>
> (Deut. 5:15)

THE SABBATH AS A MEMORIAL TO THE CREATION OF THE WORLD

What lesson is derived from such a memorial? What does it testify? Besides, what does the Torah mean to teach us when it says that "God rested"? Is He human that He tires and needs physical rest? It is to teach us that just as God stopped creating physical things on the seventh day, so is man to stop creating on this day. Man is to stop making things, to stop manipulating nature. He is to let all things run by themselves. By desisting from all such labors, we not only acknowledge the existence of a Creator, but also emulate the Divine example.

By desisting from all work on the seventh day, we testify that the world is not ours; that, not we, but God is the Lord and Creator of the universe. The fish and the animals that we don't catch, the plants or the flowers that we don't cut or pluck, the grass that we don't water on this day, the goods that we refrain from fashioning or cutting—all this inaction on the part of the individual is a demonstration of homage to the Lord, of returning all things, as it were, to His domain. On the other hand any constructive interference by man with the physical world constitutes "work," according to the

Biblical definition. Any act, however small, that involves man in physically creative acts and shows his mastery over the world constitutes *work*. It is this underlying motif which may help to explain some of the whys of the Sabbath laws. This is why acts which may not even require any physical effort, such as plucking a flower or striking a match, are still called *work*. To desist from this work on the seventh day is equivalent to recognizing God as the Creator of the world.

Samson Raphael Hirsch, in his monumental work, *Horeb*, sums up the meaning of the Sabbath laws thus:

How, above all, does man show his domination over the earth? In that he can fashion all things in his environment to his own purpose—the earth for his habitation and source of sustenance; plant and animal for food and clothing. He can transform everything into an instrument of human service. He is allowed to rule over the world for six days with God's will. On the seventh day, however, he is forbidden by Divine behest to fashion anything for his purpose. In this way he acknowledges that he has no rights of ownership or authority over the world. Nothing may be dealt with as man pleases, for everything belongs to God, the Creator, Who has set man into the world to rule it according to His word. On each Sabbath day, the world, so to speak, is restored to God, and thus man proclaims, both to himself and to his surroundings, that he enjoys only a borrowed authority.

Therefore even the smallest work done on the Sabbath is a denial of the fact that God is the Creator and Master of the world. It is an arrogant setting-up of man as his own master. It is a denial of the whole task of the Jew as man and as Israelite, which is nothing but the management of the earth according to the will of God. . . . On the other hand, every refraining from work on the Sabbath is in itself a positive expression of the fact that God is the Creator and Master of the world; that it is He who has set man in his place; that He is the Lawgiver of his life; it is a proclamation and acknowledgment of our task as men and Israelites.

Thus, doing no work on the Sabbath is an *ot*, an expressive *symbol* for all time. The Sabbath expresses the truth that the Only God is the Creator and Master of all and that man, together with all else, has been called to the service of the Only God. It is *moed*, a *time-institution*, a day singled out from other days, a summons to the ennoblement of life. It is *kodesh*, a *holy* time: if, during the six working days, man forgets that Almighty God is the Source of all power and his Lawgiver, then the Sabbath comes to elevate him by directing him once again towards his Creator. It is *brit*, a *covenant*, the only contract and basis of every relationship between God and the Jew, both as man and as Israelite. For if you consider the world and yourself as God's property, and regard your power over the earth as lent to you by God for the fulfillment of your task in life, then will your life be lived in accordance with the Torah. But if you regard the world as your own and yourself as its master, then the contract is torn up, and you are just making sport of the Torah. Finally, it is *brakha*, a *blessing*; if you thus renew your covenant with God every Sabbath, and dedicate yourself as God's servant, then on every Sabbath God will give you renewed enlightenment of the spirit, enthusiasm and strength for the fulfillment of this great task. In this way you will realize how God really calls you to an elevated state of life which is especially experienced on Sabbath. Our Sages describe this elevated state of the soul by saying that the Sabbath provides the Jew with an "extra soul" or a "super-soul."

The *melachah* which is forbidden on Sabbath is conceived as the execution of an intelligent purpose by the practical skill of man. Or, more generally, production, creation, transforming an object for human purposes; but *not* physical exertion. Even if you tired yourself out the whole day, as long as you have *produced* nothing within the meaning of the term *melachah*; as long as your activity has not been a constructive exercise of your intelligence, you have performed no *melachah* or work. On the other hand, if you have engendered, without the slightest exertion, even the smallest change in an object for human purposes, then you have profaned the Sabbath, flouted God, and undermined your calling as a Jew. Your physical power belongs to your animal nature; it is with your technical skill which serves your spirit that you master the world—and it is with this that, as a human being, you should subject yourself to God on Sabbath.[2]

THE SABBATH AS A MEMORIAL TO THE EXODUS FROM EGYPT

This motif beckons us to remember our slavery, the better to cherish freedom. If the Sabbath on the one hand emphasizes our servitude to God, it also stresses our *freedom from servitude to human masters*. It emphasizes the freedom of the human soul, the freedom of mind and of body. In this context it is important to note that the Torah forbids work to be carried on "by thy man-servant, nor thy maid-servant, nor thy cattle, nor thy stranger that is within thy gates." To be free of servitude on this day was not only for the landowner, the master, the free man—but even in those ancient, primitive times was also intended for the stranger, the servant, and the toiling beast.

Sabbath is thus a weekly-recurring divine protest against slavery and oppression. Lifting up his Kiddush cup on Friday night, the Jew links the creation of the world with man's freedom, so declaring slavery and oppression deadly sins against the very foundations of the universe. Can one be surprised that tyrants of all times did not permit Israel to celebrate the Sabbath?[3]

But slavery doesn't only consist of doing forced labor for which one doesn't get paid or gets paid very little. Slavery is not only a situation in which cruel taskmasters stand over you and tell you that you can't stop, that you must finish the assigned task before you go home and rest. Have you ever stopped to think that you yourself can be your own cruelest taskmaster, that you are capable of driving yourself in a manner that no slavemaster ever drove his slaves?

You've got to finish the job. You can't stop. There are deadlines to meet, there are obligations to fulfill, there are things which must be taken care of. There are conferences, there are business commitments. There is house cleaning, laundry, shopping, the need to get ready for an evening out. We drive ourselves day in and day out, and we think we are *free*!

Even when contemporary man doesn't actually go to his job, what does he do? He plays just as hard. He transfers the same tension, the same competitive spirit, the same frenzy and the same pressure on his nervous system, which takes such a great toll of human life, from the business office to the ball field, the golf course, the highways of our land, to mowing the lawn, and fixing the house. He thinks he's not working! He may not be getting paid for any of it. He may even enjoy some of it more than what he does for a living. He may even be having a good time. All that, yes! But the mental and emotional and physical rest, the tranquillity of mind and soul—this he doesn't have. Lewis Mumford saw the problem a little more clearly when he wrote:

In our Western culture the day of rest has now become another day of busy work, filled with amusements and restless diversions not essentially different from the routine of the work week, particularly in America. From the Sunday morning scramble through the metropolitan newspapers, to the distracting tedium of the motor car excursion, we continuously activate leisure time, instead of letting all work and routine duties come serenely to a halt.[4]

How many, in the midst of all their pressing obligations and commitments, their worries and concerns, business and personal, can just stop everything and say: "Yes, I have so many things to do. But for the next twenty-four hours, I am a free man. I will cut myself off from the world, and all its concerns, and do nothing or limit myself to spiritual pursuits"? How many can deliberately and consciously say—not "I have really finished, therefore I can rest"—but "though I have not finished, it is as though I have. I now stop for there is no such thing as *must* do"?

The Sabbath observer can and does! He has no taskmasters. For twenty-four hours, he is free. Nothing interferes with his rest, his tranquillity of mind and of soul, unless it be a matter of life and death in which he must play a decisive role. And it is precisely because the Sabbath recurs as often as every seven days, that it is the refreshing pause that a Sabbath-observant Jew finds it to be. It is not only a matter of not working physically. It is also not working emotionally. And from the positive side, it is the engendering of a completely new and different spirit. Our tradition refers to it as the additional soul, the *neshama y'tairah*. This is an attitude, a state of mind.

The great scholar of Jerusalem, Shlomo Joseph Zevin, suggests that there are two types of rest. One is rest from weariness, as a result of tiredness. Such rest is only to enable one to continue working. Though it brings relief and rest to the body (it is what Rashi calls *menuhat ara-ey*), it does not bring joy to the soul.

The second type of rest comes in the wake of completing some project, after reaching some goal. This type of rest comes at the completion of one's work, not as a "rest" during it. Here a man sits back and contemplates his achievement or his handiwork. This kind of rest is a delight to the soul. It brings a sense of release; it provides a deep satisfaction accompanied by a sense of peace and tranquillity. (It is what Rashi calls *menuhat margoa*.)

The rest that the Sabbath day is intended to reflect is the second type. "Six days shall you labor and do *all* your work." Imagine to yourself when the Sabbath arrives after six days of work that all your work has been completed in that time. The Sabbath observer feels just this way. And therein lies the meaning of his freedom from servitude.

Ahad Ha'Am was quoted as having said, "More than Israel has kept the Sabbath, the Sabbath has kept Israel." It was the Sabbath, the weekly-recurring Sabbath, that lifted the people out of the drudgery and toil of the other six days. It was the princely dignity of the Sabbath that enabled the most impoverished Jew to rise above the inferior status and conditions to which he was subjected. It was the weekly leisure of the Sabbath that enabled hardpressed people to maintain their contact with our religious source and its classics, that enabled them to remain close to Torah and Torah knowledge, each on his own level. It was the weekly Sabbath that provided resuscitation—physical, spiritual, emotional, psychological, and enabled the Jew to withstand adverse conditions. Contemporary man's need for a day of rest which is *more than physical rest, a yom menuhah,* is no less vital. To think that a more affluent society has any less need to be revived from its own forms of oppression or boredom or drudgery is to be blind to the conditions of the day.

Modern man may celebrate many holidays, but he observes few holy days. He may possess many more hours and days of leisure than those in previous generations, but he still lacks days of serenity and tranquillity.

Modern man, in fact, often has a romantic and idyllic vision of an isolated *island in the sea* as the place where just such a peaceful calm may be found. It's a romantic dream in our culture—an island to escape to with those who are dear to us. Yet the acquisition of such an island as a personal retreat is beyond the reach of most people. The Sabbath, however, serves as a precious *island in time,* removed from the mainland of the rest of the week, providing just that peaceful calm that contemporary man aspires to but never quite reaches. But the Sabbath is within our reach!

A Jewry that forgets the Sabbath—even on its own soil—will eventually dissipate and crumble spiritually. Whether we Jews live in the countries of the Diaspora, or on our own soil of Israel, the Sabbath is not less crucial today in maintaining the uniqueness of our culture, of our faith, and of our mission; it is not less crucial today in keeping Jewry everywhere conscious of itself and its faith; and in keeping it spiritually strong and dynamic.

PREPARING FOR THE SABBATH

&ce; To properly honor the Sabbath and to capture its beauty and spiritual delight, it is necessary to prepare for its coming.

ᴈ⋗ The preparations in a household should be no less elegant than the preparations the same family might make to receive a distinguished and beloved guest.

ᴈ⋗ What might a family do if a very honored guest was coming for dinner?

· A man would plan on getting home from work in plenty of time to shave, bathe, and get dressed.
· A mother would see to it that she and her children were washed and dressed in clean, fresh clothes.
· The dining table would be set in advance as on a special festive occasion; one's best dishes and tableware would be used.
· Dinner would not only be prepared in advance, but the menu would be a little more elaborate than that served at a daily meal. In a poor home, meat and fish would be reserved for the Sabbath meals. But even where meat or fish is on a family's daily menu, there are still many distinctions that a hostess makes when serving a special festive meal, both in types of dishes as well as in the number of courses.
· A house would be thoroughly cleaned, or at least straightened up.
· Every member of the family would take care of the most pressing chores before the guest arrives.
· One can also imagine that members of a household might warn friends, neighbors and business associates not to interrupt by telephone calls while their guest is visiting with them. It would not only be rude to the visitor but disturbing to all if there were constant interruptions.

All this is done *before* the honored guest arrives. This is also what must be done to prepare properly for the Sabbath.

ᴈ⋗ It is unlikely that the Sabbath spirit can be captured or made meaningful even where a festive meal is served, if children are permitted to come to a table in their play clothes or jeans; if adults sit down in their weekday workclothes, or if the necessary personal and household preparations are omitted.

THE SABBATH EVE

The Sabbath Candles

ଓ৸ Lighting of the Sabbath candles formally ushers in the Sabbath for the members of the household. (See page 74, for exception.)

ଓ৸ It is the obligation of the wife to fulfill this religious duty. Unless a woman had been living alone, she starts to observe it on the first Sabbath after her marriage.

ଓ৸ Where two or more married women are in the same household, either on a temporary or permanent basis, it is customary for each to light Sabbath candles separately.

ଓ৸ When the woman of a house is absent or is incapable of performing the ritual, or where a man lives alone, he lights the Sabbath candles himself. Although the woman is given priority in fulfilling this religious duty, lighting Sabbath candles is a requirement related to the general observance of the Sabbath and is a religious duty incumbent upon both men and women.

ଓ৸ The Sabbath candles are lighted approximately twenty minutes before sundown. In the absence of a Jewish calendar listing candlelighting time for a particular geographic area, the time of sundown can be found in the daily local newspaper and the candlelighting time determined accordingly. Once the time of sundown passes, the candles may no longer be lit.

ଓ৸ It is permissible for the candles to be lit somewhat earlier. This is often done in the summer months when the day is particularly long and the Sabbath might be ushered in an hour or so earlier.

ଓ৸ The minimum number of candles lighted is two. They symbolically represent the two forms of the fourth commandment: *Zachor—Remember* the Sabbath day to keep it holy (Exodus 20:8), and *Shamor—Observe* the Sabbath day to keep it holy (Deut. 5:12).

ଓ৸ There are some family or local traditions where three or more candles are lighted or that call for an additional Sabbath candle for every child born. One is free to light more than the minimum if one chooses to do so.

8⤳ White candles intended specifically for the Sabbath eve are generally available. If they are not available, any festive dinner candles of whatever shape, design, or color may be used instead. The only condition is that they be large enough to burn during the Sabbath meal and well into nightfall.

Although any candelabra are permissible, it is preferable to have a pair of candlesticks or candelabra reserved specifically for the Sabbath.

8⤳ Although proper ritual procedure requires that the recitation of a blessing always precedes the performance of the mitzvah, in this instance *the candles are lighted first and the benediction is recited afterward*. The reason is obvious. Recital of the blessing formally ushers in the Sabbath after which it is forbidden to light a flame. The procedure is to close one's eyes or cover them with the hands while the benediction is recited. When eyes are opened after the blessing, the sight of the Sabbath lights brings forth the delight that is actually regarded as the culmination of the mitzvah.

8⤳ The blessing recited for the Sabbath candles is:

בָּרוּךְ אַתָּה יְיָ אֱלֹהֵינוּ מֶלֶךְ הָעוֹלָם, אֲשֶׁר קִדְּשָׁנוּ בְּמִצְוֹתָיו וְצִוָּנוּ לְהַדְלִיק נֵר שֶׁל שַׁבָּת.

Baruch ata adonai elohainu melech ha-olam asher kidshanu b'mitzvotav v'tzivanu l'hadlik ner shel shabbat.

Blessed art Thou, Lord our God, King of the universe who has sanctified us with His commandments and commanded us to kindle the Sabbath lights.

8⤳ After the candles are lit, it is proper to greet the others in the household with the words *Shabbat Shalom*. Everyone responds likewise.

8⤳ The Sabbath candles should be lighted on the table where the Sabbath meal is eaten. If this is impractical, it should at least be done in the same room.

(Under exceptional circumstances, as when staying at a hotel or

73

resort, or when confined for illness, etc., this requirement is waived, and the candles may be lighted wherever it is most practical to do so.)

The Sabbath Table

&❧ The table set for the Sabbath should contain, in addition to the candles, the following special items set at the head of the table:

· Two unsliced Sabbath loaves known as *hallah*. They are covered by a napkin or cloth. (Specially decorated hallah covers are available and are recommended for use because they help beautify the Sabbath table.)
· A Kiddush Cup.

The Evening Services

&❧ The Friday evening service is known as Welcoming the Sabbath, or *Kabbalat Shabbat*. It is generally scheduled to begin in synagogues shortly after the Sabbath candles are lighted at home.

&❧ Although women are not obliged to attend these services, (and after arduous preparations for the Sabbath they may be tired and deserving of the "breathing spell" between the candlelighting and dinner time) the Sabbath spirit is enhanced if the women too welcome the Sabbath with the appropriate prayers at home. Many attend the services if they can.

&❧ The male members of the household as well as all the children should make every effort to attend the synagogue for these Friday evening services, which begin prior to sundown. These services usually last between forty and fifty minutes and possess a spiritual quality that is unique. In many synagogues, these services are conducted with much congregational singing and provide an inspiring atmosphere in which to usher in the Sabbath.

&❧ Although for the woman it is the lighting of the Sabbath candles which marks the precise moment of ushering in the Sabbath, for the male it is the recitation of the special Psalm for the Sabbath day, *Mizmor Shir L'yom HaShabbat*, during the *Kabbalat Shabbat* service which marks that precise moment.

ই় Illness, extremely foul weather, or great distance from the synagogue are legitimate reasons for not attending the services. In such
instances, the Sabbath prayers must be said at home.

ই় Where the prayers are said at home, they should be said after
the lighting of the Sabbath candles. They should be chanted by the
members of the household in much the same manner as in the synagogue. The Amidah prayer is said quietly while standing at attention
and facing in the direction of the land of Israel (*Eretz Yisrael*).

ই় The custom of "Late Friday Evening Services" has become widespread in the United States. These are generally scheduled for about
8:30 in the evening—after dinner, from late fall to early spring. There
is no objection to these "Services" if they are intended to serve as
an *Oneg Shabbat* gathering where some traditional Sabbath songs
are sung; where an address of a religious or educational nature or any
appropriate message is heard from a guest speaker or the rabbi; where
refreshments are served during a social hour. Depending upon the
community and the locality, there is a place and sometimes even
a need for such a program, especially in the winter months when
the evenings are long.

These "Services" must not, however, serve as a substitute for the
authentic sundown service which ushers in the Sabbath in the year,
nor for the regular Sabbath morning service.

But if the Sabbath is ushered in on time with due regard to the
Sabbath laws and the Sabbath day is also properly observed, the late
Friday evening hours may be made as spiritually rewarding by the
pursuit of activities other than a "late service." (See pp. 81–82.)

The Home Ritual and Kiddush

ই় Upon returning home from the synagogue following the Friday
evening *Kabbalat Shabbat* and *maariv* service (or upon concluding
these prayers at home), it is customary for the family to gather about
the Sabbath table to sing the traditional *Shalom Aleichem.**

---

* I suggest that recordings of the Sabbath melodies and other traditional songs be
used as a way of learning some of them. Several suggestions will be found in the Suggestions for Further Reading and Study (page 321).

&ᴗ It is then customary for the father to bless his children.* The mother may also perform this rite. The ritual is a simple one. The father places both his hands on the bowed head of a child (or where two children are simultaneously being blessed—one hand on the head of each child) and says:

יְשִׂמְךָ אֱלֹהִים כְּאֶפְרַיִם וְכִמְנַשֶּׁה.

To a son(s): May God make you as Ephraim and Menasheh.

יְשִׂמֵךְ אֱלֹהִים כְּשָׂרָה, רִבְקָה, רָחֵל וְלֵאָה.

To a daughter(s): May God make you as Sarah, Rebecca, Rachel, and Leah.

Followed by:

יְבָרֶכְךָ יְיָ וְיִשְׁמְרֶךָ. יָאֵר יְיָ פָּנָיו אֵלֶיךָ וִיחֻנֶּךָּ. יִשָּׂא יְיָ פָּנָיו אֵלֶיךָ, וְיָשֵׂם לְךָ שָׁלוֹם

May the Lord bless you and protect you. May the Lord shine His countenance upon you and be gracious to you. May the Lord favor you and grant you peace.

&ᴗ The Sabbath Kiddush (Sanctification) is then recited by the male head of the household while holding a full cup of wine in his hands. It should be his intention to say the Kiddush on behalf of all those present. Different customs prevail on whether everyone stands or sits during the Kiddush. Either way is correct.

It is a Torah (Biblical) requirement to sanctify the Sabbath with a verbal declaration, for it is written "Remember the Sabbath day to sanctify it" (Exodus 20:8). Our Sages taught that this "remembering" requires the recitation of a declaration of Sanctification (Kiddush) at the beginning of the Sabbath, and a declaration of Separation or Division (Havdalah) at the conclusion of the Sabbath.

&ᴗ The Sages ruled that this "remembrance" (recitation of Kiddush and Havdalah) preferably be over a cup of wine, the traditional symbol of joy and of a festive occasion.

---

* The role of the father as a spiritual guide to his children is enhanced by this ceremony. A child who steps before his or her father each week to receive a blessing is bound to view the spiritual authority and role of the father in a more positive and desirable light.

Although this traditional custom has fallen into widespread disregard in the United States, the tendency for parental authority to break down among modern families provides additional reason for its revival.

The Sabbath: An Island in Time

&⸫ If one has no wine, the Kiddush may be said over the two *whole* Sabbath loaves (*hallot*). The blessing for bread is then substituted for the blessing for wine.

וַיְהִי עֶרֶב וַיְהִי בֹקֶר

יוֹם הַשִּׁשִּׁי. וַיְכֻלּוּ הַשָּׁמַיִם וְהָאָרֶץ וְכָל צְבָאָם. וַיְכַל אֱלֹהִים
בַּיּוֹם הַשְּׁבִיעִי מְלַאכְתּוֹ אֲשֶׁר עָשָׂה, וַיִּשְׁבֹּת בַּיּוֹם הַשְּׁבִיעִי מִכָּל
מְלַאכְתּוֹ אֲשֶׁר עָשָׂה. וַיְבָרֶךְ אֱלֹהִים אֶת יוֹם הַשְּׁבִיעִי וַיְקַדֵּשׁ
אֹתוֹ, כִּי בוֹ שָׁבַת מִכָּל מְלַאכְתּוֹ אֲשֶׁר בָּרָא אֱלֹהִים לַעֲשׂוֹת.

סָבְרִי מָרָנָן וְרַבּוֹתַי.

בָּרוּךְ אַתָּה יְיָ אֱלֹהֵינוּ מֶלֶךְ הָעוֹלָם, בּוֹרֵא פְּרִי הַגָּפֶן.

בָּרוּךְ אַתָּה יְיָ אֱלֹהֵינוּ מֶלֶךְ הָעוֹלָם, אֲשֶׁר קִדְּשָׁנוּ בְּמִצְוֹתָיו
וְרָצָה בָנוּ, וְשַׁבַּת קָדְשׁוֹ בְּאַהֲבָה וּבְרָצוֹן הִנְחִילָנוּ, זִכָּרוֹן
לְמַעֲשֵׂה בְרֵאשִׁית. כִּי הוּא יוֹם תְּחִלָּה לְמִקְרָאֵי קֹדֶשׁ, זֵכֶר
לִיצִיאַת מִצְרָיִם. כִּי בָנוּ בָחַרְתָּ וְאוֹתָנוּ קִדַּשְׁתָּ מִכָּל הָעַמִּים,
וְשַׁבַּת קָדְשְׁךָ בְּאַהֲבָה וּבְרָצוֹן הִנְחַלְתָּנוּ. בָּרוּךְ אַתָּה יְיָ,
מְקַדֵּשׁ הַשַּׁבָּת.

It was evening and it was morning.

On the sixth day the heavens and the earth and all their hosts were completed. For by the seventh day God had completed his work which he had made, and he rested on the seventh day from all his work which he had made. Then God blessed the seventh day and hallowed it, because on it he rested from all his work which God had created to function thenceforth.

Blessed art Thou, Lord our God, King of the universe who creates the fruit of the vine.

Blessed art Thou, Lord our God, King of the universe, who has sanctified us with His commandments and has been pleased with us; in love and favour has given us His holy Sabbath as a heritage, a memorial of the creation—that day being also the first among the holy festivals, in remembrance of the exodus from Egypt. Thou hast chosen us and hallowed us above all nations, and in love and favour hast given us thy holy Sabbath as a heritage. Blessed art Thou, O Lord, who hallowest the Sabbath.

ৠ Although any glass or cup containing a minimum of 3.3 ounces may be used for the wine, it is preferable to use a ritual Kiddush cup, as it enhances the mitzvah.

ৠ One must be careful to use only a kosher wine. The wine must be made from grapes. The traditional blessing over wine, *borai pri hagafen*, refers only to the fruit of the vine. One cannot use for Kiddush wines made from other fruits or vegetables. In the absence of grape wine, Kiddush is said over the hallah.

ৠ A person who may not drink fermented wine for reasons of health, may use a non-fermented natural kosher grape juice. The same blessing as over fermented wine is recited.

ৠ Women are also required to fulfill the mitzvah of Kiddush. This they do by listening while it is being said and answering "Amen" at its conclusion. In the absence of a male adult in the household, the woman recites the Kiddush.

ৠ Although one male adult may recite the Kiddush on behalf of all present, if there are others at the table who wish to recite the Kiddush for themselves, they may do so.

ৠ It is proper to encourage young boys who have learned to read Hebrew to recite the Kiddush for themselves as a means of training them in the Sabbath ritual. (For the same reason, young girls may light small Sabbath candles of their own, together with their mothers.)

ৠ While the Kiddush is being recited, the hallot are kept covered with the hallah cover.

ৠ After the recitation of the Kiddush, those present respond with "Amen." The one who recited it should drink from the wine and then give some of it to all those present. The others need not recite the blessing.

ৠ Following the Kiddush, everyone ritually washes for the meal. This is done by filling a glass, cup, or other vessel with water and pouring the water over the right hand, then over the left hand. Before the hands are wiped dry on a towel, the following benediction is said:

בָּרוּךְ אַתָּה יְיָ אֱלֹהֵינוּ מֶלֶךְ הָעוֹלָם, אֲשֶׁר קִדְּשָׁנוּ בְּמִצְוֹתָיו וְצִוָּנוּ עַל נְטִילַת יָדַיִם.

Baruch ata adonai elohainu melech ha-olam asher kidshanu b'mitzvotav v'tzivanu al netilat yadayim.

Blessed art Thou, Lord our God, King of the universe who has sanctified us with His commandments and commanded us concerning the washing of the hands.

৪৯ Without further talk or interruption, the ritual washing is immediately followed by sitting down to the table. The head of the household uncovers the two hallot, lifting them momentarily while reciting the blessing over the bread:

בָּרוּךְ אַתָּה יְיָ אֱלֹהֵינוּ מֶלֶךְ הָעוֹלָם, הַמּוֹצִיא לֶחֶם מִן הָאָרֶץ.

Baruch ata adonai elohainu melech ha-olam ha-motzi lehem min ha-aretz.

Blessed art Thou, Lord our God, King of the universe who brings forth bread from the earth.

The hallah is then cut and slices distributed to all at the table. The others need not repeat the blessing over the bread if they responded "Amen" when they heard it and if the head of the household had them in mind.

৪৯ The two hallot on the table must be whole. They are known as *lehem mishne*, commemorating the double portion of the manna that the Israelites gathered on the sixth day (Exodus 16:22) which was to last them through the Sabbath.

Like the two candles, the two hallot are also said to symbolize the two forms of the fourth commandment: "*Remember* the Sabbath day" and "*Observe* the Sabbath day to keep it holy."

In the event that two whole hallot are unavailable, either rolls or matzot may be used in place of either one hallah or both hallot. It is only for the initial blessing (by the head of the household) that whole loaves (of hallot, bread, rolls, or matzot) are required. Sliced bread or sliced hallot may be used for the rest of the meal.

৪৯ The Sabbath meal should be a festive one. What is served depends upon a family's preferences. Nonetheless, the fact that the meal must be prepared in advance and may not be cooked on the spot obviously eliminates freshly fried, grilled or barbecued dishes from the Sabbath menu.

ᢡ It is customary to brighten the Sabbath dinner by the singing of *zmirot* between the courses of the meal. The zmirot are poems, most of them written during the Middle Ages, that rhapsodize the Sabbath rest and the Sabbath glory. Numerous melodies for each of these songs are extant and they lend an added dimension of cheer to the Sabbath meal. One need not limit himself to these "official" zmirot, but may choose from among many songs and melodies which have some religious or spiritual theme.

ᢡ It is obligatory to give thanks to God after having eaten, in fulfillment of the Torah requirement that "You shall eat and be satisfied and bless the Lord" (Deut. 8:10). The grace after meals (*birkat hamazon*) for which popular chants have developed should climax the meal. Unlike the rest of the week when the *birkat hamazon* is likely to be said in haste and without song, on the Sabbath it should be chanted and said without haste. Even the preschool child will soon enough learn the words of the prayer and heartily join in. (See short form of grace on page 170.)

ᢡ It is religiously praiseworthy to do those things on the Sabbath which delight the soul and which provide a measure of pleasure and joy, as long as they do not constitute a violation of the Sabbath (see pp. 89–96). Violations of the Sabbath, in spirit or in deed, can never be justified on the grounds that "they are a delight to me"; "they give me pleasure"; or "I enjoy them." Such rationalizations invite the dissipation of the unique spiritual qualities connected with the Sabbath. Since different people enjoy doing different things and favor a wide range of recreational pursuits, such rationalizations are tantamount to the total secularization of this "day of rest," and in effect, destroy the Sabbath.

Activities that "give pleasure" on the Sabbath must take place within the framework of the spiritual purposes of the Sabbath, and in consideration of the special and distinct *holiness* of the day. Such activities must not trespass into the tasks forbidden on the Sabbath by the Torah or rabbinic legislation. It is inevitable that in disregarding the halakhic discipline of the Torah, the special "Sabbath joy" and the unique "Sabbath spirit" will invariably dissipate.

LEISURE ACTIVITIES FOR THE SABBATH

ঌ The study of Torah should constitute one of the leisure activities that one pursues on the Sabbath. The association of Torah study with the purpose of the Sabbath is of ancient origin. The Midrash Tanhuma questions why the term, *vayakhel*, "And Moses *gathered together* all the children of Israel" appears only prior to the paragraph dealing with the observance of the Sabbath (Exodus 35:1) and nowhere else in the Torah. The Sages give the following answer: "It is as though God said to Moses, 'Go down and gather together great assemblies on every Sabbath to teach Torah in public.' " The Sages also said: "The Sabbath and festivals were only given to Israel to provide them with the opportunity to study Torah." Since most people are busy with their work all week, they have no time to engage in study. But on the Sabbaths and festivals they are at leisure to engage in Torah study . . . each person according to his own level and ability.

Even though the public reading of the Torah scroll during Sabbath morning services enables one to fulfill this requirement formally (this is precisely the reason the Torah is read in the synagogue on the Sabbath), it is nevertheless important for every person to advance his knowledge and understanding of every facet of Jewish faith and Jewish life continuously. The Sabbath provides an ideal opportunity to devote a few undisturbed and quiet hours each week for reading, for individual or group study. "I don't have time" is no excuse on the Sabbath.

It is a time-honored tradition that the *weekly Torah portion be reviewed* with commentaries. Those who possess the background may spend their time on Talmud or Codes. Others may prefer studying the abridged codes of Jewish law, or different books of the Bible. Still others may choose to read in Jewish history or Jewish philosophy. Whether one only reviews previously studied matter or delves into fresh material, whether one is a scholar or has only a limited Jewish education, some religious study is a vital element in the sanctity of the Sabbath.

The relationship between Sabbath observance and Jewish knowledge should not be lightly dismissed. A Jewish community which discards the Sabbath or gives it only token recognition sooner or later becomes a community that is also Jewishly ignorant, regardless of other educational programs.

ह्∾ Depending upon the time of the year and one's area of residence, one or more of the following activities may also occupy the time of different members of a family during those few leisure Sabbath hours that are left after attending the synagogue and enjoying the Sabbath meal:

· Reading and/or studying.
· Discussing and/or reviewing with children the things they have been studying and doing all week.
· Leisure stroll.
· Socializing with neighbors or nearby friends or family.
· Attending lectures, forums, or study groups organized by a synagogue or other organization.
· Getting extra hours of sleep and rest by getting to bed earlier than usual or by enjoying a Sabbath afternoon siesta.
· Home games such as chess or checkers and similar activities are permitted. Children who study all week should be permitted to devote some time to such games.
· In many communities, activities in the Sabbath spirit are organized for the children or young people. Group singing, Israeli or other folk dancing, discussion groups, refreshments and socializing are typical programs enjoyed. These are usually sponsored by youth organizations.

ह्∾ These same activities are also suitable for the Sabbath afternoon hours, following the services and the Sabbath meals.

ह्∾ Rather than feeling bored, as though one's activities are restricted, a Sabbath observer should find that the day thus spent is a tranquil delight, and that the hours at his disposal, even given the limited choice, are too few.

THE SABBATH DAY

The Morning Services

ह्∾ The Sabbath morning services at the synagogue are the most elaborate as well as the lengthiest of the week, and participating in them is important to the day's observance.

82

The Sabbath: An Island in Time

ટ≫ The length of the Sabbath service is due to several factors:

· The reading of the weekly portion of the Torah is a central feature of the Sabbath service.
· The delivery of a message or sermon by the rabbi is a commonplace and widely followed practice in most synagogues.
· It is a widespread and laudable practice for the congregation to sing many of the prayers.
· Though it enhances the enjoyment of the main service of the week, where a cantor and choir officiate, their liturgical renditions also tend to lengthen the services.
· Special ceremonies and honors sometimes accompany the observance of a Bar-Mitzvah in the synagogue.

ટ≫ In the United States most traditional congregations begin their Sabbath services sometime between 8:30 A.M. and 9:00 A.M. They usually last about three to three and a half hours, till about noon. In Israel, most synagogues begin their Sabbath morning services at about 8:00 A.M. and they usually last about two to two and a half hours.*

In some communities in the United States and Israel, some people prefer to attend an early morning Sabbath service at 6:30 A.M. which usually lasts till about 8:30 A.M.

Sabbath Morning Kiddush

ટ≫ Following the Sabbath morning services, Kiddush is again recited. This is done either at the synagogue or at home before sitting down to the Sabbath meal.

ટ≫ This Kiddush is simpler in form than the Friday evening one. The simple blessing over the wine is sufficient, although in order to lend additional significance, it is customary to precede it with one or more verses from the Torah pertaining to the Sabbath. An appropriate form for this Kiddush is:

---

* The shorter services are not due to the elimination of prayers. It is due to the fact that they are not conducted by official cantors but by members of the congregation; there are no sermons delivered, and special honors and ceremonies are held to a minimum.

וְשָׁמְרוּ בְנֵי יִשְׂרָאֵל אֶת הַשַּׁבָּת, לַעֲשׂוֹת אֶת הַשַּׁבָּת לְדֹרֹתָם בְּרִית עוֹלָם. בֵּינִי וּבֵין בְּנֵי יִשְׂרָאֵל אוֹת הִיא לְעוֹלָם, כִּי שֵׁשֶׁת יָמִים עָשָׂה יְיָ אֶת הַשָּׁמַיִם וְאֶת הָאָרֶץ, וּבַיּוֹם הַשְּׁבִיעִי שָׁבַת וַיִּנָּפַשׁ.

עַל כֵּן בֵּרַךְ יְיָ אֶת יוֹם הַשַּׁבָּת וַיְקַדְּשֵׁהוּ.

בָּרוּךְ אַתָּה יְיָ אֱלֹהֵינוּ מֶלֶךְ הָעוֹלָם, בּוֹרֵא פְּרִי הַגָּפֶן.

The children of Israel shall keep the Sabbath, to observe the Sabbath throughout their generations as an everlasting covenant. It is a sign between Me and the children of Israel forever that in six days the Lord made heaven and earth, and on the seventh day He rested and ceased from His work (Exodus 31:16–17).

. . . Therefore the Lord blessed the Sabbath day and hallowed it (Exodus 20:11).

Blessed art Thou, Lord our God, King of the universe who creates the fruit of the vine.

⁏❧ Wine is preferred, but any other alcoholic beverage may also be used for the morning Kiddush. If it is, the following blessing is substituted for the one over wine:

בָּרוּךְ אַתָּה יְיָ אֱלֹהֵינוּ מֶלֶךְ הָעוֹלָם, שֶׁהַכֹּל נִהְיֶה בִּדְבָרוֹ.

Baruch ata adonai elohainu melech ha-olam she-hakol nee-yeh bidvaro.

Blessed art Thou, Lord our God, King of the universe by whose will all things exist.

⁏❧ Since it is not permissible to eat breakfast before the shachrit morning prayers, except for some juice or a cup of tea or coffee, the Sabbath morning Kiddush serves as the entree to the partaking of other food as well, be it a light repast or a full meal.

The Three Sabbath Meals

⁏❧ It is a special mitzvah to eat three meals (*shalosh seudot*) on the Sabbath. Since one meal is on Friday evening, the other two are taken during the day. In communities where the Sabbath services last most of the morning, the second main Sabbath meal is eaten at about noon or shortly thereafter. The third meal, known as the *seudah shlishit*, is then eaten in the very late afternoon, before sundown. This meal is usually a simple meal, but should include bread or *hallah*.*

৯ The same procedure for washing, breaking bread (two Sabbath loaves), zmirot, reciting grace, etc., that were followed at the Friday evening meal are also followed for the other two Sabbath meals.

CONCLUDING THE SABBATH

The Ending of the Day

৯ The Sabbath day ends, not at sundown when the sun sets, but at nightfall when the stars come out. *Nightfall* begins when at least three stars are visible in the heavens. Calculations have, however, long replaced the visual method of determining the onset of nightfall.

The time between sundown (*shkiat hahama*) and nightfall (*tset hakokhavim*) is traditionally neither day nor night. In Hebrew it is called "between the suns" (*bayn hashmashot*). Since its status is doubtful, it is automatically attached to the Sabbath, so that there shall be no question of Sabbath violation. The *bayn hashmashot* period of Friday evening is also attached to the Sabbath for the same reason.

৯ The span of time between sundown and nightfall (darkness) depends upon the latitude. At the equator the two occur almost simultaneously, but as the distance from the equator increases, the span of time of bayn hashmashot increases. As one travels northward from the equator, nightfall gets later. As one travels southward toward the equator, nightfall comes quicker. (In the United States, along the New York City latitude, nightfall occurs about thirty to forty minutes after sundown.)

It is proper to check with the local rabbi or synagogue, or consult a local Jewish calendar as to the exact time the Sabbath ends.

---

* In many synagogues, it is customary to provide the worshippers with this *seudah shlishit* at the synagogue itself between the afternoon (*minha*) and evening (*maariv*) services.

६► Even so, many devout Jews and communities follow the principle that it is a special mitzvah "to add from the secular to the sacred, from the weekday to the Sabbath day," and just as the Sabbath is inaugurated even before sundown so the Sabbath is not concluded until some time after nightfall, with the period of time varying. The precious "guest" is detained for just a little while longer before he is allowed to leave.

Havdalah

६► Just as the recitation of Kiddush is required for Friday evening so the recitation of Havdalah is required to mark the conclusion of the Sabbath.

६► Havdalah, which means Division or Separation, may be said any time after nightfall. In the synagogue, it follows the brief evening (*maariv*) service. It should also be said at home for the benefit of those members of the household who hadn't heard it.

६► The Havdalah is said over a cup of wine, with additional blessings recited for fragrant spices (*b'samim*) and light (*ner*). The symbolic significance of the fragrant spices is that the sweet smell—regarded in rabbinic sources as a delight for the soul, rather than for the body—refreshes in some small way, making up for the loss of the "additional soul" which takes leave at the end of the Sabbath and for the loss of spiritual strength this entails.

As for the light, since it is not permitted to be kindled on the Sabbath, it was considered proper that its very first use after the Sabbath be for a religious purpose. It also symbolizes—as the first act of the week—the first act of creation which marked the first day of the week when God said, "Let there be light."

६► If wine is unavailable for Havdalah, other beverages such as beer or liqueurs may be substituted.

६► Special fragrant spice mixtures for use at Havdalah are available at Jewish religious supplies stores. The spices are generally kept in decorative and artistically designed containers of silver, brass, chromium, or wood. These containers are referred to as *b'samim boxes*.

६► The Havdalah candle is a special candle that is made of two or more braided wicks, since the flame of a torch is required and not a regular candle. They come in various sizes and colors. If a special Havdalah candle is not available, two ordinary candles may be used if they are held in an upside down v shape, like this ∧ so that the flames of the two candles come together, providing a torch-like effect.

෫ The candle is given to one member of the household to hold (usually a child) while the Havdalah is recited.

෫ After filling the cup with wine (or other beverage) to the brim and lighting the Havdalah candle, the head of the household raises the cup of wine in his right hand and says:

בָּרוּךְ אַתָּה יְיָ אֱלֹהֵינוּ מֶלֶךְ הָעוֹלָם, בּוֹרֵא פְּרִי הַגָּפֶן
(שֶׁהַכֹּל נִהְיֶה בִּדְבָרוֹ).

Baruch ata adonai elohainu melech ha-olam borai pri hagafen (she-hakol nee-yeh bidvaro).

Blessed art Thou, Lord our God, King of the universe who creates the fruit of the vine (by whose will all things exist).

· The b'samim box is then picked up and the following blessing recited:

בָּרוּךְ אַתָּה יְיָ אֱלֹהֵינוּ מֶלֶךְ הָעוֹלָם, בּוֹרֵא מִינֵי בְשָׂמִים.

Baruch ata adonai elohainu melech ha-olam borai minai b'sa-mim.

Blessed art Thou, Lord our God, King of the universe who creates diverse spices.

As this blessing is concluded, the fragrant spices are smelled.

· Turning back to look at the flame of the Havdalah candle, the following blessing is then recited:

בָּרוּךְ אַתָּה יְיָ אֱלֹהֵינוּ מֶלֶךְ הָעוֹלָם, בּוֹרֵא מְאוֹרֵי הָאֵשׁ.

Baruch ata adonai elohainu melech ha-olam borai m'orai ha-esh.

Blessed art Thou, Lord our God, King of the universe who creates the lights of the fire.

As this blessing is concluded, it is customary to momentarily examine one's hands or at least the right hand by the light of the flame so as to derive some immediate use from the light, that the blessing not be said in vain.

· The cup of wine is then picked up again and the essence of the Havdalah prayer is said:

בָּרוּךְ אַתָּה יְיָ אֱלֹהֵינוּ מֶלֶךְ הָעוֹלָם, הַמַּבְדִּיל בֵּין קֹדֶשׁ לְחֹל, בֵּין אוֹר לְחֹשֶׁךְ, בֵּין יִשְׂרָאֵל לָעַמִּים, בֵּין יוֹם הַשְּׁבִיעִי לְשֵׁשֶׁת יְמֵי הַמַּעֲשֶׂה. בָּרוּךְ אַתָּה יְיָ, הַמַּבְדִּיל בֵּין קֹדֶשׁ לְחֹל.

Baruch ata adonai elohainu melech ha-olam, hamavdil bayn kodesh l'hol, bayn or l'hoshech, bayn Yisrael l'amim, bayn yom hashvi-i leshaishet y'may hamaaseh. Baruch ata adonai, hamavdil bayn kodesh l'hol.

Blessed art Thou, Lord our God, King of the universe who makes a division between the sacred and secular, between light and darkness, between Israel and the other nations, between the seventh day and the six working days. Blessed art Thou, Lord, who makes a distinction between the sacred and the secular.

· The Siddur contains an introductory paragraph composed of selected Biblical verses that is customarily recited prior to the blessing over the wine. If one is proficient in Hebrew, this paragraph beginning with the words *Hinei ayl yeshuati* should be included in the Havdalah.

৪৯ If there is no adult male in a household to recite the Havdalah, the woman should perform the mitzvah.

৪৯ If a woman has some weekday task to do immediately after nightfall (lighting a fire, etc.) and she has not yet heard the Havdalah, she should first make the following declaration:

בָּרוּךְ הַמַּבְדִּיל בֵּין קֹדֶשׁ לְחֹל.

Baruch hamavdil bayn kodesh l'hol.

Blessed is He who divided the sacred from the secular.

This formally concludes the Sabbath for her.

TASKS FORBIDDEN ON THE SABBATH

By Biblical Law

ஓ In the Ten Commandments as well as elsewhere in the Torah, Israel is repeatedly cautioned against performing any manner of *melakha* (usually translated as *work*) on the Sabbath. Not only are there negative commandments: "You shall not do any *melakha* (work), neither you, nor your son, nor your daughter. . . ." (Exodus 20:10; Deut. 5:12–14), but there are also positive commandments "to sanctify" the day, to make it "holy," to "remember" it, to "observe" it, to "rest" on it (Exodus 23:12).

ஓ The Hebrew concept or definition of melakha is not at all identical with what is meant in English by the word "work." It is therefore preferable either to use the Hebrew term consistently or to translate it simply as a "task forbidden on the Sabbath."
The term "work" generally implies either (1) an activity that one does in the course of one's employment, profession, or occupation; or (2) an activity that involves great physical exertion. Neither of these definitions form the underlying basis for what constitutes melakha according to the Torah. If it did, and "work" meant to refrain only from such activities that come under either of these two categories, Sabbath rest would obviously differ for every person. What one does gainfully, another does for leisure. What one enjoys doing, another detests. What is hard for one is easy for another. According to such definitions, a rabbi or teacher should not be permitted to give any instruction on the Sabbath, and it should be forbidden (for the weak) to move a heavy burden from one spot to another inside one's home. Yet neither of these activities is forbidden as melakha. Furthermore, on the basis of such definitions of "work," Sabbath rest loses all its spiritual significance and implications.

ஓ The Oral Torah defines what Scripture means by the term melakha. It specifically sets forth the tasks or activities prohibited under this category. It does not leave it up to each person to define for himself what should or should not constitute melakha. If it did, there might as well be no Sabbath law at all. Any law, in any legal system, that is vague and obscure and which can be interpreted in any way one sees fit, is a useless law and serves no purpose.

Since there is a purpose to the Sabbath, and there *are* definite spiritual aims to be reached as well as spiritual concepts to be stressed, the Torah's delineation as to what does or does not constitute melakha is the key to understanding, appreciating, and observing the Sabbath.

&❧ The mere development of modern technology with its new instruments, machines, and methods, which were unknown when the Torah was given or when the Sages of the Talmud lived, does not automatically make the Sabbath laws obsolete. On the contrary, a law that is alive, and Jewish law has always been and continues to be "a living law," has within itself the built-in power and creativity that enables the "judges of the law" to continually keep applying the law to new conditions. New conditions and circumstances are continually being judged on the basis of the legal principles and concepts upon which the law rests.

New developments are thus continually brought into the framework of the Torah's commandments. If that had not been the case, Judaism would have perished a long time ago. The theoretical concepts and points of law that enable rabbis to render judgment as to whether some new development is permitted or forbidden according to the Torah—be it in questions pertaining to the Sabbath or any other area—obviously require great study. Suffice it for us to say that their authority in such matters is based on the passage in Deut. 17:9–11: "And you shall come . . . to the judge that shall be in those days . . . And you shall do according to the tenor of the sentence . . . You shall observe to do according to all that they shall teach you. . . ."

&❧ The Mishna (Shabbat 7:2) lists thirty-nine categories of activities regarded as melakha. These, as well as all other tasks that operate on the same principle or have a similar purpose are forbidden on the Sabbath by Biblical law.

&❧ Some common activities forbidden on the Sabbath because they constitute melakha, as defined by the Torah:

· Cooking and baking (even if it does not involve lighting a fire);
· Grinding, fine chopping, straining;
· Washing clothes (by hand or machine);

· Knitting, crocheting, embroidering;
· Sewing, pasting, gluing;
· Constructing or repairing—the entire range of building operations and household repair tasks;
· Writing (or erasing), drawing, painting, coloring, typing;
· Hair cutting, shaving, paring nails;
· Kindling (or extinguishing) a fire—starting a fresh fire or lighting a fire from another already burning; making a fire larger or smaller (by poking, adding or drawing off fuel, wood, oil, and paper, or by mechanical control knobs); lighting a candle, striking a match or a lighter; smoking;
· Cutting or tearing; this does not apply to the cutting of food;
· Fishing, trapping;
· Garden care or lawn maintenance—digging, planting, fertilizing, weeding, cutting, trimming, mowing, picking fruits or plucking flowers or leaves, watering (even of indoor plants);
· Carrying; pushing or moving an object more than six feet within "the public domain," or from a "private domain" into a "public domain" and vice versa.

ह‍ The Sabbath Stove:

The prohibition of cooking does not mean that we may eat only cold food on the Sabbath. On the contrary, no Sabbath is considered complete without some hot food. This result is achieved by the "Sabbath stove." This means that the stove is arranged *before the Sabbath* as follows: A sheet of tin or aluminum (or any metal conductor of heat) is placed over the burners which are lit before the Sabbath (set at a moderate or low flame, or low temperature if electric), and allowed to remain on throughout the Sabbath. Hot cooked food and an urn of hot water or tea kettle, cooked before the Sabbath, is allowed to remain on the stove from before the Sabbath, with the heat so adjusted as to keep them hot during the Sabbath until needed.[5]

By Rabbinic Law

ह‍ The rabbis and Sages, exercising their responsibility to safeguard the Torah laws from being unwittingly, carelessly, or unintentionally violated, enacted "protective legislation" known as *gezerot* (or *shvut* where it relates to the Sabbath) which are as binding upon us as the Torah itself, although the violation of these gezerot is obviously of less severity. These gezerot were designed to forbid those activities which:

· Resembled melakhot in practice, being readily confused with a Biblically forbidden task and thus easily leading to the latter melakha.
· Invariably also involved the actual melakhot, experience having shown that they actually lead to the doing of the melakha itself.

ક≫ Some common activities forbidden on the Sabbath by Rabbinic law:

· Buying and selling. (This was condemned long before by the Hebrew Prophets as a violation of the Sabbath.)
· Riding an animal.
· Boating.
· Playing a musical instrument.
· Switching on or off electric lights or any electrical apparatus such as radio, telephone, television. (Some scholars classify this prohibition as d'oraitha, i.e., derived from Biblical law.)*
· Handling of any items whose use is forbidden on the Sabbath, such as tools, money, writing equipment, various electrical gadgets or machines, candles, matches, money purses. All such items are known as muktzah, i.e., set aside or excluded from Sabbath use and handling.
· Wedding ceremonies.
· Journeying on the Sabbath, even on foot, beyond certain limits (approximately three quarters of a mile beyond the limits of the town or place in which one is spending the Sabbath). The limit is known as "Sabbath boundary" (t'hum shabbat). This is because the spirit of the Sabbath is essentially restful.

ક≫Also shunned are such activities which are not melakha by Biblical definition nor are they activities which may lead to them, but which in the opinion of the Sages constitute "a weekday task" (maasei hol) which detracts from the sanctity of the day (k'dushat hayom). Examples of some common activities in this category:

---

* However, timing devices pre-set before the Sabbath may be used to turn electric lights on or off, or control the continuous automatic operation of an elevator on the Sabbath.

- Heavy jobs such as rearranging the furniture in a house.
- Watching television even when pre-set before the Sabbath.
- Preparing for a post-Sabbath activity.
- Engaging in exercises or athletic activities.
- Reading business correspondence.

Sabbath Restrictions As Applied to Children

৫ Although very young children need not be prevented from engaging in any forbidden Sabbath activity, parents should not encourage them to do it (such as asking them to carry, tear, put on a light, etc.).

৫ As soon as a child is capable of understanding, at perhaps three or four years of age, he should be restrained from engaging in any forbidden Sabbath activity. The example set by parents is the best teacher. A simple quiet reminder, not a harsh rebuke, is the proper way of dealing with forgetfulness.

৫ Since the Sabbath should be related in the child's mind to the spirit of joy, with a sense of excitement, with getting dressed up and being taken to the synagogue, with special sweets and cakes, table hymns, Kiddush and Havdalah, with the assured presence of his parents and the greater attention that gets showered upon him— with all the things that delight the soul of a child—the restrictions are not even felt as burdensome limitations to joyous childhood activities, but rather as a natural and acceptable replacement of one set of activities by another, more delightful, set of activities.

A Word about the Automobile

৫ Of all the technological developments of the twentieth century, the issue of automobile and the Sabbath has emerged as a particular cause célèbre and as a central problem for Judaism in modern life. But among traditional Jews there is no problem at all. The fact is that contemporary rabbinic authorities have unanimously ruled that the *driving* of a motor vehicle constitutes a melakha, that it involves tasks which in essence are forbidden by the Torah. Unlike other rabbinic rulings on which there may be differences of judgment, no competent rabbinic authority and no religious scholar has ever disputed this ruling. As judgments go, it was relatively clear-cut, simple, almost self-evident.

Nor is it a current day extension of the ancient rabbinic ruling which prohibits riding on an animal on the Sabbath, as is often assumed by the masses. The ruling on the automobile has nothing in common with the ruling on riding animals. It is in fact a much graver violation. Whereas the prohibition of riding an animal is clearly a rabbinic enactment intended to serve as "a fence around the Torah," the prohibition of driving is an extension of the Biblical prohibition of kindling fire and burning. Creating sparks and *burning* gas and oil as a *direct* result of the driver's actions are but a few of the more serious objections.

&❧ It is interesting to note that those who are Sabbath observers have never objected to or revolted against this judgment. Those for whom it is unpopular and who find it difficult to observe are those whose entire way of life does not generally include the Sabbath, except perhaps for attending the synagogue. But the Sabbath is much more than going to services.

&❧ Objections do come from those who are not total Sabbath observers in the first place and who move a great distance away from a synagogue and then self-righteously proclaim their inability to get to the synagogue unless they drive there. They indifferently create the problem for themselves and then expect rabbinic authorities to sanction their transgressions on the theory that it will enable them to do a mitzvah, i.e., to attend the synagogue and pray to the Almighty.

&❧ Our Sages long ago enunciated the principle that when a mitzvah is performed by committing a transgression, an *averah*, such a mitzvah is not acceptable in the sight of God. This principle is in keeping with the entire spirit of the Hebrew Prophets.

&❧ A Sabbath observer to whom the entire Sabbath day is precious would in the first place not consider establishing his permanent residence in an area where there is no synagogue within reasonable walking distance. Just as a person might consider proximity to or quality of local schools, public transportation or convenient shopping as conditions of moving into a new area, the Sabbath observer adds the additional condition of a nearby synagogue.

&❧ Where by force of circumstances Sabbath observers are compelled to move out of established neighborhoods into newly developing areas they, like most other Jews, tend to choose areas where they know that other Jews are or soon will be living. But instead of thinking in terms of driving to their old house of worship, they set about organizing a new congregation or minyan of neighborhood people with whom to pray.

Surely, the social desire to worship with old friends, to retain membership in a prestigious congregation in the established neighborhood, to listen to a favorite rabbi or cantor, the economic consideration of a paid-up building contribution do not justify the desecration of the Sabbath and the violation of a commandment of the Lord.

&ᴇ The Sabbath observer who occasionally finds himself a great distance from a synagogue on the Sabbath—when he's vacationing or traveling—can succeed in creating for himself a Sabbath atmosphere, a Sabbath calm, and Sabbath rest no matter where he is, by observing the ritual and laws of the Sabbath as outlined and saying the Sabbath prayers privately. To think that one can, however, manage to be without a synagogue on the Sabbath on a permanent basis and still retain the full quality of the Sabbath experience would be a grave error of judgment.

&ᴇ "Isn't it better to drive to *shul* than not to go at all?" is an often-asked question.

If what the questioner means is—isn't it better for me to drive to shul (Yiddish for synagogue) thereby committing only one major transgression, and spend a few proper hours in the spirit of the Sabbath, instead of driving to the business, or to shopping, or to some recreation, or even instead of staying home and mowing the lawn, tending the garden, repairing the house or answering correspondence during the same hours, then obviously what the rabbi is being asked is to choose between the lesser of two evils. He is really being asked whether it is better to commit just one or many Sabbath violations during a certain time period. The rabbi cannot permit even one, as it is not he but the Torah that forbids it, even though it is quite obvious that it is always preferable to perform fewer transgressions rather than more, that it is always preferable to be guilty of fewer violations of the Sabbath rather than more.

In truth, "Isn't it better, Judge, to run just one red light instead of speeding, making improper turns, and running ten red lights?" would be a parallel sort of question. Obviously, it is better; but one is still guilty and can be convicted for passing the one red light, even though the punishment is less than if one were convicted for many violations or for multiple counts.

But if what the questioner means is—isn't it better for me to drive to shul on the Sabbath, there to join a congregation in public worship instead of staying home and worshipping alone and there observing the Sabbath in deed and in spirit, then the answer is still "No, it is not better!"

Suspension of Sabbath Rules

৪৶When a person's life is in danger, it is a duty to do whatever is necessary to save the life. All Sabbath laws are suspended in matters of serious illness or in any situation in which a person's life is at stake.

৪৶ A physician called upon to render emergency treatment may do all that is necessary to save a life without regard to Sabbath restrictions.

৪৶ The famous dictum that "the Sabbath was given over to man and not man to the Sabbath" (Mekhilta, Ki Tisa:5) was never intended to be exploited as a pretext for catering to one's physical and recreational pleasures nor as a rationale for abrogating or evading the Sabbath laws altogether.

৪৶ "Desecrate one Sabbath, so that he may live to fulfill many Sabbaths" (Yoma 86a).

CHAPTER

6

*The Dietary Laws:
A Diet for the Soul*

Kashrut is the Hebrew word that refers to the Jewish dietary laws. It is a variation of the word *kosher* which means *fit, proper,* or *in accordance with the religious law.* Any food that satisfies the requirements of Jewish law is *fit* for eating; it is *kosher.* The expression kosher-style is misleading and deceptive. Kosher does not stand for an ethnic way of cooking food nor for certain tastes. It is a religious term with very specific religious meaning. Its applicability is determined by set religious criteria. Either a food is kosher or it is not. Wherever the term kosher-style is used, the inference is clear that, although the reference may be to favorite Jewish dishes, they are *not* kosher.

Actually the word kosher in the religious literature is applied to any item that is prepared in accordance with the halakha. Thus we find such expressions as a *kosher Torah, kosher tefillin, kosher mezuzah, kosher talis*—meaning that they have been properly made, satisfy the requirements of Jewish law and are suitable for ritual use. A decent person who lives his life in accordance with the religious teachings in *every respect* is called a *kosher person (adam kasher).* Its colloquial usage in English as meaning "correct," "proper" (e.g., a *kosher* deal) is very true to its classical Hebrew usage. Nevertheless

97

the term is most widely used in relation to food, and it is in that context that we shall use the word kosher. For the same reason, we shall use the term *trefah* to designate everything which is not kosher (although in Jewish law, the term is technically applied only to an animal whose organs are damaged or diseased).

The Jewish dietary laws prescribe not merely a diet for the body but a diet for the soul as well; not so much a diet to maintain one's physical well-being as a diet to maintain one's spiritual well-being.

The faithful Jew observes the laws of kashrut not because he has become endeared of its specific details nor because it provides him with pleasure nor because he considers them good for his health nor because the Bible offers him clear-cut reasons, but because he regards them as Divine commandments and yields his will before the will of the Divine and to the disciplines imposed by his faith. In the words of our Sages: "A man ought not to say 'I do not *wish* to eat of the flesh of the pig' (i.e., because I don't like it). Rather he should say: 'I do wish to do these things, but my Father in Heaven has decreed otherwise.'" Although "the benefit arising from the many inexplicable laws of God is in their practice, and not in the understanding of the motives,"[1] nevertheless the Jew never tires of pursuing his quest to fathom the Divine Mind and to ascertain the reasons that prompted the promulgation of God's laws. For the man of faith is sure that reasons do exist for the Divine decrees even if they are concealed from him.

Before proceeding on this quest, let us first put to rest the very widespread misconception that the kashrut laws are just some ancient health measures. This may have been encouraged by the English translation where the terms "clean" and "unclean" are used to describe the creatures that may and may not be eaten. To the reader of the Torah in translation, the English words "clean" and "unclean" are understood in terms of physical cleanliness and uncleanliness, and the assumption is quickly drawn that it is all a matter of hygiene. The fact that the pig, a commonly-eaten domestic animal to which Jews have had a particular aversion, is an animal which is traditionally pictured as wallowing in dirt and with which the disease of trichinosis is associated only serves to strengthen the misconception. The *special* aversion to the pig is more a result of historical factors, for it was this non-kosher animal that oppressors often tried to force upon the Jew as a means of denying his faith— and our history records many martyrs who suffered death in resistance.

Simple hygiene would not explain the prohibitions against eating the camel, the horse, or the hare (commonly eaten foods in many parts of the world) which are not any dirtier than the cow or the goat. Also, the Torah permits the eating of barnyard fowl (chickens, etc.) which have no great reputation for cleanliness, either.

In fact, the terms used in Hebrew to designate the clean and unclean animals are *tahor* and *tamai*. These are terms that are never used to describe physical cleanliness or uncleanliness, but rather a spiritual or moral state of being. The term *tamai* is used only in relation to moral and religious deficiencies that contaminate the soul and character of man, particularly incest and idol worship, and to characterize the absence of ritual purity. It is often also translated as *defilement*. The creatures designated as *tamai* were not only forbidden as food, but also for sacrificial purposes. The English words *clean* and *unclean* are therefore to be understood as *purity* and *defilement* in a spiritual-ritual sense. A *clean* tongue, a *dirty* mouth or *dirty* mind, "who shall ascend unto the mountain of the Lord, a man with *clean* hands . . . ," all provide examples of how even in English *clean* and *unclean* are used in a moral-spiritual sense. It is in this sense only that the Hebrew terms *tahor* and *tamai*—used consistently in the laws of kashrut—are to be understood.

Even though some parts of the Kosher Code deal with diseases and organ injuries that make the animal trefah, for reasons that are clearly hygienic, or health-related, and while Jews have never questioned the hygienic wholesomeness of the dietary laws (the commandments of the Lord could not but be beneficial to man in every respect, physical as well as spiritual), hygienic or health considerations were not regarded as the prime purpose of kashrut. Furthermore, the limitation on the creatures that could be eaten, the requirements of ritual slaughter, the removal of the blood, the mere non-cooking of meat and milk—all these and more do not at all support the validity of the "ancient health measure" theory.

The only hint or clue that the Biblical text itself provides as to the reason for all these regulations is that in almost every instance where the food laws are referred to in the Torah, we find a call to holiness. In Leviticus, Chapter 11, for instance, following the entire section which lists what may and may not be eaten, the chapter concludes: "For I am the Lord your God; sanctify yourselves and be holy, for I am holy . . ."(Lev. 11:44). Elsewhere, "for you are a people consecrated to the Lord your God. You shall not boil a kid in its mother's milk" (Deut. 14:21), or "You shall be holy men to Me; therefore you shall not eat flesh torn by beasts in the field" (Exodus 22:30). The latter directive is in fact part of a section dealing with acts of justice and righteousness, which too have the purpose of sanctifying the people.

The idea of holiness is reinforced by the Torah's relating these laws to cautions against *defilement* (the opposite of holiness). For not only are the forbidden creatures designated as *tamai*, but Israel is repeatedly warned not to defile itself, not to make itself *tamai* with them (Lev. 11:43–44).

This emphasis upon holiness as the reason or the purpose of these kashrut regulations deserves to be better understood and appreciated; for it is an integral part of the entire picture of Judaism and has many ramifications.

To distinguish between "the beast which is to be eaten and the beast which is not to be eaten" (Lev. 11:47), is an aspect of the broader requirements that Israel learn to "distinguish between the unclean and the clean" not only in food, but in all areas of life— the sexual, the moral, the ethical, the spiritual. The laws of kashrut do not stand isolated from the purposes and goals, from the disciplines and demands that are part of the total picture of Judaism. To treat kashrut in isolation is to distort and misunderstand it.

In Judaism, holiness does not mean an ascetic, saintly withdrawal from life. Holiness does not insist upon the self-denial of any legitimate human pleasures nor the total repression of any bodily drives. But neither does it condone self-indulgence. Gluttony and drunkardness were the hallmarks of the stubborn, rebellious, incorrigible son (Deut. 21:18–21). They were regarded as abominations. The lack of self-control and the readiness to satisfy one's cravings regardless of their merit, propriety or legality were indicative of spiritual weakness and moral decay. Holiness meant and means becoming master over one's passions so that one is in command and control of them, and not they of him.

The one who has been trained to resist cravings for forbidden foods that tempt him may also have strengthened his capacity to resist his cravings for forbidden sexual involvements that may tempt him too; it may also strengthen his capacity to resist forbidden unethical actions that may hold forth the promise of tempting financial or status rewards. The transference of this religious discipline to other areas is not guaranteed, but there is no denying the inherent value in a religious discipline intended to train one to resist bodily drives and urges just to satisfy a craving or experience a pleasure.

The Biblical call to holiness is reflected by Judaism's attempt to elevate the satisfaction of all basic urges—for food, drink, sex—in which we differ not from any beast, onto a level worthy of man. Kashrut is a good example of how Judaism raises even the most mundane acts, the most routine activities, into a religious experience. What narrower minds look upon as a picayune concern with trifling kitchen matters is really an example of how Judaism elevates the mere physical satisfaction of one's appetite into a spiritual act by its emphasis on the everpresent God and our duty to serve Him at all times.

The table upon which food is served became identified in Jewish traditional thought with the Temple altar. "When the Temple stood, sacrifices would secure atonement for an individual; now his table does" (Hagigah 27a), was the way it was put by one Talmudic Sage. (This symbolic identification explains the widespread custom among Jews of not sitting down upon a table; it explains the custom among some of sprinkling salt upon the first morsel of bread eaten—just as was required of the ancient sacrifices; or of removing all knives from the table before the recitation of grace because knives and swords—symbols of war and violence—were forbidden on the altar, a symbol of peace; it is even one of the reasons given for the ritual washing before the meal—which is done not only for reasons of cleanliness but *also* to symbolize the ritual purity required of the priests when they officiated at the offerings.) Even during the meal we are directed to raise the level of the conversation, as befitting the sacred symbolism of the table. "Three who eat together and no words of Torah are exchanged, it is as though they ate from pagan offerings . . . But if three have eaten at a table and spoke words of Torah, it is as though they ate at the table of the Lord" (Avot 2:4). The *birkat hamazon*, the grace after meals is in fact a minimal satisfaction of this requirement. But the imagery is always in terms of an altar; and the very act of eating is a form of offering to God, at which appropriate prayers are recited before and after.

As the table is sanctified through blessings and prayers said around it, and by what goes on it, the Jew is taught that even as he sits down to eat, he must be aware of his Master and serve Him faithfully. As it was forbidden to bring certain animals upon the altar to God, so is it forbidden to do so upon the table. The laws of kashrut provide another example of how Judaism insists that "In *all* your ways, know Him" (Proverbs 3:6).

But this does not sufficiently explain why some things were picked for prohibition and some not. Was it just Divine caprice, and the same disciplinary and spiritual effects might have been achieved if the prohibited were permitted and the permitted prohibited? Torah scholars saw significance to the specific regulations as well. Whereas some saw some practical health benefits, others ascribed only higher moral reasons to the specific regulations, emphasizing that the purpose of holiness was also involved in the specifics. The latter saw the prohibition against the eating of blood and the eating of meat and milk together as a way by which to wean the Jew away from bloodshed and from insensitivity to the feelings of any living creature. How else to explain the prohibition against slaughtering an animal and its offspring on the same day (Lev. 22:28)? Similarly, the inculcation of more refined values was held to be the basis for the prohibition against eating "swarming, crawling things." Dr. Samuel Belkin, in his essay "The Philosophy of Purpose," contends that "the religious philosophy of purposes teaches that certain foods are forbidden not primarily for reasons of health or hygiene [although these may be a beneficial by-product of their observance], but for a higher moral reason." The "unclean foods beset the soul, preventing its moral and spiritual virtues" is the way the Sforno commentary on the Torah puts it (Sforno on Lev. 11:2).

Critics of kashrut are heard to remark that "it's not what goes into your mouth that counts, but what comes out." I hasten to add that what comes out may very well be determined in the long run by what goes in. It may be that in the long run, the food people eat—or abstain from eating perhaps even more—does have an influence over the character of a people, some of their values, and moral-ethical sensitivity.

Jewish critics, particularly among the Reformers who have cast off the disciplines of kashrut together with all our other halakhic guidelines have criticized its observance on the grounds that it tends to separate us from other peoples and other faiths by making social intercourse more difficult. Yet in addition to whatever other merits or purposes kashrut may have, for all we know this too may be part of what the Almighty intended. For barriers to total social integration in a non-Jewish environment are also barriers to intermarriage and assimilation.

We find the connection between separation and kashrut even more explicitly delineated in the following passage, "I am the Lord your God who have *set you apart* from the nations. You shall therefore separate between the clean beast and the unclean and between the unclean fowl and the clean . . ." (Lev. 20:24–25).

That the breakdown in kashrut observance has been a strong contributing factor to increased intermarriage and assimilation is all too evident. When the need to seek out kosher facilities is eliminated, especially when young people leave home for any length of time, the opportunities for meeting and developing camaraderie with fellow Jews needing the same facilities are reduced. Thus, by not asserting the distinctive Jewish norms on a day in, day out basis, the fertile conditions for assimilation are automatically set up.

While the strict observance of kashrut is not really a barrier to cordial relations with peoples of all nations and all faiths, it does provide perhaps just enough to enable Israel to remain its distinctive self. A small nation that is committed to its perpetuation and must always maintain the struggle against absorption and assimilation into larger groups should welcome observances and disciplines that set up some barriers to self-annihilation.

I like to compare kashrut to the foundations of a house. In and of itself, a foundation is not a house. One cannot take up residence there. But on the other hand, a house built without foundations or upon weak foundations has no permanance and can easily collapse upon the slightest pressure. Kashrut too, *by itself*, does not make for a Jewish home, nor for a Jewish life, nor for the holiness which is its primary purpose. But an attempt to build such an edifice without kashrut is to build weakly. The Sabbath, the festivals, the family life (the walls, the roof, the furnishings, etc., of our edifice) will be unsteady, and in danger of collapse without the proper foundation.

The religious training and the spiritual development of children is also endangered without kashrut. The non-kosher parent who thrills at the thought of a child coming home from Hebrew School capable of reciting a *brakha*, a blessing for food, may not be sensitive to the fact that the child may be thanking God for food which He commanded him not to eat. If the inconsistency and paradox is overlooked by the parents, it will soon enough become apparent to the child as he grows older. Except for the rare case, it's not the prohibited food he will give up, but the blessing that he will stop reciting. The early religious-spiritual awareness that the parents were so anxious for the child to have will become empty.

Nor does the "double standard" practiced by some Jewish families promote all the spiritual goals and purposes with which kashrut is concerned. "Keeping a kosher home" is unfortunately no longer identical with "observing kashrut." Eating like a Jew at home and like a gentile outside the home leads to the ridiculous situation where some Jews are more particular about what goes onto their household dishes than what goes into their stomachs. In what other areas of life, we wonder, are our children led to believe that one set of standards exists at home and another outside. While I wouldn't condemn this as hypocrisy but regard it as an attempt to hold on to something—a little is better than nothing, it is true—none of the reasons for observing kashrut are met by this "double standard" of "keeping kosher" only at home.

In summary, let me say that kashrut in and of itself does not make for holiness, but as an integral part of an entire pattern that makes for a distinctive life and which includes the Sabbath and the festivals, which includes ethical and moral norms, which includes sexual disciplines and guidelines, the observance of kashrut is an indispensable element.

THE FORBIDDEN FOODS

Leviticus Chapter 11 and Deuteronomy Chapter 14:2–21 list those animals, fish and fowl which are permitted to be eaten and those which are forbidden to be eaten.

Only animals that possess the dual characteristics of (1) cloven hoofs and (2) chewing the cud are permitted. All others are forbidden.

Lest the presence of only one of the characteristics be regarded as sufficient, those animals possessing only cloven hoofs or that are only cud-chewing are singled out by name as being forbidden. These include the camel, the pig, the hare, and the rock badger. Animals possessing the characteristics that designate them as "clean" are: sheep, cattle, goats, and deer.

Only fish that possess the dual characteristics of fins and scales are permitted. All others are forbidden. The common seafoods are in this prohibited category. They include: lobsters, oysters, shrimp,

104

clams and crabs. Swordfish and sturgeon have disputable scale characteristics and latter day Authorities have ruled against them.*

&ev; Among fowl, no specific characteristics to distinguish the permitted birds from the prohibited ones are given in the Torah. Instead, they are identified by name and species, twenty-four in all. From those listed in the Torah, the Talmud deduced the characteristics of the forbidden birds. Mostly, they are birds of prey or ones that treat their food as do birds of prey. They include vultures, ravens, hawks, owls, ostriches, pelicans, storks, herons, etc. The permitted fowl have traditionally been identified. They are: chicken, turkey, geese, ducks, and doves.

&ev; Amphibian creatures and insects are prohibited as are all living creatures that crawl or creep "upon the belly" (snake category); or that are "winged swarming things"; or that are in the rodent and lizard categories. "They are a detestable thing . . . you shall not defile yourselves with them . . ." (Lev. 11:42–43). Such gourmet "delicacies" as eel, snails, rattlesnakes, ants, and assorted insects are prohibited by the Torah.

&ev; All creatures permitted as food are referred to in the Torah as *tahor*, pure or clean. These are kosher, which means fit or proper in accordance with the law. All forbidden creatures are referred to as *tamai*, impure, defiled or unclean; they are also referred to as *sheketz*, a detestable thing, and as *to-ayvah*, an abomination. These are the non-kosher creatures. The term *trefah* is, however, commonly applied to them, as to any meat that is not ritually fit to be eaten according to Jewish law. There is no way of making them kosher.†

&ev; Products which come from non-kosher creatures are also not kosher. Eggs from non-kosher birds are forbidden. Milk from the non-kosher animals is forbidden. Oil from non-kosher fish is forbidden. The only exception is honey from bees which the Torah

---

* A list of commonly sold kosher fish is available upon request from the Union of Orthodox Jewish Congregations of America, 84 Fifth Ave., New York, N.Y. 10011. There are seventy-five different varieties listed.

† Vegetable products or condiments processed in such a way as to provide an artificial flavor or appearance similar to a prohibited food have been known to appear on the market. Though these foods are kosher, the use of such terms as "kosher bacon" or "kosher shrimp" is objectionable to this writer. The terms are contradictory since nothing can be done to make true bacon or shrimp kosher. Its use is deceptive and misleading and should be avoided.

specifically allows. It should perhaps be clarified that bees produce the honey from the nectar of flowers.

&. The Jewish religious code also includes some purely hygienic regulations. Any food known to be harmful to health must not be eaten even if permissible under all other kashrut rules. Such food is proscribed by the rabbis on the grounds of danger to one's well-being (*sakanah*). They base the prohibition on the Biblical passage that "for your sake, therefore, be most careful" (Deut. 4:15).

REQUIREMENT OF SHEHITAH

&. The Torah prohibits the eating of any "clean" creature (in the animal and fowl categories) which died a natural death or which had been killed in any way other than by ritual slaughter—*shehitah*. "You shall not eat anything that has died a natural death . . ." (Deut. 14:21). Such carcasses are called *nevelah* or *trefah*. "You shall slaughter of your cattle and sheep . . . as I have instructed you, and you may eat . . ." (Deut. 12:21). What is slaughtered in accordance with such instructions may be eaten; what is not, is forbidden.

&. The details of this authorized method of slaughter, known as shehitah, were transmitted through the Oral Torah. It is the only method of slaughter by which "clean" animals or birds retain their kashrut and remain fit to be eaten.

&. The requirement of ritual slaughter applies only to meat and fowl and not to fish. The Torah specifically excludes fish when it declares that "flocks and herds be *slaughtered* for them . . . the fish of the sea be *gathered* for them . . ." (Numbers 11:22).

&. This method of ritual slaughter is designed to cause the least pain to the animal and to remove as much blood as possible. It consists of the rapid to and fro cut of the throat by means of a perfectly sharpened blade of adequate length that is free from the slightest nick or unevenness. The swift movement of the knife takes a fraction of a second and quickly severs the trachea, the oesophagus, the two vagus nerves as well as both carotid arteries and the jugular veins. All available evidence indicates that consciousness is lost almost immediately, within two seconds after shehitah; that the cut itself is painless (just as when an individual is cut by a razor sharp blade, no pain is felt at the time and awareness only develops later when the blood is seen or when the wound is rubbed), and that there is no pain during the seconds that may elapse before consciousness is completely lost. The world's most eminent physiologists, pathologists and other scientists qualified to judge have declared the Jewish method to be absolutely humane.

Methods promoted by animal protection societies for stunning before slaughter would actually inflict injuries severe enough to render the animal trefah. While such stunning may be preferable to the cruelties and pain inflicted by most non-kosher slaughtering, in relation to kosher slaughtering, the shehitah cut itself may be regarded as an effective form of stunning because its effect is to produce immediate insensibility.

In addition to the humaneness of shehitah, the Jewish method carries with it another distinct advantage over most other methods. It ensures a complete and rapid draining of the blood from the animal rather than allowing the blood to congeal within the meat. This contributes to the keeping of the prohibition against the eating of blood. It is also undoubtedly true that the maximum blood drainage has many hygienic benefits.

The *shohet* is not just a Jewish slaughterman. He must be a pious person; he must possess a thorough knowledge of those portions of the Shulhan Arukh which detail the precise rules and regulations of shehitah as well as of the condition of the animal's organs which may render it trefah; he must pass a rigid examination and be duly certified by rabbinic authorities to exercise the functions of a shohet. Because of his piety, training and background, the shohet is often called upon, especially in smaller communities, to perform other duties of Jewish religious functionaries. The Jewish method goes back to the Biblical tradition (Deut. 12:21). Its details are elaborated upon in the Talmud (Hullin 1–2) and codified in the Shulhan Arukh (Yoreh Deah 1–28).

"KOSHERING" MEAT

Prohibition of Blood

8❧ The Torah forbids the eating of blood even when it comes from kosher animals and birds. It does not apply to fish blood. "You must not consume any blood, either of fowl or of animal . . . anyone who eats blood shall be cut off from his people" (Lev. 7:26–27; also 17:10–14).

ᏮᎦ To avoid violating the prohibition against eating blood, it must first be removed from the meat by one of two methods:

· The method of "soaking and salting," (commonly called "koshering").
· The method of broiling over or under a flame or in an electric oven or broiler. In this process the flame or electric heat purges the blood so that it drips out.

ᏮᎦ Either the process of broiling or that of "soaking and salting" is required for meat and fowl. It constitutes another step in rendering kosher animals and fowl that have been properly slaughtered fit to be eaten.

ᏮᎦ Where meat or fowl—even from kosher creatures that have been kosher slaughtered—is cooked or otherwise prepared without the necessary pre-requisites regarding the removal of the blood in the required manner, it becomes trefah or not kosher. During the cooking, the blood of the meat seeps out and the meat stews in its own forbidden blood, thus making trefah and prohibited the entire contents of the pot or pan.

Koshering by Broiling

ᏮᎦ The broiling must not be done in a pan, but on a grill that allows for the blood to drain off.

ᏮᎦ The grill or spit on which the "unkoshered" meat is broiled should not be used for broiling meat which had already been "koshered."

ᏮᎦ The raw meat must first be thoroughly washed down. While on the fire, it should be lightly salted.

ᏮᎦ After the meat is almost done, it must be washed off in cold water to remove the blood clinging to it. This satisfies the "koshering" requirement. It may then be reheated or the broiling continued to suit taste on another grill or spit reserved for the broiling of "koshered" meat.

103

ৡ Liver, because it contains so much blood, can only be prepared by this method. The method of soaking and salting does not work on liver and may not be used on it.

Koshering by Soaking and Salting

ৡ The meat must first be thoroughly washed down under running cold water and then placed in a pail of cool water and allowed to soak for half an hour. The meat must be entirely immersed in the water. This serves to soften the meat.

ৡ Meat which became frosted during refrigeration should not be salted until it has been allowed to thaw to room temperature.

ৡ After a half-hour period of soaking, the meat should be thoroughly covered on all sides (inside and out in the case of fowl) with a layer of medium coarse salt. Salt of the proper coarseness for this purpose is marketed in the United States as kosher salt. Ordinary table salt is too thin as it will tend to melt away and become absorbed into the meat instead of acting to absorb the blood from the meat.

ৡ The salted meat or fowl is then placed on a flat surface which is kept inclined at an angle to allow the blood to drain off. If a perforated drainboard or one with openings like a grid to allow for the draining is used, it need not be inclined.

ৡ The meat or fowl is kept in its salt for a period of *one hour*. (Under emergency conditions, the time may be reduced to a minimum of eighteen minutes.)

ৡ After the hour, the salt should be thoroughly rinsed off under running water. The meat or fowl is now ready to be boiled, fried or baked. Broiling is done on a kosher grill or spit.

ৡ The vessel or pail used for the soaking of the meat or fowl should not be used for any other purpose.

ৡ Soaking and salting must take place as soon as possible after the meat is purchased. In any case, it should not be delayed more than seventy-two hours beyond the time of slaughter or since the last time it was washed down. (See pp. 111–112.) This information may be obtained from the butcher. If a delay is unavoidable, the meat should be washed down thoroughly with cold water before the seventy-two hour interval elapses. This is to prevent the blood in the meat from drying up and congealing, which can make subsequent salting and soaking ineffective.

❧ Should meat be unavoidably kept beyond seventy-two hours without being washed down and without being "koshered," it may no longer be soaked and salted. The blood can then only be removed through broiling.

❧ An egg yolk found inside a chicken must also be soaked and salted. It should, however, lie in its salt apart from the fowl or at the upper end of the perforated board. Furthermore, such an egg yolk is not considered totally "parev" and may not be eaten together with dairy.

❧ Once the process of either broiling or soaking and salting has taken place, the excess blood has been removed. (That which still remains is regarded as "meat juice.") It is now ready to be boiled, fried, broiled, or otherwise prepared "rare" or "well-done" to suit taste.

❧ In recent years, most kosher butchers in the United States have been providing an additional consumer service. Upon request of the consumer, they will "kosher" (soak and salt) the meat for the customer. This recently introduced service eliminates much of the bother heretofore required of the housewife in the preparation of kosher meat. While in some places a small charge is made for such service, it is now generally rendered free of charge. But one must keep in mind that the butcher does not "kosher" the meat unless he is requested to do so, and that it is the duty of the housewife to do it if the butcher has not.

❧ Kosher-packaged fresh frozen meats are always soaked and salted at the processing plant and will so indicate on the package.

❧ It is advisable that all meat intended for the freezer be "koshered" by soaking and salting *before* it is frozen and stored away. This allows the housewife to prepare the meat immediately after defrosting in any way desired. If it was frozen without first being "koshered," it is best to broil the meat after defrosting.

❧ Ground meat must be "koshered" before being ground up. If meat is ground up before it is soaked and salted, it may not be eaten and is no longer treated as kosher. If cooked in a pot or broiled in a pan, it renders that utensil or vessel trefah.

&> The use of an egg with a blood spot is forbidden. Eggs used for cooking or baking should therefore be carefully checked for blood spots.

THE ROLE OF THE SHOHET AND KOSHER BUTCHER

&> Although this book does not include them, the kosher consumer should be aware that there are many other complex laws regarding conditions that would make trefah a kosher animal that was properly slaughtered. The shohet and the rabbis who supervise him must have a thorough understanding of these laws.

&> The shohet is required to carefully examine the lungs and the other internal organs of the animal after it is slaughtered, especially if there is reason to suspect that they may not meet all the many and complex criteria for sound health as set forth by the Jewish Codes of Law. Discoloration, disease, internal injuries, limb fractures, etc. will often render an animal trefah from the point of view of Jewish law.

Although the United States Government has its own set of standards and criteria for passing on the fitness of meat, and kosher slaughtered meat must also pass Government inspection, it is quite possible that meat which meets United States Government standards could be ruled trefah and unfit according to the Jewish law.

&> The kosher butcher must also possess some special skills and take special precautions if the kashrut of the meat delivered to him is to be preserved.

Fresh meat, for example, that has not yet been soaked and salted cannot be kept after slaughter for longer than seventy-two hours without being washed down. If kept for longer periods, the washing down must be repeated every seventy-two hours. This is to prevent the blood from drying up and congealing, thereby rendering useless any subsequent soaking and salting.

Unless a butcher has sold his meat within the specified time period, he must be conscientious about the washing. He must also possess the butchering skill to purge or excise certain blood vessels and fat sinews that may not be eaten; this must be done before the meat is "koshered." The butcher must be relied upon to perform such responsibilities not only skillfully but honestly.

The consumer must, therefore, be assured that the kosher butchers from whom he buys are under reliable rabbinic supervision, usually guaranteed by a "Certificate of Endorsement" that ought to be prominently displayed.

&❧ Frozen kosher meats or other processed meat products may be bought in general unsupervised food markets *only* if they come completely wrapped and packaged, and the package bears a legible endorsement of the kashrut of the product by a reliable rabbinic authority or kashrut board.

ON MEAT AND MILK MIXTURES

&❧ From the thrice-stated commandment in Scripture that "You shall not boil a kid in its mother's milk"* (Exodus 23:19, 34:26; Deut. 14:21), the Oral Torah derived the prohibition against cooking meat and milk together, against eating such a meat and milk mixture, and against deriving any benefit from such a meat and milk mixture.

(Although milk that comes from a kosher animal is permitted, it is precisely this kosher milk which, when mixed with the meat of kosher cattle, sheep, or goats that the Torah forbids. Rabbinical ordinances were enacted as "fences" to safeguard the observance of this commandment, and these are reflected in the practices followed in a kosher household.)

&❧ Although fowl was not included in the Biblical prohibition, rabbinical decree extended the prohibition of meat-milk mixing to include fowl as well. Use of the term *meat* therefore refers also to fowl in all instances.

---

* Onkelos, who usually keeps close to the Hebrew text, rendered this as "You shall not eat flesh and milk."

ક્ષ The terms *meat* (Yiddish: *fleishig*; Hebrew: *basar*) or *dairy* (Yiddish: *milchig*; Hebrew: *halav*), for the purpose of these religious laws refer not only to the actual meat and milk, and to products containing meat or milk ingredients, but also to meat and milk fats and products made from them.

A food product containing neither meat nor milk, nor derived from either is *neutral*. The Yiddish word *parev* (*parve*) or the Hebrew word *stam* is used to describe this third category. The neutral (*parev*) category includes (1) everything which grows from the soil: vegetables, fruits, nuts, coffee, spices, sugar, salt, (2) all kosher fish, (3) eggs, and (4) items manufactured from chemicals. Parev foods may be eaten or cooked with either dairy or meat products.

ક્ષ Meat and dairy products may not be cooked or served in the same vessels even if not at the same time.

ક્ષ Any vessel which has been used for the preparation of both meat and milk, even if not at the same time, (and has thus absorbed minute quantities of both meat and milk) is rendered non-kosher. It is therefore necessary to maintain separate cooking and eating utensils (dishes, tableware) for meat and dairy dishes. These must be properly marked or easily distinguished one from the other by color, design, form, or size.

ક્ષ Kosher food—meat or dairy or parev, cooked in vessels that were used for both meat and dairy—becomes non-kosher and is prohibited.

ક્ષ A specified time period must elapse after one has eaten meat before one may eat a dairy product. There are different opinions in the Codes as to the length of this waiting period. Acceptable practices range from a three-hour to a six-hour waiting period. (The reason for the waiting period is to allow time for deterioration of the fatty residue which clings to the palate and does not easily rinse out, and of the meat particles lodged in the crevices of the teeth.)

ક્ષ The reverse is not necessary. After one has eaten dairy, one may rinse his mouth with water, eat some neutral solid such as bread, and then proceed to a meat meal. (The reason is that dairy products do not possess the fatty qualities of meat or become lodged between the teeth in the same manner. Should there be a dairy product of which this is not so, such as some hard cheeses, then the same waiting period after dairy is also required.)

ક્એ A person who is ill (or a very small child) is permitted to shorten his waiting period to one hour, if necessary, provided that care is taken to cleanse the mouth and teeth thoroughly, and provided the final grace after the meat meal is said, thereby clearly designating that the second eating period is not just a continuation of the meat meal.

ક્એ A parev food cooked in a meat vessel must be served in a meat dish and *may not* be eaten *together* with dairy. One does not, however, become fleishig with it and it is permissible to eat dairy immediately afterwards.

ક્એ The kitchen sink (unless there are two separate ones) actually becomes a non-kosher vessel as it absorbs the remnants of both meat and dairy. Dishes—meat or dairy—should therefore not be soaked directly in the kitchen sink, or in the same basin. This may make the dishes non-kosher, even if the meat and dairy dishes are not soaked together at the same time. Separate basins that fit into sinks ought to be used for soaking dishes. Similarly, different colored plastic grills upon which to stack dishes in sinks should be used.

ક્એ The same dishwashing machine may be used for meat and dairy dishes if one acquires another set of racks that actually hold the dishes and utensils, reserving one rack for the meat dishes and the other for the dairy dishes, and allowing the machine to run through once while empty between meat and dairy use and vice versa. The empty run does not require a full cycle; a rinse and hold cycle using a detergent is sufficient. (Other rabbinic authorities have ruled differently and do not permit the use of the same machine even under the conditions specified.)

ક્એ It is common practice to designate towels of one color or design for the meat dishes, and towels of another color or design for the dairy dishes. This is the proper practice to follow, as it prevents a dish towel that was used for drying meat dishes from being mistakenly used the next time for dairy, and vice versa. If necessary, *any* cleanly-laundered dish towel may be used for meat or dairy.

ક્એ Where one person is served a meat meal and the other a dairy meal at the same table, a clear-cut distinction should be made between them, such as using a tablecloth or place mat (or a different tablecloth or place mat) for one of them.

114

8~ Use of butter and milk substitutes with meat: The development of pure vegetable products which "look and taste" like the dairy products they are intended to substitute (butter, cream, ice cream or sherbet, etc.) has increased the variety possible in the preparation of kosher meals. There are no halakhic objections to their use in cooking or eating with meat meals. But since they may be mistaken for their dairy counterpart and it is important to avoid what the Sages call even "the appearance of transgression," it is proper for purposes of identification that they be kept and served in the wrapper or container in which they come, or in any container which clearly designates the contents as parev.

8~ Not all coffee creams labeled "non-dairy" are in fact non-dairy, according to the rules of kashrut. Some contain sodium caseinate, which is derived from milk, making it a dairy product which should not be used at a meat meal.

8~ Glass under ordinary use has been confirmed as a non-absorbing material. Therefore, its occasional use for serving either meat or dairy is not prohibited. However, to use one set of glass dishes as a substitute for the traditional practice would be wrong and should not be permitted as a matter of policy.

8~ Water glasses may be used either at dairy or meat meals.

8~ Pyrex or similar glassware used for baking or cooking may not be used interchangeably for meat and dairy. (The presence of intense heat makes it susceptible to absorption.)

8~ When purchasing food or preparing meals, it is important to take note of ingredients, and to be fully certain as to the kashrut of the product, and as to whether it is milchig, fleishig, or parev. Food processing has become highly sophisticated today and labeling practices may be misleading to the kosher consumer. For example, mono- and di-glycerides or emulsifiers may be manufactured from either vegetable or animal fats. They may be kosher or trefah. Lactose may be manufactured from milk or from molasses. It may therefore be dairy or parev. The word "shortening" alone almost always indicates lard or other animal fats. That is why it is increasingly important to look for a reliable kashrut endorsement. While it is not the only kashrut symbol—there are some reliable local groups too—the ⓤ symbol of the Union of Orthodox Jewish Congregations of America is nationally the best known and easily the most recognized in the field.

MISCELLANEOUS PROHIBITIONS

ৰু Forbidden by Torah is the sciatic nerve, known in Hebrew as the *gid hanashe*, which runs through the hind quarter of the animal. When this sinew and its adjoining blood vessels are removed, the hind quarter of the animal may be eaten. The cutting out or purging of this sinew was done in some Jewish communities throughout history and is done in Israel today. In the United States it is not economical for the meat industry to invest many man-hours on the purging of this sinew (a time-consuming task). There are not many butchers who possess the special skills required for the task, and a vast market for non-kosher meat exists. Thus, the whole hind quarters of kosher-slaughtered animals are cut away in the packing houses and sold with non-kosher slaughtered animals. But a Jew is forbidden to eat the hind quarter of a kosher animal only when the forbidden sinew has not been removed.

ৰু Also forbidden by the Torah is the fat known as *helev*. (This is removed from the animal by the kosher butcher.) "You shall eat no *fat* of ox, of sheep, or goat" (Lev. 7:23–24). This forbidden fat surrounding the vital organs and the liver is distinguished from the permissible fat around the muscles and under the skin which is known as *shuman*. Although the Torah doesn't specify why there is this distinction between fats, it is interesting that recent bio-chemical researchers have also noted a distinction between these two kinds of fat.

ৰু Torah law prohibits the drinking of wine that had been used in connection with idolatry. Such wine is called *yayin nesekh*. Mere contact by an idolator with the wine at any stage of its preparation was sufficient to prohibit it. Aside from the fact that anything used for idolatrous ceremonies became prohibited to the Jew, the additional purpose of weaning the Jew away from convivial contact with non-Jews was also a factor in the prohibition.

While Jewish law today does not regard wine with which a non-Jew comes in contact as *yayin nesekh*, rabbinic ordinances extended the prohibition to ordinary non-Jewish wines, *stam yainam*. This restriction is lifted, however, if the wine is pre-boiled. Wines not made from the grape, but which are fermented from various fruits or grains are not included in any of the restrictions, either Biblical or rabbinic.

KOSHER FOOD IN NON-KOSHER VESSELS: ON "EATING OUT"

 relevant Any kosher food item that is boiled, baked, grilled, fried, or broiled in a trefah utensil which had been used for non-kosher meat, fowl, or fish, or which had been used indiscriminately for meat and dairy is rendered non-kosher itself and may not be eaten.

relevant Any kosher food, properly prepared in a kosher vessel, that is served *hot* in a non-kosher dish previously used for non-kosher meat, fowl, or fish, or used indiscriminately for meat and dairy is also rendered non-kosher and may not be eaten.

The basic principle of law followed in the above cases is that in the presence of heat, the kosher food absorbs traces of the absorbed forbidden food, even from an otherwise clean vessel. Though the Sages of the Talmud lived long before chemistry became a science, and before chemical theories were advanced, their ruling is today substantiated by the fact that chemical reactions and the activation and interaction of molecules of different bodies takes place only in the presence of heat.

relevant The above principle of law is also the basis for the ruling that when *cold* kosher food comes in contact with a *cold* and *clean* non-kosher utensil, the food does not become contaminated by the prohibited substances. It remains kosher and may still be eaten. (The only exception occurs when the kosher food consists primarily of very "hot" condiments such as mustard, etc.)

relevant This leniency provides eating opportunities for observant Jews who find themselves away from home or from any kosher restaurant or hotel or who may be invited to non-kosher homes. One may eat cold kosher food items that have not been boiled, baked, fried, or grilled on non-kosher utensils. These may be eaten even if served in non-kosher utensils.

(A possible menu in this category may include cold fruits, fresh vegetables, canned fruits, canned kosher fish such as tuna or salmon, some dairy products [milk, cream, butter], or even dry cereals that are easily available almost everywhere in the world.)

&> Coffee, tea, and hot chocolate are also regarded as permissible by some authorities, since the coffee or the hot water is prepared and served in vessels used exclusively for that purpose.

&> In eating places where special egg cookers are used to boil eggs the same leniency would prevail. Eggs cooked in trefah pots, however, are themselves rendered trefah. The shell of the egg is no barrier to contamination, as the shell is porous and absorbent.

&> Care should be taken when purchasing bread. Although most European breads generally contain no trefah ingredients, just flour and water, and can therefore be relied upon in case of need or emergency, American breads are usually processed with lard, which makes them trefah. Even where lard is not actually used as an ingredient, it is often used to grease the baking pans. Or the same baking pans that are used for making products with lard are used for making those without. (White breads are often also "enriched" with milk, which would make it a dairy product and of limited use, even if the problem of the lard was eliminated.) Cakes, biscuits, and pastries are often made with lard or animal fat shortening also.

&> In ordering fruit or vegetable salads in non-kosher establishments, care should be taken to ascertain that non-kosher sauces or oils derived from non-kosher fish have not been added.

&> One should be aware that this constitutes the "outer limits" of what may be eaten in non-kosher places. Devout Jews often choose not to take advantage of the permissible leniencies and restrict their eating in non-kosher places even more severely. When traveling, they take along their own food. But happily, there are kosher restaurants in many major cities. Kosher meals are also provided, upon request when reservations are made, by all domestic and international airlines and on many passenger ships.

&> The leniencies allowed should only be exercised when traveling; when visiting a private non-kosher household, Jewish or non-Jewish, or when invited to public functions of non-Jewish sponsorship. At such times and on such occasions, the individual Jew asserts his "Jewishness" and the disciplines of his faith when he limits his menu in the manner described. This is what sets him apart from those not under the terms of the Covenant.

The leniency should not be exercised when invited to a non-kosher dinner sponsored by a Jewish organization, or by any organization whose membership is limited to Jews, or which is given by a Jewish family in celebration of some occasion. Under these circumstances the observant Jew who "settles" for a fruit salad while his less observant coreligionists eat *trefah* meats, *trefah* fowl, or *trefah* fish permits himself to be treated as a "second-class citizen" among his brethren. Among Jews, he should not have to assert his "Jewishness" by keeping the Jewish values to which they are all bound by the Covenant; nor should he be subjected to the sight of fellow Jews violating sacred commandments before his eyes. Any Jewish host organization or family which shows so little consideration for the observant invitee or is so insensitive to his feelings that they arrange things so that he cannot partake *equally* by virtue of his conscience and religious duty should expect such a guest to decline any such invitation.

METHODS OF "KASHERING"

ဆ Where an error occurs and a meat vessel or utensil is unintentionally used with a dairy product or vice versa the vessel or utensil may be rendered non-kosher. This depends upon the circumstances, though it *always* is rendered non-kosher in the presence of heat, and *always* where the contact even with cold was continuous for a twenty-four-hour period. The same applies where a trefah food is unintentionally prepared in a kosher vessel or with kosher utensils.

Under such circumstances, it is sometimes possible to *kasher*, i.e., to make the vessel or utensil kosher again by various procedures.

ဆ The procedures used for kashering are varied. It may be done by immersing the utensil in (or pouring over it) boiling water, passing it through a flame until it becomes red hot, by sticking it into earth, etc. It all depends on the manner of its use and how it was contaminated. Vessels used with hot liquids are purged by boiling water; vessels used over a fire without water (frying pans, baking sheets, ovens and ranges, spits) are purged by "glowing," i.e., by subjecting the vessel to the heat of fire.

ဆ Most metal and wood utensils (Israeli rabbinic authorities also include plastic in this group) can be kashered. Earthenware, enamelware and porcelain cannot be kashered by any means. Nor is it possible to kasher utensils that possess grooves, narrow spaces, or glued-on parts with hard-to-get-to crevices, because they cannot first be thoroughly cleaned out.

꙳ The basic procedure and rules in kashering by boiling is as follows:

· The item to be kashered must first be thoroughly cleansed and scoured.
· The item to be kashered (and the vessel in which the item is to be immersed) must then not have been in use for at least twenty-four hours.
· It is then immersed into the boiling water.
· It is removed from the boiling water and rinsed in cold water.

꙳ If the item to be kashered is a pot which cannot be immersed in a larger vessel, then (instead of the third step) the pot itself is filled with water to the very brim and brought to a boil so that the water overflows.

꙳ Where kashering takes place by *glowing*, the same rules apply except that at the point of immersing, the item is instead held over a fire until it becomes red hot.

꙳ Ovens and cooking ranges previously used for non-kosher cooking may also be kashered by thorough cleansing and scouring of all visible parts followed by heating to the highest level for a half-hour. (The same procedure is followed when preparing for Passover, and kashering the ovens and range from *hametz* to *pesachdig*.)

꙳ In summary, whether the vessel or utensil can be kashered in the first place and the proper procedures to be used depends entirely upon the nature of the utensil and upon the manner in which it became trefah. It is always advisable to consult a qualified rabbinic authority on such matters to determine how best to proceed to correct the fault.

Family Life: A Key to Happiness

THE family is the core of Jewish society and a center of its religious life. If the home is strong in Jewish values, stable and healthy, then all of Jewish life and all its institutions—religious, educational, social, etc.—will be alive and vibrant. And if the home is weak, emotionally, morally, and spiritually, all else will soon mirror that weakness. The religious laws pertaining to family life therefore occupy a major part of the Jewish religious codes. These cover every aspect of family life, from its outward appearances to its most intimate relationships.

An analysis of the laws relating to this area indicates that they rest upon the following foundations:

· Respect for the integrity, individuality, and feeling of each member of the family as a human being.
· The development of a peaceful and harmonious relationship among all the members of a household (this is called *shalom bayit*).
· Recognition and acceptance of the different roles played by each member of a family.
· Maintaining spiritual purity and a wholesome attitude in the sexual relationship between husband and wife in particular and between men and women in general.

These are the underlying principles that are the basis of the Jewish laws in this area, and they are both the reasons for as well as the results of the adherence to these codes.

If a breakdown in Jewish family life is occurring in contemporary times, this may well emanate from a widespread ignorance of the rules, attitudes, and commandments relating to Jewish home life and to the sexual relationship. Jews are familiar with the *ascetic ideal* inherent in the Christian tradition, and the mood of guilt regarding sex fostered by the dominant religious thought; they have come to know the *hedonistic ideal* inherent in the secularism of our day, and the mood which rejects all guilt and every discipline in matters of sex. They have been influenced by both. Unfortunately, many Jews in our day have remained sadly ignorant of the *ideal of holiness* inherent in the Jewish tradition. The Jewish attitude has in fact stood in sharp contrast to both extremes and the Jew has maintained an age-old resistance to both views and the practices they generate.

While the Jewish ideal is intended to elevate the human being and society and to bring a happy and meaningful life to the greatest numbers, it is by no means intended solely to "make people happy." Making people happy by satisfying some immediate desire or physical urge at the expense of higher values was never the aim of Judaism. On the contrary, indiscriminate gratification was regarded as gross and vulgar, a concession to human weakness. This is nothing less than hedonism, which in its most vulgar form reduces the human being to a mere animal, possessed of no higher imperatives than the satisfaction of his physical drives and urges. Where men and women have abandoned the commandments and the Torah to "find happiness," the immediate joys and pleasures derived have invariably yielded to misery and bitterness.

There is no doubt that the observance of the Jewish family laws have contributed mightily to the stability of the Jewish family. While these laws are not an automatic panacea for personal unhappiness caused by either external factors or personality maladjustments, they do provide the formula for a stable, tranquil, harmonious, and satisfying family relationship between parents and children and between husband and wife. They do provide the formula for good, clean living and wholesome attitudes. They do provide the formula for elevating the sexual relationship from a form in which we do not appreciably differ from the animal kingdom to sacred expressions of love on a high spiritual plane, worthy of "a kingdom of priests and a holy nation."

Let us examine some of the traditional Jewish teachings about the husband-wife relationship, as this is probably less understood and appreciated by the contemporary person than the laws relating to the parent-child relationship. The growing number of family break-ups among Jews today testifies to the unfortunate fact that these laws are less widely observed.

In its general attitude toward marriage, the Jewish tradition recognizes the fact that procreation, the begetting of children, is one of the major purposes of marriage. To sire children is to fulfill a mitzvah, the Biblical commandment "Be fertile and increase." It gives meaning to the Divine blessing; it fulfills the Divine purpose; it makes us partners with the Almighty in the ongoing process of creation. The minimum number of children one must have to fulfill the mitzvah is a subject of rabbinic dispute (some say two children, others say at least one from each sex) but to avoid having children is to negate a Divine commandment. This particular purpose is not, however, what gives religious sanction or spiritual legitimacy to the marriage relationship.

Marriage has its own legitimacy, significance, and meaning apart from children. It has its own sanctity. Before God commanded, "Be fertile and increase," he set about creating a wife for Adam because "it is not good that the man should be alone. . . . I will make him a help-mate. . . ." Companionship, and the love and goodwill necessary for that relationship, is presented as the first and primary purpose of marriage. While the importance of having children is stressed, the marriage itself, the coming together as man and wife, has also been a prime target of rabbinic concern. "God waits impatiently for man to marry" (Kidd. 29b). "One who does not marry dwells without blessing, without goodness . . . without peace" (Yeb. 62b). "One who does not marry is in constant sin and God forsakes him" (Kidd. 29b, Pes. 113a). "He who has no wife cannot be considered whole." It is in having a wife that, in the opinion of our Sages, completes a man as a man. The Biblical lesson of Eve having been created as a help-mate to Adam was not lost upon them. "No man without a wife, neither a woman without a husband, nor both of them without God" (Gen. Rabbah 8: 9), sums up the Jewish concept of marriage. This is the Jewish ideal, which applies to all without distinction—rabbi and layman, priest and prophet.

The Biblical emphasis on companionship in marriage in no way implied a preference for a platonic relationship between man and woman, nor did it call for the unnatural repression of God-given physical and emotional needs. It stood to reason, then, that the sexual relationship between man and wife should be treated positively and accepted in a favorable light. The Jew is indeed forbidden from denying his wife the satisfaction of her sexual wants, apart from any consideration of procreating. Biblical law considers intercourse as a basic duty and one of the responsibilities of a married man. Just as he must provide his wife with clothing and shelter as a basic right, so he must not deny her sexual satisfaction. "Her food, her clothing and her conjugal rights, shall he not withhold" (Exodus 21:10).

These rights were recognized even when there was no possibility of conception i.e., if the woman could no longer bear children for medical reasons, or was already pregnant, or had passed her menopause. It is quite apparent that in the Jewish tradition the sexual relationship between husband and wife is not merely condoned or given a legitimacy so as to propagate the race, but possesses its own merit. Within the sanctified relationship of the marriage bond, sex is never treated as something sinful, obscene, or shameful. The contrary is the case—sex is positive, necessary, and good.

The Jewish tradition condemns in the strongest possible terms all forms of lewdness, harlotry, promiscuity, and adultery (z'nuth), and strictly prohibits these as well as all forms of incestuous sexual unions, homosexuality, and sodomy as abominable, leading to the decay of the people and the contamination of the land. However, it speaks with glowing enthusiasm for the beauty of the sexual relationship when expressed in the intimate love between a man and a woman within the sanctified union of marriage. The beauty, the character, and even the health of the offspring were thought by our Sages to be influenced by the quality of the sexual relationship. Whether or not this view will ever be scientifically validated is not important. This conviction on their part is at least a strong reflection of their healthy attitudes toward sex in marriage.

Jewish law clearly indicates its appreciation of the importance of proper attitudes prior to coitus and sets forth guiding rules.[1] It warns against approaching one's wife and forcing her to submit against her will; it warns against engaging in intercourse while under the influence of alcohol or while a couple is quarreling and "hatred divides them." Maimonides sums up the Jewish laws in this respect rather succinctly: "Sexual union should be consummated only out of desire and as a result of joy of the husband and wife."

Just as eating and drinking (through the laws of kashrut) were elevated within the Jewish faith to a level where they constituted one of the important ways by which the Jew acknowledged his Maker and served Him, so it was with regard to the satisfaction of the sex drive. Eating is necessary and good, but kashrut impresses upon us that not all food is "clean" for us, nor necessarily beneficial, nor that even good food is necessarily good for one all the time, either for health or spiritual reasons. As applied to the sexual relationship, Jewish law insists that sex, too, although necessary and desirable, may not always be good or "clean," that it too is not necessarily desirable all the time. It means that the Jew acknowledges limitations and disciplines relative to the satisfaction of these drives; it means that he is aware that a dichotomy exists between clean and unclean, pure and impure, the sacred and the defiled.

The limitations placed upon sexual expression by Jewish law and tradition in situations outside of the marriage relationship have already been alluded to. Even within marriage we have noted some of the conditions under which the Sages advised against intercourse. But there is still another area of sexual discipline that remains to be elaborated upon for it serves as the crown to what is known as "Jewish family purity."

I refer to the laws which forbid sexual relations between husband and wife beginning with the onset of her monthly menstrual period, to the end of seven "clean" days following menstruation. For the average woman, this means a period of about twelve days. During this period, the woman is in a state of separation (*niddah*), during which time she is forbidden unto her husband.

Here, too, reasons are not given in the Torah. What purpose does it serve? Several possibilities have been suggested:

> · To extend one's self-discipline to those drives and urges where passions often overcome reason and destroy elementary good judgment; where a lack of self-discipline has been known to destroy homes, bringing harm to others as well as to oneself. Strength, the Sages teach us, consists of the capacity to rule our passions, and not allow our passions to master us (Ethics of the Fathers 4:1). Holiness, in the Jewish conceptual framework, demands such strength.
> · Consideration for the emotional feelings and/or physical condition of the wife, for whom intercourse during this period might be objectionable.

125

THE DAILY WAY OF LIFE

· To minimize the element of boredom and routine in marriage which may develop with the passage of time, to keep alive the romance and tenderness so characteristic of the honeymoon period that it is necessary to recreate each month a new sense of expectation and excitement, best achieved by this required period of "separation."

· To enable one or both partners to rest up without being made to feel psychologically guilty or sexually inferior, which may plague one if disinterest or lack of vigor is felt. In this way, one does not have to bear the psychological burden of responsibility for the "rest," but can honestly attribute it to religious convictions.

Separation between husband and wife during this forbidden period does not exhaust the spiritual directives that encompass the area of "family purity." It is not just the passage of time which divides the permissive period from the prohibited period. Just looking at the calendar or glancing at a watch does not remove the woman from her state of *niddah* and return her to her husband in love and affection. A ceremonial act, a spiritually significant ritual does that. This ritual is the immersion in a ritual body of water (mikvah), without which a woman ritually remains in her state of "separation," forbidden to her husband.

Immersion in a kosher mikvah (one that ritually qualifies for that purpose) has always been the Jewish rite of purification. During Temple days, priests had to undergo immersion before being permitted to enter upon their sacred duties. Converts to Judaism, both men and women, must still undergo immersion in a mikvah, symbolizing a spiritual purification, as the final rite of their conversion without which no conversion is valid. And it is precisely this rite which a Jewish wife must fulfill each month until after her menopause.

While many writers on the subject of mikvah have marshaled impressive evidence that there are also hygienic and medical advantages that accrue from the proper observance of this rite, the primary purpose is nevertheless spiritual in character, involving a cleansing of the mind, heart, and emotions, enabling a wife to bring herself once again completely and without reservation to her husband and for her husband to receive her in like spirit.

That the immersion in a mikvah is not intended to be in lieu of a cleansing bath required by ordinary standards of hygiene is emphasized by the requirement that a bath must precede the immersion in the mikvah. In fact, all dirt or foreign matter must be scrupulously cleaned off prior to immersion.

Authentic Jewish family life cannot take place without the presence of a mikvah in a community. Observant Jewish women are known to travel great distances to a mikvah when they live far away from one. They have been known to go through great sacrifices throughout history in order to remain true to the laws of family purity. Jewish life can proceed without a synagogue; make-shift arrangements for prayer can suffice. It cannot naturally proceed without a mikvah. That is why religious kibbutzim in Israel will arrange for a mikvah almost immediately, while they delay the building of a synagogue until they can afford it. The modern, clean, tiled, antiseptic looking mikvah in use today with temperature-controlled water and hair dryer services may be a far cry from the type of mikvah built and used on top of Massada overlooking the Dead Sea, and even from those in use a generation ago, but the principle is the same. The purposes are the same and the spiritual link between the generations remains intact.

The laws of family purity are even more neglected by contemporary Jews than the Sabbath and kashrut because of total ignorance of the very existence of these laws rather than deliberate rejection. It is obviously not the kind of subject matter that is taught in the elementary Hebrew School, and therefore is not brought through the children to the attention of parents. It can be taught to Jewish children on the senior high school level, but there are too few Jewish children who continue to that level. Except for an oblique reference to the general subject called "family purity," which an unlearned listener may interpret in any number of ways, it does not lend itself to detailed teaching from the pulpit. Since the observance of family purity is confined to the intimate relationship of a husband and wife, friends and neighbors would not be aware of its observance, as they might be with kashrut and Shabbat.

Even children in a family observing family purity laws might not be aware that there is such an observance until they grow older, become aware of a mikvah, and are actually told about them. And so, except for those small adult classes or intimate private sessions a rabbi may have with a couple, or for those privileged few whose Jewish education proceeded to higher levels, most contemporary Jews have remained in total ignorance of its provisions, and if not quite that, then probably with distorted ideas as to what it is all about. What it is all about is the spiritual purity of the Jewish family and the traditional values that have brought light, happiness, and tranquillity into the Jewish home.

The values inherent in these laws cannot be disassociated from those values inherent in such rabbinic guidelines: "One who loves his wife as himself and honors her more than himself, concerning him does Scripture say: 'And you shall know that there is peace in your tent'" (Yevamot 62b, Sanhedrin 76b). "A man should always be scrupulous in the honor he accords his wife, for blessing is found in a man's home only by virtue of one's wife" (Baba Metzia 59a).

HONORING PARENTS

驼 "Honor your father and your mother" (Exodus 20:12), and "You shall revere every man his mother and his father" (Lev. 19:3), are the Biblical precepts underlying the relationship that must exist between children and their parents.

驼 The Sages equate reverence for mother and father and the respect accorded to them with the reverence due to God and the respect that must be accorded to Him.

"When a person honors his father and his mother, the Holy One, Blessed Be He, says: 'I consider it as though I were being honored'" (Niddah 31a). Disrespect for parents is tantamount to disrespect for God.

驼 Children should be taught reverence for God by the *living examples* set by their parents. Such children are also more likely to abide by the commandments to honor and revere parents. Although environmental influences are undoubtedly a contributing factor, children who disregard their parents often have before them an example set by the parents themselves in their relationship with *their* Father in Heaven.

驼 Some general principles regarding children and parents are:

> · If there is a conflict between what a father or mother says and what the Torah teaches, it is the wishes of the Father in Heaven that must take precedence, since the parents too are bidden to revere Him.
> · But even where parents disregard the Torah, never must a

son or daughter speak arrogantly or angrily to a parent; never may they be insulting or abusive. There is never any justification for such behavior no matter how objectionable or vile the behavior of a parent might be. Naturally, this applies with even greater force to routine disagreements.

· One who curses a parent, or who puts a parent to shame is considered cursed by God Himself, for it is written "Cursed be he who curses his father and mother" (Deut. 27:16).

· Where parent-child disagreements center about a child's desire to go elsewhere to study Torah because he feels he could gain more, or to enter into marriage with someone of his choice in a manner that is not contrary to religious law, and parents for whatever reason object, the child is not required to abide by such objections.

ৼ Grown children whose parents are aged and needy, have a responsibility to clothe, feed, shelter, and care for them. Whatever is done for parents must be done graciously and not grudgingly. (A married woman whose husband objects to her assuming obligations toward her parents is religiously exempt of these obligations. But if her husband has no objections, she too must do whatever she can.)

ৼ One is duty bound to honor one's parents even after their death. A son performs such an act of reverence by the recitation of the Kaddish each day for an eleven-month period. Both sons and daughters fulfill this duty by keeping the *yahrzeit*, by contributing to charity in memory of the deceased, and by living a life that reflects credit upon those who gave birth to them and raised them to adulthood.

ৼ According to the Sages, "engaging in the study of Torah and the performance of good deeds" is the greatest honor that one can bestow upon parents, living or dead, for people then say: "How praiseworthy are the father and mother who raised such a child."

THE EDUCATION AND UPBRINGING OF CHILDREN

That Judaism places great stress upon education is well known. But what Judaism means by education is not as well known. The Hebrew word for education is *hinukh*. It does not mean only formal schooling. It literally means "consecration" and refers to training a child for living, not only for a livelihood. The primary aims in the education of Jewish children are to (1) instill the moral and ethical values of the Jewish heritage; (2) encourage active observance of the Torah's commandments (mitzvot); (3) transmit knowledge of the Torah, the Talmud, and the major Jewish sources; (4) create a strong sense of identification with and concern for all Jewish people. Only then is importance attached also to acquiring knowledge in the broad secular fields and to the training needed to earn a livelihood. Jewish parents who only show concern for their children's secular education as preparation for a successful career are in fact providing only for a small part of the total education called for by Jewish tradition.

Modern Jewish parents who sincerely share the aims enumerated above have increasingly turned to the contemporary Yeshiva or Hebrew Day School for the elementary and secondary education of their children. Within the framework of a regular school day, these schools provide an intensive program of Judaic studies in addition to the required general or secular studies curriculum. Furthermore, such instruction takes place in surroundings that foster positive religious attitudes and Jewish commitment.

The tendency of some to be less concerned with the Jewish upbringing of their daughters than with that of their sons is wholly contrary to the spirit and expectations of Jewish family life. Most of the goals of Jewish education apply equally to women. The Jewish woman shares full responsibility with her husband for the many religious observances that are centered in the home. With her husband, the woman is also called upon to answer the questions of young children and guide the development of yet another generation. To leave a young woman unprepared for such a role is to invite spiritual disaster.

〜 Every parent is obligated to train his children in the observance of the commandments—the mitzvot—in accordance with the age and the capacity of the child, for it is written "Train a child according to his way" (Proverbs 22:6).

From the time children begin to talk and understand a little, short verses such as "Hear O Israel, the Lord is our God, the Lord is One," or the blessing over bread, the response of "Amen," etc., should be taught to them. Sabbath and festival songs for children, and children's rhymes with religious themes are available to young parents as aids to such training. Taking them regularly to the synagogue—once they've reached an age when they can control their behavior—adds to the training. It is inexcusable to wait until a child is of school age before beginning his religious training. To waste these very impressionable early years *solely* on fairy tales, stories, and songs that have no lasting value is irresponsible as well as foolish.

୬୭ A parent is further required to teach his children Torah, and to see to it that they receive formal instruction in Jewish religious studies. This is in fulfillment of the Biblical precept, "And you shall teach them (these words of the Torah) to your children . . ."(Deut. 11:19). No parent should be satisfied with a superficial smattering of such knowledge, but should make every effort to provide his children with quality Jewish education.

୬୭ It is the obligation of a parent to provide a child with the education or skills needed to earn a livelihood for himself when he grows up.

"A father is obligated to teach his son a skill," ruled the Talmud. To the Talmudic Sages, this injunction was based upon ethical considerations. "He who does not do so," they added, "teaches him to steal," for an unskilled person who has no means of earning a dignified livelihood may turn to theft or other criminal or immoral means of sustaining himself.

୬୭ One view expressed in the Talmud says that "it is the obligation of a parent to teach his child to swim," for this is a skill one may someday find necessary in order to save himself. One may infer from this ruling that self-defense skills are also important in the education of children.

୬୭ Never must a parent hit a child with cruelty or viciousness. Even where a beating is justified as in the case of repeated mischievousness, the dignity of the child and the possible pain inflicted should be carefully considered and proper restraint used.

୬୭ It is, in fact, forbidden for a parent to hit a *grown* child altogether. *Grown* in this instance is not determined by age but by the maturity of the child, so that even if a child is below the formal age of maturity (thirteen), and there is reason to believe that the child may react by hitting back, either by word or deed, the parent is forbidden to hit him but should chastise him verbally only, or punish him in other ways by denying certain privileges.

One who hits a grown child violates the Biblical precept: "You shall not place a stumbling block before the blind" (Lev. 19:14), i.e., not do anything that will cause the unsuspecting to fall or stumble. "Falling or stumbling" is applied also to ethical, moral, and religious failings which one is forbidden to cause or provoke in others.

ह⟩ A parent is forbidden to be supersensitive and overly demanding of his children and cause the respect due them to become a burdensome yoke, lest they thereby cause the children "to stumble" in fulfilling the precept of honoring and revering parents.

ह⟩ A parent is permitted to voluntarily yield or forgo certain courtesies or considerations due him by his children.

ह⟩ Although a boy under thirteen (and a girl under twelve) is not personally liable for the observance of religious statutes, it is forbidden to ask any child to do anything that is forbidden by religious law, even if it be for religious purposes (such as carrying the tallit or Siddur to the synagogue on the Sabbath).

ह⟩ It is important that a parent always show love for his children, and be adequately attentive to their needs and their problems.

Showering gifts upon children and acceding to their every request is not the same as showing love. Better a spanking from a parent whose child knows and feels that there is love and no rejection, than a household full of gifts from a parent whose child feels unloved, unwanted, and rejected. A request denied, while temporarily irritating to a child, may, depending upon the circumstances, be seen by the child as an indication of greater concern than indiscriminate granting of requests or a "do what you want."

ह⟩ The religious education and training of sons and daughters on every level is crucial to the perpetuation of the Jewish heritage and of world Jewry. It must be given top priority in the budgets of Jewish communities everywhere, and take second place only to efforts directed toward the saving of lives in imminent danger.

RELATIONSHIP OF HUSBAND AND WIFE

꿈 The *peaceful home* (*shalom bayit*) where harmony and good will between husband and wife reign, must be the overriding value, concern, and aim of every couple.

That which leads to *shalom bayit* has merit. Words or actions that tend to destroy the peace and harmony of the home by introducing suspicion, anger, or resentment, have no merit whatsoever, even if the words or the emotions expressed may be otherwise described as "honest," or "truthful," or "self-fulfilling."

꿈 According to Biblical precept, a husband is responsible for providing his wife with her food, clothing, and conjugal rights (Exodus 21:10). This precept teaches that it is the husband's responsibility to satisfy the physical needs of his wife.

꿈 A man must never force himself upon his wife against her will. On the contrary, conjugal relations should always be with her full consent.

꿈 If a feeling of hatred exists—he to her, or she to him—even if the physical intercourse itself may be desired, it should be avoided. If there is anger between a husband and wife, it is forbidden to engage in the conjugal act until anger has abated and tender words have replaced the harsh.

꿈 A woman must never deliberately delay her immersion in the mikvah, or otherwise make herself unavailable to her husband, just to annoy or aggravate him.

꿈 To use the conjugal act as a weapon over one's mate, as a means of punishing a mate, or as a means of getting one's way in other matters, is a most serious offense in the husband-wife relationship.

꿈 The Sages also cautioned a man to be most careful about avoiding insulting his wife, so as not to cause her pain by his words. This applies when the words between them are said in private. How much greater is the severity of the pain and the sin entailed when such insults or criticisms are made before others.

꿈 "A man must love his wife at least as much as himself but honor her more than himself" (Yevamot 62b, Sanhedrin 76b).

ૐ "A man should eat and drink with less than his means allow him; should dress according to his means; and should honor (by proper clothing and dwelling place) his wife and children with even more than what he can afford" (Hullin 84b).

ૐ "Eat and drink less and add the savings to enhance your dwelling place" (Pesachim 114a).

ૐ "In the affairs of a household and in the feeding and clothing of his sons and daughters, a man should follow the advice of his wife as peace and harmony will dwell in his home as a result" (Baba Metzia 59a).

ૐ "Our Sages said, 'A man should always flatter his wife for the sake of marital harmony'" (Midrash Yelamdenu).

ૐ "A woman of valor who can find; for her price is far above rubies" (Proverbs 31:10). A Jewish Sage once said: "This psalm is in praise of the woman who deliberately gives up her father's ways in favor of those of her husband; who smiles upon him even when he is angry; who honors him in poverty as well as in wealth, in old age as in youth. She is slow to leave home but quick to give bread to the poor. Though she may have many servants, she does not sit idly by, but works with them. She is attentive to those who address her, but not hasty in response. She is happy with her husband's happiness, and a source of hope to him when he is burdened with woe. Her ways are seemly and she is clad in modesty."[2]

ૐ "Who is rich?" Rabbi Akiva said: "He who has a wife whose ways are pleasant" (Shabbat 25b).

ૐ "A man should be kindly and not demanding in his house" (Midrash Bamidbar Raba 89).

ૐ "Anger in a household is like a worm among sesame seeds" (Sotah 3). Because sesame seeds are so small, when a worm spoils some of them all must be discarded, as it is impossible to separate the good seeds from the worm-eaten ones. "Through anger the wise man loses his wisdom" (Pesachim 66). But should anger come to pass, it is better to be angry and then contrite, with due apologies and humility, than to try to justify the anger by insisting that it was right.

ૐ One must learn to listen patiently and attentively to the wishes, the claims, or the arguments of a wife and children before responding, so that the response be considered and appropriate, and not hasty or thoughtless.

DIVORCE

৵ Where, despite every effort to preserve the peace of the home and the harmony of the husband-wife relationship, bitterness, continuous strife, and the flames of dissension nevertheless prevail, it is better that the couple should be parted and not continue to live together. In such instances, the Torah provides for the bonds of marriage to be dissolved by a divorce.

৵ The law allowing divorce is based upon Biblical precept. Its procedure is strictly governed by the halakha. The Hebrew term for a Jewish divorce is *get*.

A religious marriage that is consecrated "according to the Law of Moses and Israel" is not dissolved by the decree of a judge in a civil court who acts in accordance with the secular laws of the State but must be severed also "according to the Law of Moses and Israel."* Without a *get*, the marriage status of the couple remains in force.

৵ Any marriage or relationship that might therefore be contracted following a civil divorce without benefit of a religious divorce has no validity according to Jewish religious law, and is regarded as an adulterous relationship.

৵ Where a husband and wife have parted ways and no longer consider themselves to be husband and wife, or have arranged for a civil divorce in the secular courts, it is a religious transgression of the gravest magnitude to neglect to arrange for a *get* out of indifference, or to refuse to do so out of misguided spite. Such neglect affects not only the man and the woman themselves in the sight of God, and whatever subsequent partners they may take unto themselves, but also puts an unfortunate stigma of illegitimacy upon children who may be born from subsequent unions.

---

* The State assumed jurisdiction in the area of divorce because classical Christianity had no provision for it in its religious statutes. The indissoluble everlasting bond of the marriage was central to Christian teaching. The "till death do us part" was not merely a romantic ideal enunciated by lovers in a marriage ceremony, but a church law which tolerated no divorce and made no provisions for it.

If divorce is the only solution to the unhappiness of a relationship, then it should be a complete divorce, properly carried out and recognized in the sight of God under the precepts of the faith under which the marriage was first consecrated. If this not be done, what moral merit is there in arranging for a divorce that satisfies only the civil authorities and the secular law?

&❧ Even though the Torah permits divorce and makes provision for it on grounds no more severe than simple incompatibility, it must never be carried out arbitrarily or hastily, but only where every hope of healing the breach is gone and strife and bitterness continue to prevail. "Then, the law of divorce is given for the peace of man and the unity of the family. Those who divorce when they must, bring good upon themselves, not evil."[3]

Still, the human tragedy inherent in any divorce, especially when there are children to be considered, cannot be more poignantly portrayed than by the Talmudic adage which says that whenever a divorce takes place, "even the altar of God sheds tears."

For a description of the procedure and rules governing a *get*, see Divorce Proceedings, pp. 292–294.

SEXUAL DISCIPLINE IN MARRIAGE

&❧ The Biblical precept: "You shall not come near a woman while she is impure by her uncleanness to uncover her nakedness" (Lev. 18:19), is the basis for the sexual discipline and rules that govern the Jewish marriage relationship. These laws are generally referred to as family purity (*taharat hamishpaha*).

&❧ For a full seven-day period from the onset of the monthly menstrual period, the Torah prohibits all sexual relations between husband and wife. The technical term for the state in which the wife is in during the menstrual period is called *niddah* (literal meaning: to be removed or separated).

&❧ By rabbinic edict, the Talmud extended this period of separation (niddah) to "seven clean days" following the menstrual period. Since the menstrual period lasts about five days for the average woman, the total period of separation that is in force each month is about twelve days.*

&❧ During the period of separation the husband and wife may not sleep in the same bed as a precaution lest they forget themselves. It is for this reason that twin beds rather than double beds have been the adopted style in the Jewish home.

&❧ A woman remains in the state of niddah until she has immersed herself in a ritual body of water (*mikvah*). This immersion is the ritual act which divides the two periods of time—the period of separation when marital relations are forbidden and the period of union when such relations are not only permissible but regarded as essential to physical and mental health.

&❧ It is the responsibility of the wife to note carefully the day on which she last saw blood and to count the seven "clean" days that follow, so that her visit to the mikvah is neither too soon nor unnecessarily delayed.

&❧ The proper time for the immersion is after nightfall,† following the seventh clean day. Unless her husband is out of the city, a wife should not delay her visit to the mikvah.

&❧ At the mikvah, supervised by a woman attendant, the woman prepares herself for the ritual immersion by first cleansing herself thoroughly in a hot bath and removing *all* articles, such as bandages, hairpins, rings, even nail polish, that would constitute a barrier between the water and *all* parts of her body. The hair is also washed and combed.

&❧ Since rabbinic opinion was divided as to whether the dirt accumulated beneath fingernails and toenails constituted a "barrier," the custom became widespread to crop the nails of fingers and toes closely before immersion so as to effectively remove all particles of dirt. When this custom is not followed, the immersion is not disqualified, since it is the opinion of some authorities "that from the Mishna and many *poskim* it is clear that as long as the nail is clean, it [in principle] constitutes no barrier" (Yoreh Deah 198, Shakh 25).

---

* It is of interest to note that the natural fertile period in a woman which lasts about three days, generally falls at the conclusion of this twelve-day period.

† It is for this reason that ritualariums (*mikvaot*) are usually open to the public only during the evening hours.

&~ In our day, the widespread practice to wear nails long, and to take great effort in caring for them with cosmetic instruments (nail files, nail brushes, etc.) that are effective in removing accumulated dirt and in thoroughly cleansing under the nails should prove no deterrent to going to the mikvah. Nevertheless if at the time of immersion, the nails are due to be cut because they are too long, they should be cut down to their desired length prior to the immersion (Teshuvot HaBach 11).

&~ After the woman has once immersed herself completely while in an upright position, the following blessing is recited:

בָּרוּךְ אַתָּה יְיָ אֱלֹהֵינוּ מֶלֶךְ הָעוֹלָם, אֲשֶׁר קִדְּשָׁנוּ בְּמִצְוֹתָיו וְצִוָּנוּ עַל הַטְּבִילָה.

Baruch ata adonai elohainu melech ha-olam asher kidshanu b'mitzvotav v'tzivanu al hatvilah.

Blessed art Thou, Lord our God, King of the universe who has sanctified us with His commandments and commanded us concerning the immersion.

After the blessing, the woman totally immerses herself once again.

&~ The first time that a woman is obliged to immerse herself in a mikvah, thereby removing herself from a state of niddah, is *prior* to her wedding. Every effort should therefore be made to plan a wedding during that period of the month when it is permissible for the bride and groom to have marital relations.

&~ According to Biblical law, a woman is also considered in a state of impurity (*tumah*) for seven days following the birth of a son and for fourteen days following the birth of a daughter. In both cases a period of "seven clean days" are then counted, followed by the proper immersion.

In many communities, it became a widespread practice for the woman not to immerse herself until a period of forty days has elapsed after the birth of a son, or eighty days after the birth of a daughter. This custom, however, is not a binding one on all communities, in the opinion of the Sages.

&~ In a strongly traditional Jewish community, the establishment of a mikvah is considered even more necessary for the physical as well as spiritual life of the community than a synagogue, and takes priority over it.

MODESTY

&ᴥ Modesty should be the byword in the behavior of every member of a family. It should mark the relationship of husband and wife, of parents and children, and of every member of the family in all their social relationships outside the family.

&ᴥ Modesty means moderation in speech, in dress, in eating and drinking, in seeking pleasures and entertainment.

&ᴥ Nothing is as gross as vulgar speech (or signs of the hand implying vulgar acts or thoughts). The use of curse words and uncouth expressions is a violation of the standards of behavior demanded by the Torah.

&ᴥ It is important to be modest in one's dress. Immodest dress for a woman consists in exposing parts of herself that are generally covered. To wear clothes that unduly expose oneself because of some faddish fashion is no less improper than if it were done in order to deliberately titillate every male passerby. Being smartly dressed need not mean immodesty.

&ᴥ Modesty in behavior calls for not being overly aggressive and forward, but also not overly shy and withdrawn.

&ᴥ Modesty implies moderation in all things. This does not mean that one is to desist from joyous participation at happy occasions, but it does mean that one ought not to overindulge to the point of becoming intoxicated.

&ᴥ "You shall not commit adultery" is a Biblical commandment which forbids any relationship with another man's wife. Both the wife and the man with whom she commits such an offense are equally guilty. This violation is among the gravest of offenses. The sin is not so much against the husband of the unfaithful wife as it is against God Himself whose precept and law is violated.

&ᴗ Even where adultery is not involved, the Torah forbids sexual promiscuity and condemns it as *z'nut*, the sort of immoral behavior which was common among the nations in whose midst the Israelites lived and which practices they were bidden to resist.

Against this and all forms of sexual perversions, the Torah strongly cautions. "And you shall not walk in the customs of the nation which I am casting out before you; for they did all these things, and therefore I abhorred them" (Lev. 20:23).

&ᴗ The Jewish moral norms clearly insist that the sexual relationship be reserved for the sanctity of the marriage bond. "And you shall be holy to me; for I the Lord am holy . . ." (Lev. 20:26).

&ᴗ Vulgarity in all its forms, whether in art, literature, movies, theater, television, or newspapers and magazines, is the very antithesis of Judaism. Public display of nudity, sensual lust, and the promotion of sexual license constitute the sort of vulgarity against which Judaism set itself apart from its very inception. The Jewish objections to the manners and morals in the days of the pagan deities of Baal and Astarte, and in the heyday of Greek and Roman hedonism, are just as applicable to contemporary "swinging" America.

The fact that the moral attitude of the masses is changing—that they are becoming tolerant and indeed receptive to license—does not mean that these new standards should now be condoned. What it should mean for us is that the struggle to maintain the traditional sacred Jewish values has now become harder than it has been for a long time. What it means is a renewal of the same spiritual struggle that has had to be waged over the centuries. If once again it were to mean Israel engaged in a moral struggle, that would certainly be nothing new.

ABORTION AND BIRTH CONTROL

Abortion

Although the decision on aborting a birth must be made separately in each case, and authoritative rabbinic opinion should be sought in each instance, there are religious guidelines regarding abortions which are derived from Biblical and Talmudic sources. All halakhic scholars agree that therapeutic abortions—namely, abortions performed in order to preserve the life of the mother—are not only permissible but mandatory. The stage of pregnancy does not matter. Wherever there is a question of the life of the mother or that of the unborn child, Jewish law rules in favor of preserving the life of the mother. The status of the fetus as human life does not equal that of the mother.

There is also general agreement among rabbinic authorities that abortions for reasons of convenience, economics, or other personal reasons are clearly prohibited. This applies from conception onward. While a fetus is not regarded as a living soul until birth, it does have a status of *potential life*, the destruction of which is a serious offense.

Opinions among halakhic authorities differ, however, in such instances where there is a strong possibility that the child will be born deformed, in cases of incest, or where there are possibilities of serious emotional and psychological disturbances to the mother even if there is no actual threat to her life. Permissive rulings for abortions before the fortieth day—and in some instances up to three months—will be found in such instances. Opinions in this area range from the stricter views of the current Chief Rabbi of Israel, Isaac Unterman, to the more liberal views of the late rabbinic scholar and halakhic authority, Yehiel Yaacov Weinberg (see Responsa—Sridai Eish, Vol. 3:127 and Noam, Vols. 6, 7, and 9).

Birth Control

As long as families do plan to have children and do in fact fulfill the mitzvah of "be fertile and increase," the concept of planned parenthood or spacing of births does not constitute a religious problem.

The halakha is more concerned with the religious permissibility of the method used in birth control. Contemporary rabbinic authority has expressed no objection to the use of "the pill," since it does not appear to violate the injunction against "the destruction of seed."

It must nevertheless be said that rabbinic tradition has always encouraged having many children. Maimonides writes "Even if a person has fulfilled the commandment of 'be fruitful and increase,' he is still enjoined not to refrain from fruitfulness and increase as long as he is able, for he who adds a life in Israel is as he who built a world" (Ishut 15:16).

CHAPTER

8

Signs of the Covenant:
Love and Reverence

The mitzvot of *tefillin, mezuzah,* and *tzitzit* are all intended to serve as signs, as reminders of the presence of the Lord, of His commandments, and of our duties to Him. "And remember all the commandments of the Lord and do them" (Num. 15:37–41). Like prayer, called *service of the heart,* these rituals too reflect our love and reverence for God.

The call to love God is almost as pervasive as the command to obey Him. The twice-daily affirmation of God's unity—*Hear O Israel, the Lord is our God, the Lord is One*—is immediately followed by the reminder, *And you shall love the Lord your God with all your heart, with all your soul, and with all your might.* But it does not stop there, for *these words which I have commanded you this day upon your hearts,* i.e., to love your God, etc., must be diligently taught to the children, it must help to mold one's thought and action when arising and when going to bed, and when walking on the street and going about one's affairs. Reminders to that effect must be visibly placed upon one's hand and head, and upon the gates and doorposts of one's home.

Although "fear of God" (reverence for God)* appears to be stressed in all religious sources, and each day's prayer begins with Proverbs' reminder that "The beginning of wisdom is the fear of the Lord," the Talmud has indicated that "Greater is he who serves in love than the one who serves in fear" (Sotah 31a).

Maimonides, in his *Guide to the Perplexed,* emphasizes the greater merit involved when drawing near to God and observing His precepts out of love for Him rather than out of fear. Love is of a much higher category, demanding greater intellectual capacity and much deeper insight. Since not everyone can discipline himself to observe the precepts by rising to the level of Love, "the beginning of wisdom" demands that it be done at least out of fear (reverence-awe) of God.

Whatever the greater merit of and preference for serving God out of love rather than fear, there is no doubt but that both feelings are necessary within the consciousness of the *average* individual. Each comes into play depending upon time and circumstance in maintaining devotion and duty. Both feelings must be present, with one becoming dominant when the other tends to become lax.

Consider the relationship of a parent and child. A child whose only feeling for mother and father is love, while fear of punishment plays no role, is more apt to disobey than the child who harbors some fear as well. This is particularly true of a younger child who does not comprehend all the implications of his actions or desires and is still dominated by selfishness. "Learning to share" is part of the training

---

 * It ought to be made clear that the English translation for the Hebrew concept *Yirat Hashem,* which is generally translated as *fear of God* does not really convey its true meaning. For it certainly does not mean *fear* in the sense of *being afraid,* as one might be afraid of a fierce beast or a dangerous situation. For such a feeling, the proper Hebrew word is *pachad.*

Although man is often described as possessed of *pachad* in relating to God, God is described by such a term only when Jacob refers to the Almighty as "The Fear of Isaac." (See Genesis 31:42, 53.) While *Yirah* does contain the notion of fearing punishment for wrongdoing, it generally connotes a sense of awe or deep reverence as one might feel when coming before a powerful ruler or before a great and famous personality. The extra care that one exerts regarding his dress, speech, and behavior at such an occasion results from this sense of awe, reverence and "fear." To become nervous or shy on such an occasion is not uncommon. We sometimes hear of someone being *dumbstruck* when suddenly coming into the presence of such a person. This is not necessarily the result of fear. It is rather the result of awe. And it is precisely this feeling that is meant by the term *Yirat Hashem.* Nor does the term *Reverence for God* do justice to the term *Yirat Hashem.* It is too tepid, too lukewarm. It implies courtesy, politeness, and respect which—however required—does not reflect the depth of feeling conveyed by the term *Yirah.*

in "learning to love." On the other hand, when a child's only reason for obeying is fear of punishment, he is apt to break out of his disciplines the moment his parents are not looking, or he feels he can get away with it, while the child who also loves his parents would avoid doing anything that might hurt them. In the relationship between human beings and God, as between children and parents, the most effective ties are based on a balance between love and fear.

Though the ritual acts of *tefillin, mezuzah*, and *tzitzit* were required of us in the framework of love of God, the purpose is not to encourage just sentiment or abstract feelings. It is rather to remind us "to walk in the ways of the Lord."

"You shall love the Lord your God" was interpreted by the Sages to mean "that you cause the name of the Lord to be beloved" (Sifre Deut. 6:4). In other words, even the commandment to love was geared to action, doing, and activity, rather than just to feeling. We are called upon to *demonstrate* our love of God by behaving in such a way toward our fellow men as will invite their love and respect for the God who thus instructed us. This requires ethical and moral standards of the highest caliber.

TEFILLIN

Hear O Israel the Lord is our God the Lord is One. And you shall love the Lord, your God with all your heart, with all your soul, and with all your might . . . And these words which I command you this day . . . *bind them as a sign on your hand and as a symbol* (frontlets) *between your eyes, and write them on the doorposts of your house and on your gates.*

(Deut. 6:4-9)*

These passages from the Torah are the basis for the observance of two unique Jewish symbols that since ancient times testified to the eternal Covenant between God and Israel: the tefillin and the mezuzah

---

* Other Biblical references to the observance of this mitzvah of *tefillin* include Exodus 13:9; 13:16, and Deut. 11:18.

(see pp. 152–155). Both are capsule sized reminders of the entire Torah which the Jew is bidden to observe. Whereas the mezuzah is placed at the entrances to a dwelling place and in the home to designate it as Jewish in character and to serve as a reminder of the Divine Presence and of the obligation to observe *all* His commandments, the tefillin are worn on the person, on the hand and head.

ह The tefillin (translated as *phylacteries*) consist of two small black boxes, containing small scrolls of parchment upon which are written four Biblical passages. They are: Exodus 13:1–10 ("Consecrate every first born to Me . . ."); Exodus 13:11–16 ("When the Lord will bring you into the land . . ."); Deut. 6:4–9 ("Hear O Israel, the Lord is our God, the Lord is One . . ."); and Deut. 11:13–21 ("If you will diligently obey my commandments . . .").

ह These four passages from the Torah all include the commandment to don tefillin as a sign, as a symbol of Jewish faith and devotion.

ह Each of the black boxes comes with leather straps (Hebrew: *retzuot*) so designed as to enable one to be bound upon the hand and for the other to be worn above the forehead.

ह The leather straps, the boxes and the parchment are all made from kosher animals. The writing must be handwritten by a scribe.

ह The word *tefillin* reminds one of the Hebrew word *tefilah*, which means prayer. Both words are derived from the same root (פלל) meaning "judgment." Prayer and the ritual objects associated with it testify to our faith in the presence and judgment of the Almighty, while also providing the opportunity for self-examination and self-judgment.

ह Since the observance of tefillin is restricted to specific times, women are exempt from this obligation and do not put on tefillin. (See page 163 for an explanation of the rule exempting women from some observances.)

ह Since a minor male (under thirteen) does not put on tefillin until he becomes of age, putting on tefillin has become the most visible religious ritual that "sets the men apart from the boys." It is *the* religious symbol and ritual obligation that is most closely identified with becoming Bar-Mitzvah, i.e., of age.

145

• This mitzvah is fulfilled only during the day, preferably in the morning in conjunction with the recitation of the *shachrit*, morning prayers.

• It is observed only on weekdays. Tefillin are not worn on Sabbaths or festivals.

The reason is that the tefillin were to serve as a symbol, as a reminder to the Jew of all the commandments at a time when he is occupied and burdened by multiple concerns and may possibly forget. For such times, it is also considered an adornment. But the Sabbath and the festivals are also called reminders of the Covenant between God and Israel. The very Sabbath day itself and the very festival itself is intended to serve as an everpresent reminder of God's Presence and of His commandments. The Sabbath and festival days are themselves a special adornment to the life of the Jew. To add the observance of tefillin in the context of its meaning and purpose would not only be superfluous but would imply downgrading the Sabbath. Strange as it may sound, the sacred tefillin may not even be handled on the Sabbaths and festivals.

• On the Intermediate days (*hol hamoed*) of Pesach and Succot, different practices prevail as a result of the different rulings on this question by the Early Authorities (*Rishonim*). Sephardic Jews do not put on tefillin at all on these days, while among Ashkenazic Jews there are those who also do not; there are those who put them on without reciting the blessings; and those who recite either the first blessing only or both blessings while putting them on, but do so inaudibly. Unless one has a family tradition in this matter, it is proper to follow the tradition of the congregation among whom one prays. In any one synagogue, everyone should follow the same practice.

• The procedure for putting on and taking off the tefillin:

  • The tefillin are put on after the tallit. This is because we follow the general principle that "that which occurs more often precedes that which occurs less often" (Zvahim 89a). The mitzvah of *tzitzit* (tallit) is in force on the Sabbath as well as on weekdays and tefillin is only in force on weekdays.

  • One should stand while putting on or taking off the tefillin.

  • While the tefillin are being put on, one may not divert his attention from the task at hand by either engaging in conversa-

146

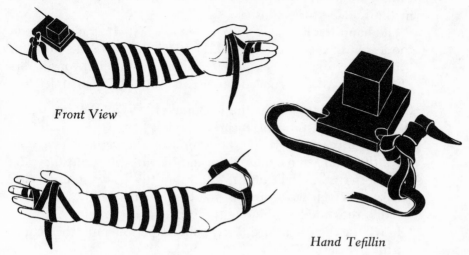

Front View

Hand Tefillin

Back View

Correct Tefillin Position on Hand

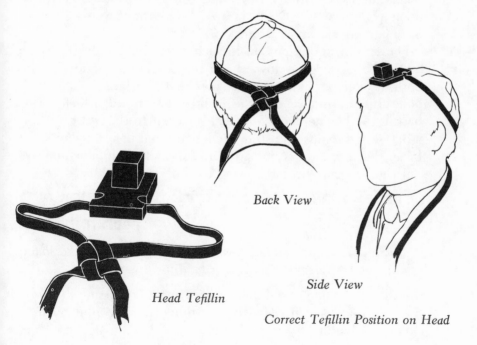

Back View

Head Tefillin

Side View

Correct Tefillin Position on Head

FIGURE 1   Tefillin

147

tion or by joining the congregation in such prayer responses as in the Kaddish or Kedusha.

· The hand tefillin (*shel yad*) is put on first. It is placed upon the left arm. One reason for the left hand is that the word for "your hand" in the verse "and it shall be a sign upon your hand" (Exodus 13:16), is spelled in such a way יָדְכָה that led the

Sages to also read into it the meaning of יָד כֵּהָה "the weaker hand" which in most instances, is the left hand.

Another reason is the juxtaposition of the verses "*You shall bind them* on your hands . . ." and "*You shall write them* on the doorposts . . ." (Deut. 6:8–9). From this it was inferred that the hand which writes is also the hand which binds. The right hand is thus used for binding the tefillin on the left hand.

· For both these reasons, a left-handed person puts the tefillin on his right arm.

· The tefillin box is set on the biceps of the arm, which is the area of the arm closest to the heart. It thus lends additional symbolic emphasis to the verses "And you shall place these words upon your hearts" (Deut. 11:18); "And these words shall be . . . upon your hearts" (Deut. 6:6).

· The tefillin box is put on in such a way that the broad side of the lip or ledge is toward the top of the arm and not the bottom. This arrangement provides that the knot, which symbolically is fashioned like the Hebrew letter *yud*, which forms part of the Divine name *Shaddai*, is closest to the heart.

· Before tightening the strap around the biceps, care should be taken that the knot is immediately adjacent to the box and has not slid away, and the following blessing is recited:

בָּרוּךְ אַתָּה יְיָ אֱלֹהֵינוּ מֶלֶךְ הָעוֹלָם, אֲשֶׁר קִדְּשָׁנוּ בְּמִצְוֹתָיו וְצִוָּנוּ לְהָנִיחַ תְּפִלִּין.

Baruch ata adonai elohainu melech ha-olam asher kidshanu b'mitzvotav v'tzivanu l'hanee-ach tefillin.

Blessed art Thou, Lord our God, King of the universe who has sanctified us with His commandments and commanded us to put on tefillin.

· The strap is then tightened, and wound seven times around the forearm below the elbow. The length of strap remaining after the seven times around is then wrapped around the palm of the hand.

· The head tefillin (*shel rosh*) is then put on. Before fixing it firmly upon the head the following blessing is recited:

בָּרוּךְ אַתָּה יְיָ אֱלֹהֵינוּ מֶלֶךְ הָעוֹלָם, אֲשֶׁר קִדְּשָׁנוּ בְּמִצְוֹתָיו וְצִוָּנוּ עַל מִצְוַת תְּפִלִּין.

Baruch ata adonai elohainu melech ha-olam asher kidshanu b'mitzvotav v'tzivanu al mitzvat tefillin.

Blessed art Thou, Lord our God, King of the universe who has sanctified us with His commandments and commanded us concerning the mitzvah of tefillin.

This blessing is followed by the following declaration, said immediately after the tefillin has been fixed firmly upon the head.

בָּרוּךְ שֵׁם כְּבוֹד מַלְכוּתוֹ לְעוֹלָם וָעֶד.

Baruch shem kvod malchuto l'olam va-ed.

Blessed be He whose glorious Majesty is forever and ever.

· The head tefillin is placed above the forehead. The lowest point of the tefillin box should not be below the hairline (or where the natural hairline might be in case one is bald-headed). It should also be adjusted *on the head* in such a way that it is on a line *between the eyes*, for it is written "And they shall be for a sign between your eyes" (Deut. 6:8).
· The knot of the headstrap should be centered behind the head at the base of the skull; the straps are brought forward across the chest and left hanging loosely, with the black side in front.
· After properly adjusting the tefillin on the head, the strap around the palm is unwrapped and wound three times around the middle finger—once around the middle part of the finger and twice around the lower part closest to the knuckle. The remainder of the strap is then carried around the ring finger and rewound around the palm. While doing so the following is said:

וְאֵרַשְׂתִּיךְ לִי לְעוֹלָם, וְאֵרַשְׂתִּיךְ לִי בְּצֶדֶק וּבְמִשְׁפָּט וּבְחֶסֶד וּבְרַחֲמִים. וְאֵרַשְׂתִּיךְ לִי בֶּאֱמוּנָה, וְיָדַעַתְּ אֶת יְיָ.

149

I will betroth you to me forever; I will betroth you to me in righteousness and in justice, in kindness and in mercy. I will betroth you to me in faithfulness; and you shall know the Lord (Hosea 2:21-22).

· At the conclusion of the service,* the tefillin are removed in the reverse order:

> The strap around the fingers is unwound.
> The head tefillin is taken off.
> The strap around the forearm is unwound and the hand tefillin is taken off.
> The tallit is not removed until after the tefillin.

· There are various ways to wrap the tefillin neatly. There is no religious significance to these methods. One may use whichever way is easiest and most suited for the size tefillin in use.

ૐ The tefillin should be placed directly upon the flesh of the arm and the hair of the head. There may not be any intervening material. If a person's hand is bandaged, he is exempt from putting on the tefillin. If it is the head that is bandaged, there are views that permit the tefillin to be put on, but without reciting the blessing.

ૐ If for any reason (a bandage, cast, physical impairment, loss of one of the tefillin) a person is not able to put on either the head tefillin or the hand tefillin, he is still required to put on the other one. Tefillin are reckoned as two separate mitzvot or religious duties and the inability to perform one does not exempt one from the obligation to perform the other.

ૐ If only the hand tefillin is put on, only the first blessing, לְהָנִיחַ תְּפִלִּין "to put on tefillin," is recited. If only the head tefillin is put on, both blessings, לְהָנִיחַ תְּפִלִּין "to put on tefillin" and עַל מִצְוַת תְּפִלִּין "concerning the mitzvah of tefillin" are recited.

---

* On Rosh Hodesh, the tefillin are removed just prior to the *musaph* Amidah. On hol hamoed, where tefillin are put on, they are removed right after the *shachrit* Amidah, just prior to Hallel.

Signs of the Covenant: Love and Reverence

&❧ It is customary and proper to begin to put on the tefillin one to three months prior to the Bar-Mitzvah, and not to wait until the actual birthdate.

&❧ If a person has no tefillin and enters a synagogue to join the congregation in prayer, it is preferable that he wait until after the services and borrow a pair of tefillin from another worshipper so that he may at least read the *Shema* and the *Amidah* while wearing tefillin, rather than pray with the congregation without tefillin.

&❧ The tefillin is part of the religious uniform worn by adult males during the weekday morning services. To engage in morning weekday prayers without them is a mark of disrespect. It is to approach the Lord, as a soldier in the army of God, improperly attired. No private would appear before a commanding officer, no subject before his ruler, improperly attired or wearing only half a uniform. To deliberately refuse to put on tefillin while reciting the Shema, where the commandment to put on tefillin appears twice, is looked upon as an act of arrogant contempt before the Lord. The Sages said: "Whoever recites the Shema without tefillin, it is as if he bears false witness against himself," i.e., accuses himself of falsehood (Brakhot 14b).

Putting on a tallit for the prayers (thereby fulfilling the mitzvah of tzitzit) is no substitute for the mitzvah of tefillin, and does not minimize the seriousness of neglecting the latter.

The few minutes of instruction required in order to learn how to put on tefillin should never deter an adult male who has never learned to put them on or who through years of neglect may have forgotten. He should seek out a rabbi, a teacher, or a fellow worshipper and ask for guidance. Nor should personal embarrassment in using a ritual object unique to Judaism and unknown to other faiths ever prove a deterrent. On the contrary, tefillin should be donned with pride and dignity. Their very antiquity and their basis in Scripture testify to the unbroken continuity of our faith for almost three and a half thousand years, and to the strength of Jewish conviction in the One God throughout all those generations. When the tefillin are put on, a male Jew testifies to his identification with the Jewish past, its present, and its future. Whether one prays in the synagogue or in the privacy of one's own home, tefillin is a required daily weekday observance.

&❧ While he who does not put on tefillin violates eight affirmative Biblical precepts, it is said of whoever puts on tefillin regularly that he will enjoy a long life, for it is written "The Lord is upon them, they shall live" (Isaiah 38:16).

MEZUZAH

&❧ "And these words which I command you this day . . . you shall write them on the doorposts of your house and on your gates" (Deut. 6:9). (See Tefillin, page 145.)

&❧ Although *mezuzah* is the Hebrew word for doorpost, the parchment scroll (*klaf*) which is placed upon the doorpost is also referred to as *mezuzah* after the place where it is put.

&❧ The mezuzah is a small scroll of parchment on which are written two Biblical passages. They are: "Hear O Israel, the Lord is our God, the Lord is One . . ." (Deut. 6:4–9), and "And if you will carefully obey my commandments . . ." (Deut. 11:13–21).

&❧ The parchment scroll is rolled up, enclosed in a case of a wood, metal or plastic material,* and attached to the doorpost. It is also permissible to hollow out a cavity in the doorpost and to insert the mezuzah or parchment scroll into it.

&❧ If a house has more than one entrance, even if only one is regularly used for coming and going, a mezuzah must be attached at each entrance.

&❧ Courtyards, fenced-in, or walled-in estates also require a mezuzah at their entrances, if the entrances are built according to the specifications listed below, since it is also written "upon your gates."

&❧ It is required to affix a mezuzah also at the entrance to each of the interior rooms of a house.

&❧ A mezuzah should not be affixed to such rooms as toilets and bathrooms, or to such buildings as bathhouses, as dignified use of the premises is a prerequisite.

---

* The mezuzah case has become an object of modern artistic creativity. One can find many differently designed mezuzah cases in a wide range of expensive and inexpensive materials.

ϑ∾ The house, or the room for which a mezuzah is required must be built for permanent use. (The reason a succah does not require a mezuzah is that it is built as a temporary residence.)

ϑ∾ A mezuzah is required for all openings built with two doorposts and an overhead lintel.

ϑ∾ The mezuzah may be put on by any member of the household, by women as well as by those who have not reached the age of Bar- or Bat-Mitzvah but are old enough to understand the nature and significance of this mitzvah.

ϑ∾ When one moves into a rented home, the law provides a thirty-day period in which to affix a mezuzah. If the home is one's own, it should be done immediately. Although it should not be delayed and ought to be taken care of as soon as possible, one is not in violation of the commandment until after the thirty-day period.

ϑ∾ If one moves out of a home, what should be done with the mezuzot—remove them or leave them? If one knows that another Jew will be moving in, it is proper to leave the mezuzot.

If one knows or has reason to believe that a non-Jew may be moving into the premises, it is best to remove the mezuzot. The reason is that the non-Jew may not treat the mezuzah as a sacred object and may himself possibly remove it or desecrate it.

Should a non-Jew request that the mezuzah be left on since he regards it as some sort of "lucky charm" that might bring him good fortune, this is an unworthy attitude toward the mezuzah and the mezuzah should still be removed.

If, however, it is only the mezuzah case that finds favor in the eyes of the non-Jew as a decorative piece, this may be left on as long as the sacred parchment scroll (*klaf*) is removed.

ϑ∾ According to Maimonides, those who look upon the mezuzah as an amulet, a lucky charm for the household, are ignorant. "Those fools not only fail to fulfill the mitzvah itself, but they have taken a great mitzvah, which involves the Oneness of God and the reminder to love Him and worship Him, and treat it as though it were an amulet designed to benefit them personally . . ." (Hil. Mezuzah 5:4).

ϑ∾ One notes the prevailing custom these days of wearing small mezuzah-like charms. If these are intended merely as jewelry in the

153

form of a Jewish symbol, similar to the Star of David or the Ten Commandments, or to identify the wearer as a Jew, there are no objections, although an actual mezuzah should not be so worn. If, however, they are worn as an amulet or a "lucky charm," it is a most unworthy use of the mezuzah even if a non-kosher (religiously invalid) mezuzah is used.

&❧ From time immemorial, the mezuzah has marked the Jewish home and made it identifiable as a residence wherein Jews live. But for the Jew himself, it should serve as a reminder upon entering or leaving his household of the Divine Presence and His unity, and of his own duties to abide by all the laws and precepts set forth in the Torah.

&❧ Procedure for affixing a mezuzah:

· Before attaching a mezuzah to a doorpost, the following blessing should be recited:

בָּרוּךְ אַתָּה יְיָ אֱלֹהֵינוּ מֶלֶךְ הָעוֹלָם, אֲשֶׁר קִדְּשָׁנוּ בְּמִצְוֹתָיו וְצִוָּנוּ לִקְבּוֹעַ מְזוּזָה.

Baruch ata adonai elohainu melech ha-olam asher kidshanu b'mitzvotav v'tzivanu likboa mezuzah.

Blessed art Thou, Lord our God, King of the universe who has sanctified us with His commandments and commanded us to affix a mezuzah.

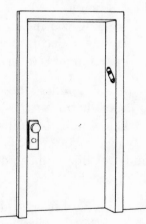

FIGURE 2

154

· The mezuzah, in its case, is then nailed or screwed or glued to the right side of the door, as one enters the house or room.
· The mezuzah is placed at the beginning of the upper third of the doorpost (a height of a little less than a third of the way from the top of the doorpost). If one is in doubt about the estimated height, better somewhat higher than lower.
· If the doorpost is a wide one, it should be placed no further in than three and three-quarter inches from the outside.
· The mezuzah is tilted at an angle with the upper part of the mezuzah slanted inwards toward the house or room, and the lower part away from the house.
Should the doorpost be too narrow to permit the mezuzah to be slanted, it may be attached vertically. This is preferable to attaching it behind the door inside the house.

TZITZIT AND TALLIT

ક્ષ The commandment in the following passage calls for the attachment of fringes (*tzitzit*) to four-cornered garments as a reminder of all the commandments of the Lord:

> And the Lord spoke unto Moses, saying: "Speak unto the children of Israel, and bid them that they make them throughout their generations fringes in the corners of their garments, and that they put with the fringe of each corner a thread of blue. And it shall be unto you for a fringe, that ye may look upon it, and remember all the commandments of the Lord, and do them; and that ye go not about after your own heart and your own eyes, after which ye use to go astray; that ye may remember and do all My commandments, and be holy unto your God. I am the Lord your God, who brought you out of the land of Egypt, to be your God: I am the Lord your God."
>
> (Numbers 15:37-41)

ક્ષ Garments not possessing four or more corners are not required to have the special fringes.

ક્ષ The observance of this mitzvah is limited to the day. Because it emphasizes "and you shall look upon them" (i.e., see them), the

Sages taught that at night (when in pitch darkness one cannot see) the mitzvah of tzitzit is not in force.*

§ Although in ancient times four-cornered garments or robes were common, the development of clothing not having four corners would have rendered this mitzvah totally obsolete, with the full sanction of the law. To prevent the total disappearance of a mitzvah that possessed such great symbolic significance (since it serves as a reminder to observe all the commandments), the Sages encouraged the wearing of specially-made four-cornered garments so as to provide the opportunity to observe and implement this commandment.

Says Maimonides: "Although one is not obligated to buy a garment and wrap himself in it just so as to provide it with fringes, it is not proper for a devout or pious person to exempt himself from observing this precept. He should strive to wear a garment that requires fringes so as to perform this precept. And during times of prayer, one should take special care to do so" (Hil. Tzitzit 3:11).

§ The *tallit,* a four-cornered robe with the required tzitzit, has thus become the garment traditionally worn by men during morning prayer services. In English, it is commonly called a "prayer shawl."

Before wrapping the tallit about oneself, it is held in both hands while standing, and the following blessing is recited:

בָּרוּךְ אַתָּה יְיָ אֱלֹהֵינוּ מֶלֶךְ הָעוֹלָם, אֲשֶׁר קִדְּשָׁנוּ בְּמִצְוֹתָיו וְצִוָּנוּ לְהִתְעַטֵּף בַּצִּיצִת.

Baruch ata adonai elohainu melech ha-olam asher kidshanu b'mitzvotav v'tzivanu l'hit-atef b'tzitzit.

Blessed art Thou, Lord our God, King of the universe who has sanctified us with His commandments and commanded us to wrap ourselves in the tzitzit.

§ It is the fringes (tzitzit) on the four corners of the tallit that provide it with its religious significance. The rest of its design, whether simple or elaborate, colorful or plain, rich in embroidered Jewish religious symbols or lacking them, is only incidental to its

---

* It is for this reason that a tallit is never worn at evening services. The only exception is on Yom Kippur night for Kol Nidre services because of the extraordinary sanctity of the night.

primary use for the observance of the mitzvah of "putting tzitzit on the corners of your garments so that you may look upon them and remember to do all the commandments of the Lord . . . ."

&❧ The shorter fringes found along the two sides of many *tallitot* (plural) are not tzitzit, but only ornaments and have no particular significance.

&❧ In order for the tallit to qualify as a garment, it should be large enough to cover the greater portion of one's torso. A proper tallit is not a narrow neck scarf, which certainly does not qualify.

&❧ It is not only through the tallit worn during prayer that the mitzvah of tzitzit is observed. A devout or pious person will also acquire a small tallit (*tallit katan*). This is a four-cornered garment which fits over the shoulders, covering chest and back and usually worn under the shirt. Thus the mitzvah is observed not only during prayer but all day as well.

&❧ The *tallit katan* is sometimes referred to as an *arba kanfot*, which means four corners and is descriptive of the type of garment it is.*

&❧ The blessing recited before putting on the tallit katan is:

בָּרוּךְ אַתָּה יְיָ אֱלֹהֵינוּ מֶלֶךְ הָעוֹלָם, אֲשֶׁר קִדְּשָׁנוּ בְּמִצְוֹתָיו וְצִוָּנוּ עַל מִצְוַת צִיצִת.

Baruch ata adonai elohainu melech ha-olam asher kidshanu b'mitzvotav v'tzivanu al mitzvat tzitzit.

Blessed art Thou, Lord our God, King of the universe who has sanctified us with His commandments and commanded us concerning the mitzvah of tzitzit.

This, too, is said only during the day and not at night.

&❧ Where the tzitzit on even one of the four corners of a tallit or tallit katan are cut or torn (off), it should be removed and the

---

* The tallit katan, like the regular tallit and all other ritual items and sacred books can be purchased in any Jewish Religious Supplies store.

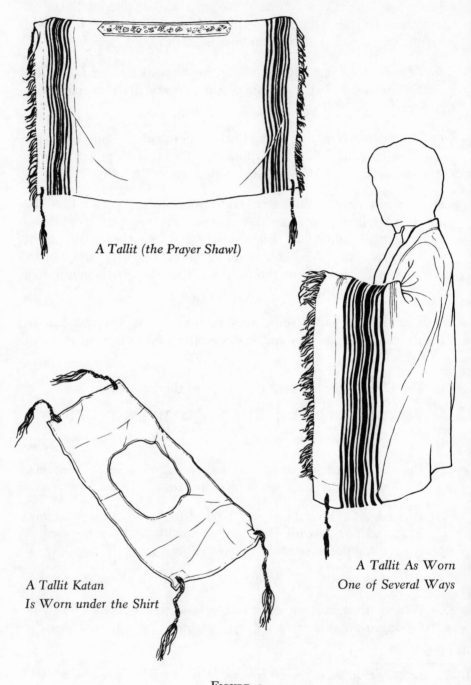

A Tallit (the Prayer Shawl)

A Tallit Katan
Is Worn under the Shirt

A Tallit As Worn
One of Several Ways

FIGURE 3

158

tzitzit replaced. A person who knows how to tie the tzitzit onto their four corners should be asked to do it.

కు The specific instructions as to how the tzitzit are tied to the tallit are not found in the Written Torah, but have been handed down by the Oral Torah. The Shulhan Arukh describes it in detail. There is much mystical as well as symbolic meaning attached to the procedure. For example, the thirty-nine windings that go into the making of each of the four fringes equals the numerical value of the Hebrew words for "The Lord is One."

PRAYER

కు To engage in prayer is the most obvious and the most universal reflection of man's relationship with God. Prayer in its highest form and at its most sincere levels is called a "service of the heart," (*avodah she'blev*), and constitutes one of the many ways by which *love of God* is expressed.

కు "And you shall *serve* the Lord your God" (Exodus 23:25). According to Maimonides, this refers to prayer for he relates it to "And you shall *serve* the Lord your God *with all your heart*." According to the Sages, the latter part of the verse is a reference to *prayer* (tefilah). This religious duty is equally incumbent upon men and women.

కు Originally prayer was unstructured and informal. To engage in prayer at least once a day, however short or long, was the minimal obligation, although many did so more often.

కు Although prayer in its most ideal expression should be spontaneous, expressing in words what the heart feels and the mind believes, the inability of people "to express themselves adequately and accurately," the lack of command of language by the average person "to adequately express needs or to praise God," led Ezra and the Men of the Great Assembly "to institute the Eighteen Benedictions in their present order. The first three of these Eighteen Benedictions contain praise to God; the last three, thanksgiving; and the intermediate petitions are prayers for the most essential needs of the individual and the community. They were set on everyone's lips and learned, so that men of inarticulate speech might offer prayer as clearly as those who speak an eloquent Hebrew. For this reason, they instituted all other blessings and prayers which are arrayed on the lips of all Israel, to make each blessing readily available to the stammerer or the one who is unfamiliar with the language" (Hil. Tefilah 1:4).

ৡ Although the "service of the heart" was always considered to be the most natural expression of faith, the prayer services became also the official substitute for the central Temple worship (which had taken the form of sacrificial offerings of either meal, flour and/or animals), after the Temple had been destroyed and the sacrificial service eliminated.*

ৡ The morning (*shachrit*) service is thus said to correspond to the *shachrit* offering; the *minha* service to the daily afternoon offering; the *musaf* service on Sabbaths and festivals to the additional *musaf* offering required on those special days. Furthermore, the time when these services may be held corresponds to the time periods when their corresponding offerings could be brought.

The exception to this parallel relationship is the daily evening service (*arvit* or *maariv*) for there was no corresponding evening offering. It is for this reason that the obligatory status of this worship service was always questionable and a matter of dispute. Although precedent, tradition, and usage finally established the *maariv* as a standard service, its "non-statutory" status is indicated by the fact that it is the only service where the Amidah does not have to be repeated by the Reader.

ৡ The tradition of prayer among Jews as a "service of the heart" extends to a period of time long before the Temple was destroyed. The practices of the Patriarchs set the example. "And Abraham prayed unto God" (Genesis 20:17) was an act of faith that was repeated by his descendants after him. This explains why three, rather than only two daily services developed, as might have been expected if the reason for the daily services was only that they substituted for the Temple sacrifices.

---

* According to the Torah, the sacrificial service was limited to the Beit Hamikdash and to the Temple Mount. It was forbidden to offer a sacrifice at any other place.

The tradition of three daily services is ascribed to the practices of the Patriarchs. The morning prayer is ascribed to Abraham, the afternoon prayer to Isaac, and the evening prayer is credited to Jacob.

ào Since the various worship services are nevertheless regarded as also being in lieu of the sacrificial offerings (*korbanot*), prayer also assumed the obligatory qualities (and character) of the *korbanot*. The bringing of korbanot was to indicate loyalty and devotion to God. It was also a means of bringing the Jew closer to God. (*Korban*— literally *sacrifice*—is actually a derivative of the word *karov*, which means *to approach, to come closer*.) So was the "worship of the heart" to reflect these qualities.

ào Whatever formal prayers represent or symbolize, one thing must be borne in mind: prayer, tefilah, involves talking to God. It does not mean to watch a service *performed*; it does not even mean to just sit while others pray. It means to involve oneself in an experience where one attempts to address the Almighty Himself.

ào Although prayers said daily may tend to deteriorate into routine recitations, the Sages stressed the importance of avoiding this danger. "And when you pray, make not your prayer routine, but (a plea for) mercy and supplication before God" (Avot 2:18). "He who makes his prayer routine, his prayer is not considered as supplication" (Brakhot 4:4).

ào To assure meaningfulness in prayer, the Sages insisted upon conditions conducive to concentration (*kavanah*). They called for purity of thought and sanctity of place. They called for proper and respectful behavior during prayer. Thus:

- It is forbidden to talk or chatter during prayer.
- It is forbidden to introduce distractions during prayer.
- It is forbidden to condone levity, playfulness, and similar disrespectful practices.

These are among the specific rules intended to *assist* the worshipper in attaining a sense of spiritual depth when engaged in prayer. The rest is, however, up to the person himself.

ào The daily morning prayers should be said upon arising, immediately after washing and dressing. It is considered an act of disrespect before the Lord to sit down to eat before praying. If one, however, requires some nourishment upon arising, particularly on the Sabbath when the morning prayers are lengthier, it is permitted to have some tea or coffee or juice before the services.

ह्ल The core of every worship service is the Amidah. It is also called the *Shmoneh Esrai*, because its daily form originally consisted of eighteen benedictions. This prayer constitutes the essence of the daily morning, afternoon and evening services, as well as of all of the Sabbath and festival services.

The Amidah is said quietly while standing at attention (feet together). A sick person or invalid may say this prayer while sitting or even lying down.

ह्ल One should not allow oneself to be interrupted during the recitation of the Amidah, or to have one's attention diverted from the prayer. One should try to clear one's mind of all distracting thoughts.

ह्ल The Amidah should not be said while facing a painting or any sculptured work. It is also expressly forbidden to say it in front of a mirror.

ह्ल The Amidah should be said while facing in the direction of the land of Israel. Those in Israel face in the direction of Jerusalem. Those in Jerusalem, face in the direction of the Temple Mount. If one is unsure about his directions, "let him then direct his heart to his Father in Heaven."

ह्ल In public worship, the Amidah is repeated in its entirety by the Reader at every service except at the evening maariv service. The purpose is to enable those who cannot pray at all or whose Hebrew prayers are full of errors to listen carefully and answer "Amen" after each blessing. This response credits the respondent with the merit of having properly recited the Amidah prayer.

ह्ल "Know before whom you stand," is a favorite reminder inscribed on the walls of synagogues and holy arks. It emphasizes the awareness that each worshipper must have while praying.

ह्ल The widespread custom of taking three steps back upon the conclusion of the Amidah was adapted from the ancient customs followed in the relationship between master and servant, and between sovereign king and subject. This was the manner in which a servant or a subject would take leave of his master or sovereign. The Jew saw fit to take leave of the King of Kings, the Holy One, Blessed Be He, in like fashion to emphasize their status as His subjects or servants.

৯৬ The morning Amidah (shachrit) may be said anytime from sunrise until one-third of the day (a day is reckoned from sunrise to sunset). In case of unavoidable delay—although the proper time has passed—it may still be said until the half-day mark.

The afternoon Amidah (minha) may be said anytime from a half-hour past the half-day mark until sundown.

The evening Amidah (maariv) is said all evening beginning with nightfall. It may, however, be said earlier.

৯৬ Women are not bound to the formal prayer service nor to the set times designated for the three daily services, nor are they required, as are the men, to join in public congregational worship. The established principle that women are generally exempt from those positive ritual observances that need to be done at a set time (*she-hazman grama*) takes into consideration a woman's primary responsibility as wife and mother. A woman nursing a child, for example, was not expected to drop everything in order to attend set prayer schedules. The man is expected to arrange his schedule and his work to conform to religious requirements. And while not all women have such responsibilities throughout their lives, the law cannot distinguish between those who do and those who don't— and so the leniency with regard to some observances is extended to all.

While women are required to pray, they can do so at any time convenient to them and can do so privately without attending a public service. While it is praiseworthy of them to make every effort to attend the synagogue on Sabbaths and festivals—and observant Jewish women usually do—their attendance is not a religious statutory requirement.

Shema

৯৬ Every Jew is required to recite the Biblical passage known as the *Shema* (Hear O Israel) twice a day, morning and evening, in fulfillment of the precept: "And you shall talk of them . . . When you lie down and when you rise up." The morning and evening prayer service incorporates the passage.

שְׁמַע יִשְׂרָאֵל, יְיָ אֱלֹהֵינוּ, יְיָ אֶחָד.

בָּרוּךְ שֵׁם כְּבוֹד מַלְכוּתוֹ לְעוֹלָם וָעֶד.

וְאָהַבְתָּ אֵת יְיָ אֱלֹהֶיךָ בְּכָל לְבָבְךָ וּבְכָל נַפְשְׁךָ וּבְכָל

מְאֹדֶךָ. וְהָיוּ הַדְּבָרִים הָאֵלֶּה, אֲשֶׁר אָנֹכִי מְצַוְּךָ הַיּוֹם, עַל

לְבָבֶךָ. וְשִׁנַּנְתָּם לְבָנֶיךָ, וְדִבַּרְתָּ בָּם בְּשִׁבְתְּךָ בְּבֵיתֶךָ, וּבְלֶכְתְּךָ

בַדֶּרֶךְ, וּבְשָׁכְבְּךָ וּבְקוּמֶךָ. וּקְשַׁרְתָּם לְאוֹת עַל יָדֶךָ, וְהָיוּ

לְטֹטָפֹת בֵּין עֵינֶיךָ. וּכְתַבְתָּם עַל מְזוּזוֹת בֵּיתֶךָ וּבִשְׁעָרֶיךָ.

*Shema yisrael, adonai elohainu adonai ehad. Baruch shem kvod
malchuto l'olam va-ed. V'a-havta et adonai elohecha b'chol
l'vavcha uv-chol naf-sh'cha uv-chol m'odecha. V'hayu hadvarim
ha-aileh asher anochi m'tzav-cha ha-yom al l'vavecha, v'shee-
nantam l'vanecha v'dee-barta bam, b'sheev-t'cha b'vaitecha
uv-lech-t'cha va-derech, uv-shach-b'cha uv-kumecha. Uk-shartam
l'ot al yadecha, v'hayu l'totafot bayn aynecha uch-tavtam al
mezuzot baytecha u-vish-arecha.*

Hear, O Israel, the Lord is our God, the Lord is One. Blessed
be the name of his glorious Majesty forever and ever. Love
the Lord your God with all your heart, with all your soul,
with all your means. And these words which I command you today shall be upon your heart. Teach them diligently to your children, and talk of them when you sit in your house, when you walk
on the road, when you lie down and when you rise up. Bind them
for a sign upon your hand and for frontlets between your eyes.
Write them upon the doorposts of your house and upon your gates.

&❧ Even though the Shema is an integral part of the morning and
evening services, the Shema is not, technically speaking, a prayer.
It is a declaration of faith. It is an affirmation of the unity of God
that reminds us of our obligations to Him, that recalls the signs of
the Covenant and cautions against turning astray to follow the vain
desires of the heart and the immoralities for which the eyes may long.

Blessings When Called to Torah

&ᴗ The Jewish tradition also regards *religious study* as a form of Divine worship.

&ᴗ To provide the average worshipper with the opportunity to satisfy the minimum requirements of daily Torah study, portions of the preliminary daily service include selections, not only from the Torah but also from the Mishna and Gemara (Talmud).

&ᴗ *Reading from the Torah* constitutes a central part of the Sabbath and festival services. The Torah is also read at the Monday and Thursday morning services, the Sabbath afternoon services, as well as on all special occasions, such as Rosh Hodesh and the fast days.

In ancient times, the Torah Reading was accompanied by a Translator (*meturgeman*) who rendered it into the colloquial tongue, verse by verse. Where the Hebrew is not easily understood, the rabbi's sermon elaborating on the meaning of selected portions of the Torah Reading or the use of a text with a translation serves a comparable purpose.

&ᴗ When a person is called up to the Reading of the Torah (it is called an *Aliyah*), he recites two blessings; the first one just before the Reader reads the portion, the second one immediately following. The two blessings are as follows:

בָּרְכוּ אֶת יְיָ הַמְבֹרָךְ.

Congregation responds:

בָּרוּךְ יְיָ הַמְבֹרָךְ לְעוֹלָם וָעֶד.

He repeats the response and continues:

בָּרוּךְ אַתָּה יְיָ אֱלֹהֵינוּ מֶלֶךְ הָעוֹלָם, אֲשֶׁר בָּחַר בָּנוּ מִכָּל הָעַמִּים וְנָתַן לָנוּ אֶת תּוֹרָתוֹ. בָּרוּךְ אַתָּה יְיָ, נוֹתֵן הַתּוֹרָה.

Barchu et adonai hamvorach. Baruch adonai hamvorach l'olam va-ed.

Baruch ata adonai elohainu melech ha-olam asher bachar banu mikol ha-amim, v'natan lanu et torato. Baruch ata adonai, notain hatorah.

Bless the Lord who is blessed. Blessed is the Lord who is forever blessed.

Blessed art Thou Lord our God, King of the universe who has chosen us from among all peoples by giving us Thy Torah. Blessed art Thou Lord, giver of the Torah.

The Torah is read. Then he recites:

בָּרוּךְ אַתָּה יְיָ אֱלֹהֵינוּ מֶלֶךְ הָעוֹלָם, אֲשֶׁר נָתַן לָנוּ תּוֹרַת

אֱמֶת וְחַיֵּי עוֹלָם נָטַע בְּתוֹכֵנוּ. בָּרוּךְ אַתָּה יְיָ, נוֹתֵן הַתּוֹרָה.

Baruch ata adonai elohainu melech ha-olam asher natan lanu torat emet, v'hayai olam nata b'tohainu. Baruch ata adonai, notain hatorah.

Blessed art Thou, Lord our God, King of the universe who has given us Thy Torah of truth and thereby planted among us life eternal. Blessed art Thou, Lord, giver of the Torah.

ଅ❧ As a sign of affection for the Torah, it is customary just before reciting each of the benedictions to touch the Torah with the tallit at the place where the individual portion begins, and then to kiss the tallit.

ଅ❧ While the first blessing is recited, it is proper that the Torah scroll remain open; while the second blessing is recited, the scroll is rolled together.

ଅ❧ Although it is permissible to worship in private (*tefilat yahid*), our religious tradition has always considered public worship (*tefilat tzibbur*) preferable and more laudatory. Every effort to join a congregation in prayer should thus be made.

ଅ❧ Public worship cannot take place if there are fewer than ten adult male Jews present. The reason why a female, a male child under 13, or a non-Jew cannot qualify for the quorum, although they may join in the public worship once a quorum is established, is that the persons in these categories do not have the same religious obligation under the law to join in public worship. According to principles of Jewish law, persons with lesser obligations *in any particular religious area* do not in *that same area* enjoy its inherent privileges. For why women are exempt from the obligation of attending public worship, see page 163.

ౝ The quorum of ten needed for the conduct of public religious worship is called a *minyan*. Literally, the word means "a number," or "a few." The basis for ten as the quorum is the Biblical passage in Numbers 14:27, where the term *eidah* which means a congregation or a community is used. According to rabbinic tradition, the reference here is to the ten scouts who brought back to Moses the pessimistic report of their expedition into the land of Canaan.

That any number less than ten is not regarded as a community is alluded to in the Torah elsewhere as well. Abraham stopped his bargaining with God for the fate of Sodom and Gomorrah after he reached the figure of ten (Genesis 18:16–33). As long as ten righteous men could be found, the merits of the righteous community, though small, could be weighed against the sins of the wicked community. With less than ten, they could be regarded only as a handful of individuals whose personal merits could not offset the collective wickedness of the community.

ౝ The following portions of the service are never said unless a minyan is present:

· Kaddish, the Sanctification of God's name.
· Kedusha, a prayer in the Amidah, the Eighteen Benedictions.
· Borchu, the call to bless God.
· Birkat Kohanim, the Priestly Benediction.
· Reader's repetition of the Amidah, the Eighteen Benedictions.
· Reading of the Torah.

The basis for requiring a minyan for prayers that sanctify God's name is the Biblical passage from Leviticus 22:32: ". . . that I may be sanctified in the midst of the Israelite people." The sanctification of God's Name is not a private matter, but a public act in the midst of a community.

ౝ If less than the necessary quorum gathers, the people may proceed to recite all other prayers (excluding those enumerated) privately as individuals, or in unison under the leadership of a Reader.

Blessings for Various Foods and Occasions

ౝ In addition to the formal worship services, a sense of the Divine Presence is maintained by the prayers and blessings that are recited daily for many things—foremost being those in connection with the daily meals.

&ᴗ The blessing for bread is:

בָּרוּךְ אַתָּה יְיָ אֱלֹהֵינוּ מֶלֶךְ הָעוֹלָם, הַמּוֹצִיא לֶחֶם מִן הָאָרֶץ.

Baruch ata adonai elohainu melech ha-olam hamotzi lehem min ha-aretz.

Blessed art Thou, Lord our God, King of the universe who brings forth bread from the earth.

When bread is served with a meal, only the blessing for the bread is said. When not eating bread, or when partaking of a food at times other than at regular mealtime, other blessings are used. A few that one should know by heart:

בָּרוּךְ אַתָּה יְיָ אֱלֹהֵינוּ מֶלֶךְ הָעוֹלָם, שֶׁהַכֹּל נִהְיֶה בִּדְבָרוֹ.

Baruch ata adonai elohainu melech ha-olam she-hakol nee-yeh bidvaro.

Blessed art Thou, Lord our God, King of the universe through whose word all things were called into being.

(This is said before drinking any liquid except wine, or eating meat, fish, eggs, cheese, etc.)

בָּרוּךְ אַתָּה יְיָ אֱלֹהֵינוּ מֶלֶךְ הָעוֹלָם, בּוֹרֵא פְּרִי הָעֵץ.

Baruch ata adonai elohainu melech ha-olam borai pri ha-etz.

Blessed art Thou, Lord our God, King of the universe who creates the fruit of the tree.

(This is said before eating a fruit which grows on a tree.)

בָּרוּךְ אַתָּה יְיָ אֱלֹהֵינוּ מֶלֶךְ הָעוֹלָם, בּוֹרֵא פְּרִי הָאֲדָמָה.

Baruch ata adonai elohainu melech ha-olam borai pri ha-adamah.

Blessed art Thou, Lord our God, King of the universe who creates the fruit of the earth.

(This is said before eating any vegetable or fruit which grows from the ground.)

בָּרוּךְ אַתָּה יְיָ אֱלֹהֵינוּ מֶלֶךְ הָעוֹלָם, בּוֹרֵא מִינֵי מְזוֹנוֹת.

Baruch ata adonai elohainu melech ha-olam borai minai m'zonot.

Blessed art Thou. Lord our God, King of the universe who creates various kinds of food.

(This is said before eating a food, other than bread, prepared from any of the five grains [wheat, barley, rye, oats, spelt] and rice.)

ه A blessing that is appropriate for special joyous occasions in one's life, upon hearing good tidings, acquiring new possessions, tasting of a new fruit:

בָּרוּךְ אַתָּה יְיָ אֱלֹהֵינוּ מֶלֶךְ הָעוֹלָם, שֶׁהֶחֱיָנוּ וְקִיְּמָנוּ וְהִגִּיעָנוּ לַזְּמַן הַזֶּה.

Baruch ata adonai elohainu melech ha-olam sheheheyanu v'kee-y'manu v'hee-gee-anu lazman hazeh.

Blessed art Thou. Lord our God, King of the universe who has kept us in life and sustained us and enabled us to reach this season.

This last blessing is also said at candlelighting and at Kiddush on the first two days of each of the major festivals (Pesach, Shavuot, Succot, Shmini Atzeret and Rosh Hashana) as well as for lighting the *menorah* on the first day of Hanukah.

ه Blessings were instituted to provide awareness of God's role in nature and the life of man. A selection of such blessings follow:

On seeing a person of profound Torah wisdom:

בָּרוּךְ אַתָּה יְיָ אֱלֹהֵינוּ מֶלֶךְ הָעוֹלָם, שֶׁחָלַק מֵחָכְמָתוֹ לִירֵאָיו.

Blessed art Thou, Lord our God, King of the universe who has imparted of His wisdom to those who revere Him.

On seeing a person of profound secular learning:

בָּרוּךְ אַתָּה יְיָ אֱלֹהֵינוּ מֶלֶךְ הָעוֹלָם, שֶׁנָּתַן מֵחָכְמָתוֹ לְבָשָׂר וָדָם.

Blessed art Thou, Lord our God, King of the universe who has imparted of His wisdom to flesh and blood.

On hearing bad tidings:

בָּרוּךְ אַתָּה יְיָ אֱלֹהֵינוּ מֶלֶךְ הָעוֹלָם, דַּיַּן הָאֱמֶת.

Blessed art Thou, Lord our God, King of the universe, the true Judge.

On hearing good tidings:

בָּרוּךְ אַתָּה יְיָ אֱלֹהֵינוּ מֶלֶךְ הָעוֹלָם, הַטּוֹב וְהַמֵּטִיב.

Blessed art Thou, Lord our God, King of the universe who is good and does good.

On seeing beauties of nature:

בָּרוּךְ אַתָּה יְיָ אֱלֹהֵינוּ מֶלֶךְ הָעוֹלָם, שֶׁכָּכָה לוֹ בְּעוֹלָמוֹ.

Blessed art Thou, Lord our God, King of the universe who has such as these in His world.

On seeing the wonders of nature:

בָּרוּךְ אַתָּה יְיָ אֱלֹהֵינוּ מֶלֶךְ הָעוֹלָם, עֹשֶׂה מַעֲשֵׂה בְרֵאשִׁית.

Blessed art Thou, Lord our God, King of the universe who hast made the works of creation.

Selected Forms of Grace after Meals

SHORT FORM OF GRACE

בָּרוּךְ אַתָּה יְיָ אֱלֹהֵינוּ מֶלֶךְ הָעוֹלָם, הַזָּן אֶת הָעוֹלָם כֻּלּוֹ בְּטוּבוֹ בְּחֵן בְּחֶסֶד וּבְרַחֲמִים. הוּא נוֹתֵן לֶחֶם לְכָל בָּשָׂר, כִּי לְעוֹלָם חַסְדּוֹ. וּבְטוּבוֹ הַגָּדוֹל תָּמִיד לֹא חָסַר לָנוּ וְאַל יֶחְסַר לָנוּ מָזוֹן לְעוֹלָם וָעֶד. בַּעֲבוּר שְׁמוֹ הַגָּדוֹל, כִּי הוּא אֵל זָן וּמְפַרְנֵס לַכֹּל וּמֵטִיב לַכֹּל וּמֵכִין מָזוֹן לְכָל בְּרִיּוֹתָיו אֲשֶׁר בָּרָא. בָּרוּךְ אַתָּה יְיָ, הַזָּן אֶת הַכֹּל.

נוֹדֶה לְךָ יְיָ אֱלֹהֵינוּ, עַל שֶׁהִנְחַלְתָּ לַאֲבוֹתֵינוּ אֶרֶץ חֶמְדָּה
טוֹבָה וּרְחָבָה, בְּרִית וְתוֹרָה וְלֶחֶם לָשׂוֹבַע. בָּרוּךְ אַתָּה יְיָ,
עַל הָאָרֶץ וְעַל הַמָּזוֹן.

רַחֵם יְיָ אֱלֹהֵינוּ, עַל יִשְׂרָאֵל עַמֶּךָ וְעַל יְרוּשָׁלַיִם עִירֶךָ,
וְעַל צִיּוֹן מִשְׁכַּן כְּבוֹדֶךָ וְעַל מַלְכוּת בֵּית דָּוִד מְשִׁיחֶךָ,
וְתַגְדִּיל מְהֵרָה כְבוֹד הַבַּיִת וּתְנַחֲמֵנוּ בִּכְפְלַיִם. בָּרוּךְ אַתָּה
יְיָ, בּוֹנֵה בְרַחֲמָיו יְרוּשָׁלַיִם, אָמֵן.

בָּרוּךְ אַתָּה יְיָ, אֱלֹהֵינוּ מֶלֶךְ הָעוֹלָם, הָאֵל אָבִינוּ מַלְכֵּנוּ
הַמֶּלֶךְ הַטּוֹב וְהַמֵּטִיב לַכֹּל. הוּא הֵטִיב, הוּא מֵטִיב, הוּא
יֵיטִיב לָנוּ.

(On Sabbath add:

וְיַנְחִילֵנוּ יוֹם שֶׁכֻּלוֹ שַׁבָּת)

וִיזַכֵּנוּ לִימוֹת הַמָּשִׁיחַ וּלְחַיֵּי הָעוֹלָם הַבָּא. עוֹשֶׂה שָׁלוֹם
בִּמְרוֹמָיו, הוּא יַעֲשֶׂה שָׁלוֹם עָלֵינוּ וְעַל כָּל יִשְׂרָאֵל, וְאִמְרוּ
אָמֵן.

Blessed art Thou, Lord our God, King of the universe. Thou sustainest the whole world with Thy goodness, loving favor and kindness. Thou givest food to all flesh, for Thy mercy endures forever. In Thy great goodness, our sustenance has never failed us. May it never fail us for the sake of Thy great name. Thou art God who provides nourishing food for all and art beneficent to all, preparing food for all Thy creatures whom Thou hast created. Blessed art Thou, Lord, who provides food for all.

We thank Thee, Lord our God, for the desirable, good and ample land which Thou didst grant to our fathers as a heritage. We thank Thee for the Covenant and the Torah, for life and sustenance in plenty. Blessed art Thou, Lord, for the land and for the food.

Have compassion, Lord our God, upon Israel Thy people, upon Jerusalem, Thy city, and upon the royal house of David Thine anointed. May Thou soon exalt the glory of Thy Temple,

171

and doubly comfort us. Blessed art Thou, Lord, who in Thy mercy rebuilds Jerusalem. Amen.

Blessed art Thou, Lord our God, God, our Father, our King, who is kind and deals kindly with all; Thou hast dealt kindly, dost deal kindly, and wilt deal kindly with us.

(On Sabbath say: Let us inherit the day which shall be wholly a Sabbath; and)

(On Festivals say: Let us inherit the day which is altogether good; and)

Make us worthy of the days of the Messiah, and the life of the world to come. May He who creates peace in His celestial heights create peace for us and for all Israel; and say, Amen.

FORM OF GRACE

After cake or Holy Land fruits (grapes, figs, pomegranates, olives and dates)

בָּרוּךְ אַתָּה יְיָ אֱלֹהֵינוּ מֶלֶךְ הָעוֹלָם,

Cake and wine	Cake	Fruit	Wine
עַל הַגֶּפֶן וְעַל	עַל הַמִּחְיָה	עַל הָעֵץ	עַל הַגֶּפֶן
פְּרִי הַגֶּפֶן	וְעַל הַכַּלְכָּלָה וְעַל הַגֶּפֶן	וְעַל פְּרִי	וְעַל פְּרִי
וְעַל הַמִּחְיָה וְעַל	הָעֵץ,	הַכַּלְכָּלָה,	הַגֶּפֶן, וְעַל פְּרִי הַגֶּפֶן,

וְעַל תְּנוּבַת הַשָּׂדֶה, וְעַל אֶרֶץ חֶמְדָּה טוֹבָה וּרְחָבָה שֶׁרָצִיתָ וְהִנְחַלְתָּ לַאֲבוֹתֵינוּ לֶאֱכֹל מִפִּרְיָה וְלִשְׂבֹּעַ מִטּוּבָהּ. רַחֶם־נָא, יְיָ אֱלֹהֵינוּ, עַל יִשְׂרָאֵל עַמֶּךָ, וְעַל יְרוּשָׁלַיִם עִירֶךָ, וְעַל צִיּוֹן מִשְׁכַּן כְּבוֹדֶךָ, וְעַל מִזְבַּחַךְ וְעַל הֵיכָלֶךָ. וּבְנֵה יְרוּשָׁלַיִם עִיר הַקֹּדֶשׁ בִּמְהֵרָה בְיָמֵינוּ, וְהַעֲלֵנוּ לְתוֹכָהּ וְשַׂמְּחֵנוּ בְּבִנְיָנָהּ, וְנֹאכַל מִפִּרְיָהּ וְנִשְׂבַּע מִטּוּבָהּ, וּנְבָרֶכְךָ עָלֶיהָ בִּקְדֻשָּׁה וּבְטָהֳרָה.

On Sabbath:

רְצֵה וְהַחֲלִיצֵנוּ בְּיוֹם הַשַּׁבָּת הַזֶּה.

On Rosh Ḥodesh:

זָכְרֵנוּ לְטוֹבָה בְּיוֹם רֹאשׁ הַחֹדֶשׁ הַזֶּה.

Signs of the Covenant: Love and Reverence

On Rosh Hashana:

זָכְרֵנוּ לְטוֹבָה בְּיוֹם הַזִּכָּרוֹן הַזֶּה.

On festivals:

שַׂמְּחֵנוּ בְּיוֹם חַג

Shmini Atzeret	Succot	Shavuot	Pesach

הַמַּצּוֹת הַשָּׁבֻעוֹת הַסֻּכּוֹת הַשְּׁמִינִי, חַג הָעֲצֶרֶת

הַזֶּה. כִּי אַתָּה, יְיָ, טוֹב וּמֵטִיב לַכֹּל, וְנוֹדֶה לְּךָ עַל הָאָרֶץ

Fruit	Wine

וְעַל פְּרִי הַגָּפֶן. בָּרוּךְ אַתָּה   וְעַל הַפֵּרוֹת. בָּרוּךְ אַתָּה

יְיָ, עַל הָאָרֶץ וְעַל פְּרִי הַגָּפֶן.   יְיָ, עַל הָאָרֶץ וְעַל הַפֵּרוֹת.

Cake

וְעַל הַמִּחְיָה, בָּרוּךְ אַתָּה יְיָ, עַל הָאָרֶץ וְעַל הַמִּחְיָה.

Cake and wine

וְעַל הַמִּחְיָה, וְעַל פְּרִי הַגָּפֶן. בָּרוּךְ אַתָּה יְיָ, עַל הָאָרֶץ

וְעַל הַמִּחְיָה וְעַל פְּרִי הַגָּפֶן.

Blessed art Thou, Lord our God, King of the universe, for the food and the sustenance, for the produce of the field, for the desirable, good and spacious land that pleased Thee to give to our forefathers as a heritage to eat of its fruit and be sated from its goodness. Be merciful, Lord our God, to Thy people Israel, to Thy city Jerusalem and to Zion, the dwelling place of Thy glory, to Thy altar and Thy temple. Rebuild Jerusalem, the holy city, soon in our days; bring us to it and gladden us with its restoration; we will eat of its fruit and be sated with its goodness and we will bless Thee for it in holiness and purity; (on Sabbath or festival, appropriate verse is inserted here) for Thou, O Lord, art good and do good to all; we will thank Thee for the land and for the food. Blessed art Thou, O Lord, for the land and for the food.

FORM OF GRACE

After any food or liquids requiring the blessing *she-hakol nee-yeh bidvaro*

בָּרוּךְ אַתָּה יְיָ אֱלֹהֵינוּ מֶלֶךְ הָעוֹלָם, בּוֹרֵא נְפָשׁוֹת רַבּוֹת
וְחֶסְרוֹנָן עַל כָּל מַה שֶּׁבָּרָאתָ לְהַחֲיוֹת בָּהֶם נֶפֶשׁ כָּל חָי. בָּרוּךְ
חֵי הָעוֹלָמִים.

Blessed art Thou, Lord our God, King of the universe, who creates many living beings and the things they need [to survive]. For all that Thou hast created to sustain the life of every living being, blessed [be Thou], the Life of the universe.

&❧ Whenever one hears another recite a blessing, he should answer "Amen" at its conclusion. The "Amen" constitutes an "endorsement," and affirmation that the blessing is true, that I believe it, or that "it should soon come to pass" where the blessing is in the form of a prayer petition.

&❧ A person does *not* answer "Amen" after a blessing he recites himself (unless it is part of the formal structure of the prayer itself as in *boneh Yerushalayim* in the grace after meals or in Kaddish).

&❧ So that God's name is not used in vain, it is customary to refrain from saying *Adonai* (the Lord) except in prayer and during the actual recitation of blessings. When reference is made to God in the course of conversation, even when quoting passages, the term *HaShem* (The Name) is used instead. (*Adoshem* is a distortion and should not be used as it is not respectful usage.) Other commonly used terms that refer to God are: *HaKadosh Baruch Hu* (The Holy One, Blessed Be He); *Ribbono Shel Olam* (Master of the Universe); *Avinu She'ba Shamayim* (Our Father in Heaven).

Selected Morning Prayers

&❧ When arising in the morning, it is also appropriate to begin the day with a prayer of thanks. Immediately after having washed one's hands, one says:

מוֹדֶה אֲנִי לְפָנֶיךָ, מֶלֶךְ חַי וְקַיָּם, שֶׁהֶחֱזַרְתָּ בִּי נִשְׁמָתִי בְּחֶמְלָה;
רַבָּה אֱמוּנָתֶךָ.

I thank Thee, O King, who lives for always and who, as I
awaken, has in mercy returned my soul to me; we can ever
trust in Thee.

וְהַעֲרֶב־נָא יְיָ אֱלֹהֵינוּ, אֶת דִּבְרֵי תוֹרָתְךָ בְּפִינוּ וּבְפִי עַמְּךָ
בֵּית יִשְׂרָאֵל, וְנִהְיֶה אֲנַחְנוּ וְצֶאֱצָאֵינוּ, וְצֶאֱצָאֵי עַמְּךָ בֵּית
יִשְׂרָאֵל, כֻּלָּנוּ יוֹדְעֵי שְׁמֶךָ וְלוֹמְדֵי תוֹרָתְךָ לִשְׁמָהּ. בָּרוּךְ אַתָּה
יְיָ, הַמְלַמֵּד תּוֹרָה לְעַמּוֹ יִשְׂרָאֵל.

Cause the words of the Torah to be sweet in our mouths, Lord our
God, and in the mouths of Thy people, the House of Israel, so
that we and our offspring and the offspring of Thy people, the
House of Israel, may all know Thy Name and study Thy Torah.
Blessed art Thou Lord, who teaches the Torah to His people Israel.

אֱלֹהַי, נְשָׁמָה שֶׁנָּתַתָּ בִּי טְהוֹרָה הִיא. אַתָּה בְרָאתָהּ, אַתָּה
יְצַרְתָּהּ, אַתָּה נְפַחְתָּהּ בִּי, וְאַתָּה מְשַׁמְּרָהּ בְּקִרְבִּי, וְאַתָּה עָתִיד
לִטְּלָהּ מִמֶּנִּי וּלְהַחֲזִירָהּ בִּי לֶעָתִיד לָבוֹא. כָּל זְמַן שֶׁהַנְּשָׁמָה
בְקִרְבִּי מוֹדֶה אֲנִי לְפָנֶיךָ, יְיָ אֱלֹהַי וֵאלֹהֵי אֲבוֹתַי, רִבּוֹן כָּל
הַמַּעֲשִׂים, אֲדוֹן כָּל הַנְּשָׁמוֹת. בָּרוּךְ אַתָּה יְיָ, הַמַּחֲזִיר נְשָׁמוֹת
לִפְגָרִים מֵתִים.

My God, the soul that Thou placed within me is pure. Thou
created it; Thou fashioned it; Thou breathed it into me. Thou
preservest it within me, and will one day take it from me, and
restore it to me in the hereafter. So long as my soul is within me,
I give thanks before Thee, Lord my God and God of my fathers,
Master of all creation, Lord of all souls. Blessed art Thou, O
Lord, who restorest the souls to the dead.

175

וִיהִי רָצוֹן מִלְפָנֶיךָ יְיָ אֱלֹהֵינוּ וֵאלֹהֵי אֲבוֹתֵינוּ, שֶׁתַּרְגִּילֵנוּ
בְּתוֹרָתֶךָ וְדַבְּקֵנוּ בְּמִצְוֹתֶיךָ. וְאַל תְּבִיאֵנוּ לֹא לִידֵי חֵטְא וְלֹא
לִידֵי עֲבֵרָה וְעָוֹן וְלֹא לִידֵי נִסָּיוֹן וְלֹא לִידֵי בִזָּיוֹן. וְאַל תַּשְׁלֶט־
בָּנוּ יֵצֶר הָרָע. וְהַרְחִיקֵנוּ מֵאָדָם רָע וּמֵחָבֵר רָע. וְדַבְּקֵנוּ בְּיֵצֶר
הַטּוֹב וּבְמַעֲשִׂים טוֹבִים. וְכֹף אֶת יִצְרֵנוּ לְהִשְׁתַּעְבֶּד־לָךְ.
וּתְנֵנוּ הַיּוֹם וּבְכָל יוֹם לְחֵן וּלְחֶסֶד וּלְרַחֲמִים בְּעֵינֶיךָ
וּבְעֵינֵי כָל רוֹאֵינוּ וְתִגְמְלֵנוּ חֲסָדִים טוֹבִים. בָּרוּךְ אַתָּה יְיָ,
גּוֹמֵל חֲסָדִים טוֹבִים לְעַמּוֹ יִשְׂרָאֵל.

May it be Thy will, O Lord our God and God of our fathers, that we become accustomed to walk in the way of Thy Torah, and to cling to Thy precepts. Lead us not into sin or transgression and iniquity, or into temptation or disgrace; let not the impulse to evil rule over us; keep us far from evil men and worthless companions; and help us cling to the will to do good and to good deeds. Bend our will to Thine. Give us this day and every day grace, favor, and mercy—in Thy sight and in the sight of all men, and bestow upon us Thy lovingkindness. Blessed art Thou Lord, who bestows lovingkindness upon His people, Israel.

לְפִיכָךְ אֲנַחְנוּ חַיָּבִים לְהוֹדוֹת לְךָ וּלְשַׁבֵּחֲךָ וּלְפָאֶרְךָ
וּלְבָרֵךְ וּלְקַדֵּשׁ וְלָתֵת שֶׁבַח וְהוֹדָיָה לִשְׁמֶךָ. אַשְׁרֵינוּ מַה טּוֹב
חֶלְקֵנוּ וּמַה נָּעִים גּוֹרָלֵנוּ וּמַה יָּפָה יְרֻשָּׁתֵנוּ. אַשְׁרֵינוּ
שֶׁאֲנַחְנוּ מַשְׁכִּימִים וּמַעֲרִיבִים עֶרֶב וָבֹקֶר וְאוֹמְרִים פַּעֲמַיִם
בְּכָל יוֹם: שְׁמַע יִשְׂרָאֵל, יְיָ אֱלֹהֵינוּ, יְיָ אֶחָד.

It is our duty to thank Thee, to praise and extol Thee, to bless, sanctify and render praise and thanksgiving to Thy Name. We are fortunate—how goodly is our portion, how pleasant is our lot and how beautiful is our heritage. We are fortunate that we arise and retire, at eve and at morn, declaring twice each day: Hear O Israel, The Lord is our God, The Lord is One.

For the full text of the Shema, the Amidah, the grace after meals, and other sections of the different prayer services obtain a daily prayer book, preferably one with an English translation. No Jew should be without one.

&☙ Although the halakha has ruled that prayer can be said in any language, and an individual is permitted to do so when saying his own prayers, it is most important that a community or a congregation does not deviate from the practice of conducting its public religious services in Hebrew, the sacred tongue. The reasons are manifold. (1) A religious community should not descend to the level of its most unlearned members by adopting the lowest common denominator as its standard. (2) To do so removes whatever incentive there might otherwise be for persons without any Hebrew training at all to invest the little time and effort needed to master Hebrew reading. (The average adult can easily do so with ten to twelve hours of instruction.) It also makes it unnecessary for the younger generation to learn Hebrew, even in its most elementary form. On the contrary, a community should encourage its membership to rise to greater heights by establishing higher expectations and continuously demanding higher standards. (3) Total estrangement from the Hebrew tongue represents estrangement also from the Hebrew Bible and all the other classical sources. It means the loss of understanding of Hebraic concepts and Jewish values best conveyed through the Hebrew idiom, and not through the translations. (4) Historically, the severance of an organic bond with the Hebrew tongue by a Jewish community has ultimately led to the total disappearance through assimilation of that community. (5) It is only through a relatively uniform Hebrew service (though variations in worship practices from community to community do exist, the basic pattern of the traditional service as well as the basic prayers are common to all) that the unity of the Jewish people throughout the world is strengthened. Not only does it tie the simplest Jew ever closer to the Holy Land where Hebrew is today the spoken tongue, but it enables a Jew to feel at home in any synagogue anywhere in the world, even where one is unable otherwise to communicate with his coreligionists because they speak other languages.

If all Jews were to conduct their worship services in their respective vernaculars, an American or British Jew who was trained to participate in an English service would be completely lost in France, South America, Germany, Russia, Poland, Denmark, Greece, Italy, etc., where he would find synagogues whose services were conducted respectively in French, Spanish, German, Russian, Polish, Danish, Greek, Italian, etc. Estrangement from the synagogues of fellow Jews about the world would be a hard and damaging blow to the sense of Jewish unity.

ह्ण How can one pray if one does not understand the meaning of the words? Isn't it hypocritical to utter senseless words? Doesn't even the Talmud teach us that he who prays should concentrate on what his lips are saying? To an individual asking these questions, the answers are many:

· By all means, say the prayers in the language you best understand. God understands every language! (But don't demand that the standard of an entire community be watered-down to your level. Demand of yourself the effort needed to rise higher in knowledge.)
· Better still, obtain a Siddur with a translation on one side, and as you say the Hebrew prayers, glance at and study the translation thus slowly learning to understand the meaning of the prayers. In the course of time, the Hebrew words themselves will become more intelligible.
· If you find that even this is beyond your capacity, understand that prayer is not only words, but also a mood, a feeling. The spirit also counts! If a person recites prayers he does not fully understand, but his heart is humble before the Lord and his thoughts are directed to his Father in Heaven, can it be said that his Father in Heaven does not understand his intent nor deem his heartfelt *thoughts* less worthy of consideration?

&c "I will pray only when I am moved to pray" is the argument heard from those who object to regular prayer. Suffice it to recall the proverbial story of the soldier in the foxhole who, when he wanted to pray, did not know what to say or how to say it. To pray with true sincerity, to reach spiritual heights as a result of true prayer is not easy. It requires training and practice. It is an art in itself.

While it is true that not every time an observant Jew fulfills his prayer obligations does he reach these noble heights, the likelihood of such experiences, and the occasions on which he *will* experience such heights are always greater for him than for the one who *waits* to be inspired.

Who is more likely to write the master novel, the masterpiece in music, the inspiring work? Is it the one who has had no training in writing or in music and who waits to be inspired to write or compose, or the one who has worked hard at it, trained himself well, and who continuously writes and composes, even if often with mediocre results?

A WORD ABOUT THE PRAYER BOOK

The Hebrew prayer book (*Siddur*) is more than just a book of prayers. Properly studied and understood, it becomes a vast repository of all the principles of Jewish faith, a record of both the great victories and tragic defeats Israel has known in its long history. It is a testimony of the aspirations and hopes of the Jewish people throughout time. It is witness to the ethical and moral heights to which Jewry aspired and attained. It is a reminder of laughter and gaiety, of celebration and rejoicing as well as of sorrow and grief, of mourning and bemoaning that takes place in the life of the individual as in the life of an entire people. It provides insights into daily Jewish living as well as into all the special occasions and festivals in the Jewish calendar. It contains Biblical passages that date as far back as 3300 years; prayers composed by the Sages as long as 2500 years ago. While most of the prayers are hallowed by their Biblical and Talmudic origins, there will also be found passages, prayers and selections that have been written since. Not only are the Middle Ages well represented, but newer editions even contain authorized selections composed by the Chief Rabbinate of Israel.

The Siddur is study as well as prayer. It is moral instruction and ethical guidance as well as pleas for personal needs. It emphasizes *man's duties* as well as his *rights*. It is the record *par excellence* of Israel's relationship with God.

ON WEARING A HEADCOVERING

§⤸ "It is a custom not to walk under the heavens bareheaded" (Orach Hayim 2:6). Though never legislated by the Sages, the custom of not going about bareheaded at any time—at home, in the synagogue and outdoors—extends back several thousand years in time. In many ways, it has today become a mark of Jewish piety.

To wear a headcovering was the ancient Roman stigma for a servant. Free men went bareheaded. The Jews adopted this practice in a House of God and in prayer or whenever God's name was mentioned in blessings (such as during meals which are preceded and followed by blessings) to emphasize that they were the servants of the Lord. Gradually, the practice was extended to wearing a headcovering also under the open skies. It became the Jewish way of showing reverence for God. "Cover your head, so that the reverence of Heaven be upon you" (Shabbat 156b).

In our own day, especially when living and working in a non-Jewish environment, and where the mark of respect in public buildings or Christian institutions consists in removing one's headcovering, the liberties taken with this custom can be justified. Nevertheless, the wearing of a headcovering, at least in a Jewish house of worship, in any consecrated area (such as a cemetery), and whenever one says his prayers or recites a blessing is a requirement that should be strictly adhered to, for it has remained the distinctive Jewish way to show reverence for the Lord.

§⤸ The headcovering that is usually worn, especially indoors, is a skullcap known in Yiddish as a *yarmulke* and in Hebrew as a *kippah*. No religious significance is attached to this particular type of headcovering. Its light weight and convenience is the basis for its wide-spread use.

While a white skullcap is preferred for the High Holydays because white is the symbol of purity, there is otherwise no special significance to the wide array of colors and designs in which these skullcaps are now made.

PERSONAL GROOMING

• "You shall not . . . destroy the corners of your beard" (Lev. 19:27). The halakha (by relating this verse to Lev. 21:5) clearly understood this prohibition as one which prohibited the use of a razor blade or knife to shave the beard of one's face. (Technically it's only the five corners that are thus forbidden: at the chin; in front of but just above and just below the ears.)

This law, as well as several others which forbid tattooing and other forms of self-mutilation, were directed against practices common to idolatry and associated with pagan customs. "It was the practice of pagan priests to destroy (shave) their beards. Therefore did the Torah forbid it. . . . But one is not culpable for it unless it is done with a razor . . . therefore if one cut the beard of his face with scissors, one is not liable" (Hil. Avodat Kochavim 12:7).

This prohibition had an obvious impact on the historical style of Jewish grooming; hence the traditional image of the Jew as a full-bearded person.

It is only since this past century when it became possible to use means other than a razor with which to remove facial hair that even observant Jews began to appear clean-shaven. At first, clippers (which operate on the principle of a scissors rather than a knife), powder and similar depilatories came into use. The modern electric shaver (which operates on the scissors principle rather than as a blade) was ruled permissible by religious authorities. This made it possible for even the pious Jew to be clean-shaven or partially bearded without violating the Torah law. Nevertheless, the bearded face probably still reflects an image of greater piety.

• The first part of this same Torah sentence states "You shall not round the corners of your head. . . ." The reasons are the same as

181

given above. Because of this, it is not permissible to totally remove the sideburns. While halakhic rulings permit the use of scissors or clippers to trim the sideburns, the custom of refusing to take advantage of such rulings prevailed among Hasidic Jews and they do not touch the sideburns at all; hence their dangling side-curls (*payos*), most noticeable on the children and young boys whose beards are not yet fully grown.

The Synagogue: Where Jews Assemble

> And they shall build for me a Sanctuary that I may dwell in their midst.
>
> (Exodus 25:8)

A SYNAGOGUE is any building or room that is set aside for prayer. This has always been and still remains its primary purpose. Yet in all of rabbinic literature, only once (Gitin 39b) has it ever been referred to as a House of Prayer (*Beit Tefilah*). From its very inception after the destruction of the First Temple in 586 B.C.E. to this very day, it has generally been referred to as a *Beit Knesset*, which literally means a House of Assembly, or a House of Gathering. The Greek term for a Jewish house of worship—from whence we derive the word synagogue—is in fact a literal translation of *Beit Knesset*. Its very name emphasizes the fact that the synagogue served purposes beyond that of being only a center for public worship.

Its most notable additional role has been as a center for religious study, especially by adults. Thus the term *Beit Midrash*, House of Study, became almost synonymous with *Beit Knesset*. The Beit Midrash may have been a separate room attached to the Beit

Knesset, or was the same place, used for both purposes. Since lifelong study of Torah was always encouraged, ranking even higher than prayer itself ("and the study of Torah is equivalent to all the commandments"), the study of Torah not only became an integral part of the prayer service* but study groups would gather prior to or immediately following the services for the purpose of studying Torah. The role of the synagogue as a Beit Midrash, a place for the continuing, lifelong education of Jews has remained constant.

Quite often the synagogue also served as a center for the formal education of children and youth. The Talmud relates that "there were 480 synagogues in Jerusalem and each and every one of them had an elementary school (*Beit Sefer*) and a secondary school (*Beit Talmud*). The *Beit Sefer* was to teach Scriptures and the *Beit Talmud* was to teach Mishna." This function, however, varied through the centuries and differed from country to country and community to community.

As an extension of its educational functions, the local synagogue also provided the services of a library to the community. Thus we find the definitive law that "dwellers of a city may compel each other . . . to buy a scroll of the Torah and the books of the Prophets and the Writings, so that whoever of the public wishes to read in them may do so. And in our own days when books are printed . . . one may compel the purchase of necessary printed books such as the entire Hebrew Bible with a Rashi commentary, Mishnayot, the entire Talmud, Rambam, the four sections of the Shulhan Arukh, so that whoever desires to do so, can come and study from them." The synagogue, or the Beit Midrash, was the place where this religious library was kept for public use.

Whether by design or because the synagogue building was usually the only public building in a community, it was also the place where community meetings and gatherings were held and where the routine affairs of the community were deliberated.† It usually also housed the local rabbinic court (Beth Din).

---

* The public reading of the Torah, the weekly delivery of a sermon (*drasha*) or lecture on the part of the Sages, a practice which goes back to early Talmudic times, are all part of the *study* program that became an integral part of the service. Furthermore, the worship service itself contains passages intended to enable one to fulfill his minimum duty to study Torah.

† The synagogue also served as the community social welfare agency, collecting funds and dispensing charity to the poor, loans to the needy, and organizing or providing hospitality to the traveler.

Although the name Beit Knesset, House of Assembly, reflects more accurately than does the term Beit Tefilah, House of Prayer, the broader scope of activities traditionally carried on in the synagogue, tradition ascribes to the synagogue not only great importance but also great sanctity. The Sages looked upon it as second only to the Temple, and referred to the synagogue (and study halls too for that matter) as the *mikdash me'at,* the small sanctuary (Megillah 29a). They derived this term from Ezekiel 11:16 where it says "yet have I been to them as a little sanctuary." The Divine Presence in the synagogue was stressed over and over again. Typical is the interpretation given to Psalms 82:1, "God standeth in the congregation of God," which they took to mean that God's Presence is to be found in the synagogues. Praying in a synagogue was regarded as of greater merit than praying anywhere else. The synagogue was held in high regard and in great affection by the Sages. It undoubtedly played a vital role not only in promoting and strengthening the faith of Israel but also as a cohesive social force in the Jewish community.

However central an institution the synagogue has always been in Jewish life, it has never been synonymous with Judaism. While there are synagogues, one cannot speak of The Synagogue as the authoritative institution of the faith. Judaism is not embodied in any institution but in the Torah, Written and Oral. At one time, the Sanhedrin, a Supreme Religious Court, exercised a centralized authority. But for the past eighteen centuries, that authority was diffused among the rabbinic heads of their respective communities.

The synagogue is a place which is sacred only by virtue of the use to which it is put, prayer and religious study. As an institution, it provides for certain functions required by the faith—namely, prayer, study, community affairs, and welfare activities. It also serves to promote and encourage the religious life of the Jewish community and contributes to its cohesiveness. The synagogue is only an *instrument* of the Jewish faith.

Furthermore, the functioning of a synagogue is not dependent upon a clergy. Every aspect of a religious service may be and usually is conducted by the laymen themselves, if they possess the knowledge and training to do so. The management and maintenance too of the institution is usually the responsibility of lay people, who either volunteer or are elected to their posts of leadership. Although it is desirable and usual for a congregation to engage the services of a rabbi to provide religious guidance, direction, and leadership to a community, there are synagogues, particularly small ones, that function without one. Traditionally the rabbi served a community, not a synagogue.

The religious ideals of Judaism and its social consciousness need not be expressed through the institution of the House of Worship. It can just as well, and very often does, express itself through other organs of the Jewish community. Nor is it necessary that it be expressed by an official synagogue leader or religious functionary for it to be a legitimate expression of Judaism.

The extent to which a synagogue is even representative of Judaism —apart from its function as a gathering place for prayer—is determined very much by the caliber of the people who are at its helm at any particular time (be they rabbis or laymen), and also by the caliber and commitment of the congregation itself.

THE SYNAGOGUE AS INSTITUTION

Synagogues are autonomous institutions. They are established, organized, maintained and controlled locally by any group of Jews who wish to have a synagogue in their midst. Each synagogue is independent of the other and is governed by an elected group of officers and Board of Directors. Although each synagogue is essentially bound by the Codes of Jewish Law in its ritual practices, there is nothing to prevent any synagogue from establishing its own policies and its own procedures in both ritual as well as general matters. There are national synagogue bodies with which most synagogues are identified, but these associations are purely voluntary and have no power of enforcing decisions on the local congregations. (The situation differs in Britain where the central synagogue agency does possess greater powers of enforcement.) Orthodox Jews, in their synagogues' rituals and procedures, feel bound by the laws of prayer and synagogue procedures formulated in the Jewish Codes of Law. The rulings of their rabbis in all ritual matters are accepted as binding. The synagogue practices of those Jews who do not submit to such guidelines will depend on the degree of their own "feel" for or against the traditional patterns. Thus synagogues officially belonging even to the same "denominational" grouping may differ considerably one from the other in their religious policies and in the way their respective worship services are conducted. While the influence and attitude of the rabbi is almost always a strong factor, the freedom to choose a rabbi who is sympathetic to the views of the congregation means that such influence is sometimes, though not always, more theoretical than actual.

While the Placement Bureaus of rabbinical schools serve as clearing houses for the placement of rabbis, and establish the ground rules for interviewing candidates and for the terms of their contracts, they cannot impose a rabbi on a congregation, and the contract is between the rabbi and the congregation. As congregations are free to elect their own rabbis, they are also free not to renew a contract by vote of the congregation. Where a rabbi serves a congregation for more than ten years, he is usually regarded as having tenure, although this too is not universal.

Any Jew is free to enter, worship in, and join any synagogue, regardless of his own level of observance or religious commitment.

In the framework of the American experience, the difference between *joining* a synagogue and *worshipping* in a synagogue should, however, be understood by the uninitiated. It is possible for one to join and be a member of a synagogue without ever going there to worship; and it is possible for people to worship quite regularly in a synagogue without ever being a member of it. Membership in an American synagogue is reckoned in terms of *joining* rather than *worshipping*. Membership involves the payment of a specified fee as annual dues. Dues are the prime source of income for most synagogues, enabling them to operate on a year-round basis. Membership in a synagogue reflects a willingness to support and maintain the religious institution financially (a self-imposed tax, if you will), and to be regarded as a member of a religiously-oriented community. It is not necessarily an indication of personal piety or level of religious commitment. This is judged by other criteria, including the regularity with which one worships at the synagogue, by the extent of observance of the wide range of mitzvot, and by one's ethical and moral standards.

But since membership involves dues, there are always those who either cannot afford such payments or who do not wish to spend for such matters. Where Jewish communities had taxing power, part of the taxes collected from all but the most indigent maintained the local synagogue and direct membership dues were never involved. But in the United States, it is estimated that half the Jewish families in the country are not members of any synagogue, even though dues rates vary from synagogue to synagogue, from insignificant amounts to rather substantial sums, depending on their size and their budget.

Except for the two days of Rosh Hashana and the one day of Yom Kippur when almost every synagogue member attends services and the limited number of seats in each synagogue restrict the number of people who can be accommodated (thus restricting the accommodation to the supporting membership),* even those who do not affiliate with a synagogue and who do not exert themselves to contribute to the maintenance of the institution on a year-round basis are not barred and may still worship at no cost to them on the other 362 days, including each of the fifty-two Sabbaths and all the other major festivals. Since Jewish law does not permit handling money on the Sabbaths and festivals, collections (or plate-passing) is not practiced. At morning weekday services, it is traditional, though not obligatory, for worshippers to contribute some coins in a charity box.

Persons of other faiths are always welcome to enter a synagogue at any time, if they wish to observe a service. Except for the High Holydays (Rosh Hashana and Yom Kippur) no special arrangements need to be made.

RESPONSIBILITY OF SYNAGOGUES TODAY

While its principal purpose is to serve as a place where Jews can assemble for worship, such assembly will in the long run only be meaningful if those who manage the synagogues will also serve effectively in those broader areas where it has historically been involved.

The synagogue can and must be an instrument for the religious and spiritual education of its membership, from the very young to the very old, so that they may learn to appreciate better the meaning and significance of the Jewish faith and reflect it in the daily pattern of their lives—in the observance of the ritual law as well as in the implementation of Judaism's ethical and moral imperatives. Such education can be provided directly or indirectly by encouraging active

---

* Membership in some congregations is reckoned on the basis of those who purchase reserved seating for the High Holyday services, rather than in terms of annual dues.

There is hardly any synagogue anywhere that does not make special provisions to accommodate the indigent person even at these services.

support and identification with other educational institutions. Programs for youth provide informal education and training.

It is the responsibility of the synagogue to encourage the support of every endeavor and every project that is crucial to the survival of our faith or of our people. The role of Eretz Yisrael as an element in the faith of Israel must be recognized and a living relationship with the Holy Land must be encouraged, while the security of the embattled country must be supported in every way.

It is the responsibility of the synagogue to promote the true center of Jewish life, which is the Jewish home. If the home is Jewishly strong, there will always be a need for a synagogue. But if the Jewish home is weak, even the synagogues are in danger of crumbling.

It is the responsibility of the synagogue to strengthen loyalty, not to itself as an institution, but to God whom it serves, and to Torah as the Divine command. It is loyalty to the mitzvot, to the teachings of the Torah, that is the measure of the faith of the Jew, and not loyalty to an institution.

Synagogue leadership must therefore regard the institution not only as a gathering place for worship, but as an instrument to promote actively all the values of the faith. In other words, the modern synagogue must be a vehicle for Jewish education (formal and informal), the spiritual-religious growth of its membership, and for encouraging the daily translation of the values of Judaism in every area of life. A synagogue's success or failure should be judged by how effectively it fulfills these responsibilities. ·

These roles must be filled by synagogues especially in the Diaspora, where even the not-so-devout Jew, who neglects to pray regularly and for whom a House of Worship plays a relatively minor role, will join a synagogue and become part of a congregation. He may do so in order to identify himself as a Jew, an identification that he desires and seeks. Affiliation with a synagogue is the most obvious way to express such an identification in the Diaspora, no matter how assimilated one may be. Or one may join a synagogue to enable his children to take advantage of the educational and cultural opportunities provided there for the children and the young people. Or he may join a synagogue because the social life of that particular community revolves around the synagogue and he does not wish to be excluded. Or he may join a synagogue in order to keep up a family attachment to a particular synagogue even if it has otherwise lost all religious significance for him. This is precisely why the responsibilities imposed upon synagogues in the Diaspora are all the more crucial, for this relationship even with the non-religious Jew provides the leadership of this religious institution with opportunities to encourage a return to God on the broadest and deepest levels (*teshuvah*). It provides opportunities to transform a vague desire for identification, or some ulterior motive (to take advantage of certain facilities or services) into a more meaningful and stronger attachment to Judaism.

But even the devout Jew who attends the synagogue faithfully for religious services has every right to expect that the synagogue help him keep his children loyal to the faith, that it help him in educating his children Jewishly and religiously, that it help him guide his children to resist assimilationist forces; he has every right to demand that the synagogue provide not only books in its library or Beit Midrash so that he can come to study or peruse them, but that it provide a teacher and conduct classes to enrich his own understanding, and that it provide opportunities for socializing with other Jews apart from the casual meetings before and after services.

In Israel, where the very life of the society is Jewish, where one can find Jewish cultural and religious values and mores reflected in most public institutions and ceremonies, where religious schooling is provided by government, where Jewish books are available in public libraries and courses in Jewish studies are offered at universities, and where most social welfare is a responsibility of government and not of synagogue-based communities, the synagogues are perforce limited to worship and continuing adult study. Since the forces that encourage even non-religious Jews to join a synagogue in the Diaspora are obviated by the Jewish character of the entire country, only Jews who attend a synagogue regularly for at least Sabbath and festival services will tend to join them formally in Israel.

But even in Israel there would be tremendous opportunities for spreading the influence of the religious faith and its way of life if the synagogues were to become active, aggressive institutions instead of remaining passive. If they were to provide additional facilities and services to young people during after-school hours or periods of school vacation or initiate other programs, they might attract those elements who currently find no interest either in the synagogue or the religious way of life. There is no doubt that even in Israel the synagogue can serve as a more effective instrument for the training of Jewish children in the ways of faith and mitzvot and as a vehicle for encouraging those who have strayed to return; that it can serve as a vital force in the integration of new Jewish immigrants into the social and cultural life of the community. Rabbinic and lay leadership sensitive to the possibilities can achieve much.

BEHAVIOR IN THE SYNAGOGUE

෪ Any community inhabited by at least ten male Jews should have a specially designated place where they can assemble for prayer. This place is called a synagogue (Beit Knesset). The Yiddish term is shul. Residents of a town may compel one another to build a synagogue for themselves and to buy a Torah and other sacred books.

In a place where there is no permanent daily minyan or quorum for services, members may compel each other to attend the services.

෪ Synagogues and study halls (where religious study takes place) must be treated with respect and reverence. The holiness of a Beit Knesset, a synagogue sanctuary, and that of a Beit Midrash, a study hall, is great indeed. We are cautioned to be aware of the Divine Presence who always dwells therein, and to behave and dress, as well as pray accordingly.

As the ancient Temple in Jerusalem was the Great Temple in the Jewish faith, so is every synagogue and house of study considered a *mikdash me'at*, a small Temple, a sanctuary in smaller spiritual replica. ". . . Yet have I been to them as a little sanctuary . . ." (Ezekiel 11:16).

෪ One may not eat or drink in a sanctuary.

෪ One is not permitted to run about in a synagogue, but should walk with dignity and respect.

෪ It is a great mitzvah to worship in a synagogue or a house of study, for these places are sanctified. One should make a special effort to do so even when one prays alone.

THE WORSHIP SERVICES

෪ Public worship services are conducted daily in synagogues each morning and evening. While the afternoon *minha* and evening *maariv* prayers are generally conducted just prior to and shortly after sundown, the schedule of the daily morning services and those of the Sabbath day may differ slightly from congregation to congregation so that one should familiarize himself with the schedule of the local congregation.

৯ A complete public prayer service cannot be held unless at least six out of the ten or more who are present are active participants in the worship. If this is not the case, the Reader does not repeat aloud the entire Amidah but only the first three benedictions—enabling all those present to recite the Kedusha. He then proceeds to complete the Amidah silently.

৯ Many centuries of geographic dispersion and the separation of Jewish communities has led to slightly different patterns of traditional prayer and to a variety of customs followed by traditional synagogues of different communities. The basic order of the service is, however, the same everywhere, based upon Talmudic guidelines and principles. That they resemble one another as much as they do despite centuries-long separation is the real source of amazement. The differences, though quickly apparent to one who is familiar with the worship service, are superficial. There is no basic clash of halakhic or religious legal principles in the variety of the customs that prevail. They only add to the colorful variety of Jewish synagogue life.

৯ The two basic synagogue traditions and prayer liturgies are called *Ashkenazic* (referring to the practices followed by the Jews in Central, Eastern and Western Europe and all who came from there) and *Sephardic* (the practices followed by Spanish Jewry and those around the entire Mediterranean seacoast, and their descendants).

The differences between the two synagogue liturgies can be traced back to the differences of opinion between the ancient scholars of Eretz Yisrael and Babylonia. Ashkenazic Jewry was influenced by the tradition of Eretz Yisrael, whereas Sephardic Jewry adopted the Babylonian tradition. But even among Ashkenazic Jews, Hasidic communities adopted some features of the Sephardic Order of Service, and so there developed a Sephard liturgy *(nusach Sephard)* even among Ashkenazim. (A difference quickly noted is in the recitation of the Kaddish, which in the Sephardic version contains four more words, *v'yatzmach purkanai v'karev m'shihai.* The opening sentence of the *Kedusha* also differs slightly.)

 familiar with the traditions of that

కు The disciples of the great Ashkenazic scholar, Elijah, Gaon of Vilna, followed his halakhic rulings in matters of prayer and synagogue procedures, which differed in many respects from the practices prevailing in the Ashkenazic synagogues of his time. Thus, a liturgy of the HaGaon Reb Eliyahu developed (*nusach Hagra*). Because the disciples of the Vilna Gaon played such a tremendous role in the early resettlement of Eretz Yisrael (early 1800's), their influence upon Israel's synagogues has been profound and a goodly number of Ashkenazic synagogues in Israel follow that liturgy.

కు There are many rules and regulations governing the order of the service for various occasions. These should be followed in accordance with the directions and instructions of the rabbi; or in his absence, in accordance with the guidance of a layman knowledgeable in the laws pertaining to prayer and familiar with the traditions of that congregation.

THE RITUAL ITEMS

కు A synagogue, whether large or small, designed elaborately or simply, must contain the following basic ritual items:

· Holy Ark (*aron kodesh*)—a cabinet, or a recess in the wall in which are kept the scrolls of the Torah (*sifrei Torah*). The curtain covering the *aron kodesh* is called a *parokhet*. The aron kodesh is generally set on the wall in the direction of Eretz Yisrael (in Israel, toward Jerusalem).

· Eternal Light (*ner tamid*)—a lamp that is placed above and somewhat in front of the Holy Ark. It is allowed to burn continually. It is symbolic of the Biblical directive to "cause a lamp to burn continually in the tabernacle outside of the parokhet which is before (the Ark of) the testimony . . ." (Exodus 27:20–21).

· *Bimah* is the platform, traditionally set apart from the Ark, on which stands a table (*shulhan*). From this table, the Torah is read to the congregation and the Reader or cantor leads the congregation in services.

In Ashkenazic synagogues, there will be an additional lectern, *amud*, between the bimah and the aron kodesh, on a lower level, in deference to the verse "From out of the depths did I cry out to Thee, O Lord," (Psalms 130:1) and from which some of the services are conducted.

· Though not essential, a candelabrum (*menorah*) reminiscent of the seven-branched menorah of the Temple, will generally be placed in a prominent place near the aron kodesh or the bimah. (So as not to duplicate the one in the Temple, either a six- or eight-branched menorah is used.)

· Aside from these items, whatever other Jewish religious and historical symbols may be displayed depends upon the taste and/or wealth of the congregation, or upon the advice of the architect of the particular synagogue. Stained glass windows, wall inscriptions, carvings, paintings, etc., can express many religious themes, and can reflect a wide range of religious symbols and ritual objects, or historic events in the life of the Jewish people from its very inception over 3800 years ago. The major restriction in these art forms is that no human figures are permissible in the synagogue.

﮲ A women's section (*ezrat nashim*), is an ancient and distinctive feature of the traditional synagogue. It follows the pattern established in the ancient Temple of Jerusalem which provided an ezrat nashim so as to prevent light-headed levity, immodest and unbecoming behavior between the sexes that might take place in the freely mingling crowds coming to the holy Temple.

At times the ezrat nashim took the form of a balcony; at other times, of a distinctly divided section on the side or to the rear of the men's section, on the same or slightly raised level. Rabbinic opinion differs only as to the proper heights of such a divider (*mehitzah*), ranging from 38 inches to over 60 inches.*

﮲ Other than the restrictions governing the interior arrangement of a synagogue necessitated by the requirement of an ezrat nashim, and the relative positions of the aron kodesh and bimah, there are no other distinct architectural patterns required for the interior or

---

* See article by Norman Lamm, "Separate Pews in the Synagogue," *Tradition*, vol. 1, no. 2 for fuller treatment of this question in contemporary times. Copies can be obtained from the Rabbinical Council of America. See also *The Sanctity of the Synagogue*, edited by Baruch Litvin (New York: The Spero Foundation, 1959).

the exterior of the building. Synagogues have thus often provided opportunities for artistic and architectural creativity.

SYNAGOGUE PERSONNEL

The Rabbi

ह‌‌‌‌ The rabbi (or the *rav*, as he is called in Hebrew) is the religious head of the community. His traditional ordination is called *semikha*. His rigorous training in and expert knowledge of the Torah, the Talmud, and the Codes of Law, and his personal faith and piety is the basis of the authority which a traditional community recognizes and accepts.

ह‌‌‌‌ In our day, Jewish communities in the Diaspora are religiously organized around synagogues so that each rabbi is the head of that community of Jews associated with that particular congregation. This development has forced the rabbi to become concerned also with the synagogue institution itself and become involved in its purely administrative concerns. As long as such institutional leadership is not permitted to take priority over and displace the rabbi's traditional and basic responsibility for spiritual leadership there is much to be said in favor of this contemporary development.

ह‌‌‌‌ The rabbi must not only teach the Torah and the Jewish way of life by what he says, but also by the example he sets. He must not only teach Judaism and provide leadership to the religious institutions of Judaism, he must personally reflect the values and the ways of the faith that he wishes to instill in others.

Since the Torah confers authority on the spiritual leader to act as judge in deciding religious questions brought before him, the rabbi must in that capacity possess the expertise in the law that such decision making powers necessitate. He must himself be loyal and faithful to that law, and be committed to its underlying principles and axioms of faith.

The Cantor

ह‌‌‌‌ The cantor (or *hazzan* as he is called in Hebrew) fills the role of the emissary of the congregation (*shaliah tzibbur*). It is he who represents and leads the congregation in prayer before the Almighty. In larger or more affluent congregations, the position of cantor will be a full time position. Although generally responsible for conducting only the main Sabbath service of the week and all the holiday services, he will also have other duties relating to the music and choral programs of the synagogue and the religious school. In addition, he will be called upon to assist the rabbi in officiating at weddings and funerals, where appropriate vocal chanting contributes immeasurably to the services. Depending upon the needs of the congregation, there are duties and responsibilities in other areas of synagogue work and religious education that he might be called upon to fulfill if he has the qualifications. At the daily services, however, and on such occasions when the cantor is absent, a qualified worshipper in the congregation may be called upon to serve as *shaliah tzibbur*.

&❧ In smaller congregations where no official cantor is engaged, qualified members of the congregation are called upon to conduct the services. In Judaism, any layman who possesses the educational background and the religious merit (and every Jew should) is privileged to conduct all parts of the religious service.

&❧ Jewish law sets forth the qualifications expected of one who serves as the permanent shaliah tzibbur, or as the *hazzan* of a congregation:

> · He must be a worthy and suitable person who is not tainted by any reputation for religious or moral transgressions. One who is known to commit religious or moral transgressions is disqualified and must not be chosen.
> · He must be a modest person and personally acceptable to the congregation. After all, he represents them before the Lord, and they must concur in that representation.
> · He should possess a pleasant voice, one that is sweet to the ears. This not only makes the prayer experience a more pleasant one for the worshippers, but is deemed to be an expression of great honor to the Lord. Where an unsuitable or unworthy person is permitted to act as shaliah tzibbur on account of his pleasant voice alone, his prayers are regarded by our religious tradition as unacceptable to the Holy One, Blessed Be He. It is, in fact, considered an abomination. "Those who do this, withhold good from Israel" (Mishne Berurah: 12 on Orakh Hayim 53:4).

· The cantor should be a person who understands what he is saying. He should know the meaning of the Hebrew prayers, and possess the faith to say them with sincerity.

· He must not be a dull or foolish person, but one who can intelligently discuss and participate in the affairs of the community.

· He should be well-versed in the various melodies and chants that are appropriate for different services. In the past, one obtained such training by apprenticing oneself to an experienced hazzan. In our day, there are Institutes where such cantorial training is offered.

Voice and music training is also valuable to the contemporary hazzan and enhances his professional stature and qualifications.

8~ If there cannot be found one who possesses all of these qualifications, the one with the most wisdom and good deeds should be chosen. Should the choice be between an unlearned mature person who has a pleasant voice, and a lad of but thirteen who *understands what he is saying* but whose voice is not pleasant, the young man should be preferred.

8~ One should not be elected as permanent shaliah tzibbur unless he has reached a level of maturity equivalent to the late teens. It is a matter of respect for the community. Maturity is considered an asset for filling this role, but a congregation may waive this honor due it if it sees fit to do so. If it is only on occasion, anyone who has passed the age of thirteen may officiate.

8~ A hazzan who unduly prolongs the service is not acting properly, for it places an excessive burden upon the congregation.

The Sexton

8~ The sexton (or *shamash* as he is called in Hebrew) is a religious functionary who attends to many duties in a synagogue. He generally is charged with supervising the daily services, with the care and maintenance of the ritual items of the synagogue—the prayer books, Bibles, scrolls, etc. He will often serve also as the Torah Reader (*Baal-Koreh*), or as a substitute for the cantor. He works with and assists the rabbi in many ways. While there are no formal religious requirements for one to serve in this capacity, and special schooling beyond that which a well-educated Jew is expected to possess is not required, the sexton is expected to be a pious person and to reflect a fairly sound level of Jewish education. The better his background in Jewish studies and the more competent he is in many religious skills, the more valuable will he be in service to a congregation and the more varied the tasks and responsibilities which can be assigned to him.

The Gabbai

క⋗ The terms *gabbai* and *parnas* have traditionally been applied to the lay head of a Jewish religious community. In our day, the President and the other lay officers of a congregation act in that capacity. They, assisted by the Board of Directors, have primary responsibility for the financial maintenance of the synagogue, for setting its fiscal policies, and for conducting the general affairs of the congregation.

ROLE OF THE KOHEN

In ancient Israel, the religious leadership and supervision of worship in the Tabernacle and Temple was entrusted to Aaron and his descendants from the tribe of Levi. They were to be the *kohanim*, the priests in Israel. The rest of the tribe of Levi were assigned secondary functions in the "sacred work." It was a privileged position, awarded them as a reward for the steadfastness of their tribe to God when all the rest of the children of Israel fell wayward in the incident of the Golden Calf.

Although the priests and Levites were not to share in the division of the land among the tribes of Israel, thus being denied a source of self-support, their sustenance was assured by the Biblical commandments which call for the setting aside of tithings (*terumoth* and *maaseroth*) from the produce of the land for the support of the kohanim and Levites.

The role and function of the kohen varied during the course of Jewish history. At the very minimum, the kohen was charged with performing the various rites in the Temple in connection with the daily and holiday offerings and with the worship assemblies as on Yom Kippur. They were also charged with quasi-medical responsibilities, being trained in the recognition of various diseases and skin conditions. Whether or not to quarantine was a decision that the kohen had to make.

They were also to serve as spiritual guides, as judges and teachers, and as interpreters of the Torah to the people, although these functions were not exclusively confined or limited to them. But as the spiritual quality of the priesthood waned, the kohanim as a class, confined themselves to their Biblically-mandated functions, while prophets, sages and rabbis arose to fulfill the other spiritual responsibilities. But in the Temple worship itself, the Torah commanded that "no stranger shall approach," and by stranger was meant anyone who was not a kohen.

The privileged position of the kohen in the religious hierarchy also called for special disciplines and responsibilities. Not everything that was permitted to the rest of Israel was permitted to the kohen. Specifically, he was forbidden to defile himself with the dead or to take a divorcee as a wife.

With the destruction of the Temple in 70 c.e., the primary responsibilities of the kohen became obsolete. General religious leadership was based upon scholarship and personal merit rather than the privilege of birth. The kohen now had to compete equally with all other Jews for religious leadership.

Still, even after the Temple's destruction there remained certain rites that only the kohen was permitted to perform. No stranger— not even the greatest Jewish scholar and saint—dared replace him in violation of Torah law. Thus, the redemption of the first born and the priestly benedictions (*dukhenen*) remain to this day the prerogative of the kohen.

Additional honors and forms of respect continued to be extended to him within the ritual framework. By the same token, the special disciplines imposed upon the kohen have also remained in force to this day, thus assuring the continuation of the special role first assigned to Aaron and to his descendants.

Maintaining the lineal descent and ritual integrity of the priesthood not only serves the purpose of retaining qualified people for the performance of the above-mentioned ritual services, but also keeps alive the institution of kohen for whatever expansion of his duties might someday occur as a result of that ultimate of all miracles—the coming of the Messiah and the total redemption of Israel.

CEREMONY OF THE PRIESTLY BENEDICTION

And the Lord spoke to Moses, saying: Speak to Aaron and his sons: Thus shall you bless the children of Israel; *Say to them*:

May the Lord bless you and protect you.
May the Lord cause His Countenance to shine upon you and be gracious to you.
May the Lord bestow His favor upon you and grant you peace.

Thus shall they put My name upon the children of Israel, and I* *will bless them.*

(Numbers 6:22–27)

ક• It is a commandment of the Torah that the kohanim bless the people, as it is written "Thus shall you bless the children of Israel . . ." (Numbers 6:23). The rite has popularly come to be known as *dukhen* after the term for the *platform* upon which the kohanim stood when they uttered the blessing in Temple days. In Hebrew, the rite is called *nesiat kapayim* (raising of the hands). A kohen who blesses is himself blessed. And one who does not bless is not blessed, as it is written "And those who bless you, I shall bless" (Genesis 12:3).

ક• Any kohen (not otherwise disqualified—see below) who does not ascend the bimah to recite the Priestly Benediction, transgresses a positive commandment of the Torah.†

---

* "I" is emphasized so that it should not occur to the kohanim to say, "We will bless Israel," for it is written: "For the Lord your God will bless you, as He promised you" (Deut. 16:6 and 21:5); "And the priests, the sons of Levi, shall come near—for them the Lord, your God, has chosen to minister to Him, and *to bless in the name of the Lord.*"

"The priest was no Mediator; and no priest could say, *I* bless the children of Israel. God is the source of, and He alone can give effect to the blessing pronounced by the priests. They were merely the *channel* through which the blessing was conveyed *to* the Israelites" (Commentary of J. H. Hertz, Pentateuch, Numbers 6:27).

† Rabbi Joshua Ben Levi was of the opinion that a qualified kohen who does not ascend to the bimah for the blessing transgresses three positive commandments. (1) "Thus shall you bless"; (2) "Say unto them"; (3) "Let them put My Name . . ." (Sotah 38b).

&ᴥ The commandment is violated only if the kohen is present when called upon to dukhen and fails to do so. This is the reason for the custom among kohanim who are disqualified or who for personal reasons feel reluctant to perform their duty to step out of the synagogue before the Reader reaches that point in the service when they would have to ascend the bimah.

&ᴥ It is as much a mitzvah for a kohen to perform the rite of the Priestly Benediction as it is for any Jew to observe any of the positive mitzvot such as eating matzah on Pesach, sitting in a succah on Succot, putting on tefillin each day, etc. Although the kohen technically avoids the violation of the mitzvah by stepping out of the synagogue, he is guilty in *spirit* if he deliberately avoids it.

&ᴥ A kohen is disqualified from dukhenen for any of the following reasons:

> · If he is in violation of the priestly laws by having contracted a marriage forbidden to him or by regularly disregarding the restrictions forbidding "defilement with the dead."
> · If he is a *halal*, the offspring of a marriage that his father was not permitted to contract because he was a kohen.
> · If he has at any time committed murder, even if he has since served his punishment and repented.
> · If he is physically disabled, deformed, or possessed of a physical blemish (see Lev. 21:16–24) that might distract the congregation.
> · If he is an *onan* (a mourner before burial takes place), or a mourner for his father or mother during the twelve month period of mourning, or a mourner for other relatives during the *shloshim* (the 30 day period). If there are no other kohanim in the synagogue the mourner may dukhen; only during the week of shiva may he not do so at all. (In Israel, only the latter restriction prevails.)
> · If he is intoxicated or has drunk any intoxicating beverages prior to the dukhenen.
> · If he despises the congregation or is in turn despised by them (see note on page 204).

&ᴥ The transgression of religious commandments, other than those referred to above does not disqualify a kohen from performing the rite of the Priestly Benediction. Just as one who violates the Sabbath is not disqualified from putting on tefillin, sitting in a succah or eating matzah on Pesach, neither is a kohen halakhically disqualified from fulfilling this priestly mitzvah.*

In an extremely observant congregation where one who is not a devout, observant person is regarded with disdain and is not accorded other honors, it may be that a kohen who does not observe the Sabbath laws or dietary laws or other religious duties may be barred from ascending the bimah based upon the last disqualification mentioned above.

Where, however, religious laxity is prevalent among a congregation and non-observant individuals are not only tolerated but play leading roles in the affairs of the congregation and are honored by being called to the Torah, etc. it is an act of misplaced piety to discourage a none-too-observant kohen from performing the rite of the Priestly Benediction. Under such circumstances, it is in fact meritorious to encourage him to do so, in order to credit him with an additional mitzvah and prevent this central rite of a traditional service from becoming forgotten. Properly performed, it is not only meaningful, but awe-inspiring and beautiful as well.†

ဆ So as not to nullify the mitzvah of dukhenen, the halakha rules that if the Reader himself is a kohen and there are no other kohanim present, he may go up to dukhen even though he is otherwise not required to do so.

ဆ A kohen who cannot or does not ascend to dukhen should step out of the synagogue before the prayer r'tzai, and remain outside until after the Priestly Benediction is completed.

ဆ In the Diaspora, kohanim perform the rite of the Priestly Benediction during the repetition of musaf Amidah on Rosh Hashana,

---

* While it may be that a kohen who does not observe the Sabbath or the dietary laws or other religious duties will feel himself unworthy to dukhen, or feel that he will slight the congregation if he ascends before them and does therefore of his own accord step out of the synagogue and refrain from dukhenen, the privilege and the duty may not be denied him should he insist on doing it.

† To say, "We don't have any religiously worthy kohanim among the worshippers" to explain the elimination of the entire rite of dukhenen from the services of some contemporary congregations in the United States is not halakhically sound. Suppose a Sabbath-observing kohen joins the congregation? Will he be permitted to ascend for the Priestly Benediction? Suppose a pious kohen visits the congregation? Will he be permitted to perform his Biblical duty?

Yom Kippur and the sacred days of each of the three major festivals.*

In Israel, the rite is also performed every Sabbath during both the shachrit and musaf Amidah. In Jerusalem, it is performed every day of the year during the shachrit and (when applicable) the musaf Amidah (and on fast days even at minha, in some communities).

৯১ In some communities in the Diaspora, it is customary not to dukhen on a Yom Tov which falls out on a Sabbath day. There is no basis for this practice. It is proper to dukhen on a Yom Tov even if it coincides with the Sabbath.

৯১ Prior to the Priestly Benediction, the kohen is prohibited from drinking wine or other intoxicating beverages.

৯১ Before ascending to dukhen, the kohen must wash his hands up to the wrists, as was the practice in the Temple in preparation for the Avodah (Divine Service), as is written "Lift up your hands to the sanctuary, and bless the Lord" (Psalms 134:2). No blessing is recited.

৯১ It is proper for a Levite to pour the water over the hands of the kohanim (Numbers 18:2). If no Levite is present, any first-born son may pour the water. If neither a Levite nor a first-born son is present, the kohen should do it himself.

৯১ Just as the kohen was forbidden to enter the Temple area wearing shoes (Berakhot 9:5), so the Sages decreed after the destruction of the Temple that a kohen may not ascend the bimah for the Priestly Benediction wearing his shoes (Sotah 40a). They should be removed or loosened before washing the hands so that there is no need to touch them after the washing. The kohen should wear socks or slippers made of cloth, rubber or straw instead of going completely barefoot.

৯১ The kohanim ascend the bimah when the Reader begins the blessing of *r'tzai*. When they first ascend, they face the Holy Ark

---

* The reason given for the limitation to these days is based upon the Scriptural interpretation that only one who is of good heart, cheerful and content should bless (see Proverbs 22:9). On Yom Tov, when the *simha* of the festival and even on Yom Kippur when the *simha* of forgiveness is paramount, these criteria of joy were met even in the hard-pressed Jewish communities of the Diaspora.

(aron kodesh). When the reader or someone designated for that purpose calls out "Kohanim," the kohanim begin to recite in unison the following blessing:

בָּרוּךְ אַתָּה יְיָ אֱלֹהֵינוּ מֶלֶךְ הָעוֹלָם, אֲשֶׁר קִדְּשָׁנוּ בִּקְדֻשָּׁתוֹ
שֶׁל אַהֲרֹן ...

Baruch ata adonai elohainu melech ha-olam asher kidshanu bikdushato shel Aharon . . .

Blessed art Thou, Lord our God, King of the universe who sanctified us with the sanctity of Aaron . . .

At this point, with the prayer shawls over their heads (to prevent distraction), their hands lifted to shoulder height, fingers spread in the appropriate manner, they turn around to face the congregation and conclude the blessing with the words:

... וְצִוָּנוּ לְבָרֵךְ אֶת עַמּוֹ יִשְׂרָאֵל בְּאַהֲבָה.

. . . v'tzivanu l'varekh et amo Yisrael b'a-hava.

. . . and commanded us to bless His people Israel with love.*

ટ≈ The Reader then calls out each word of the blessing to the kohanim, and they in turn recite the blessing, word for word.

While the kohanim utter the words of the blessing, the worshippers should not say anything at all, but should listen carefully to the words.

At the end of each of the three sentences of the blessing, following the words *veyishmarekha, vihuneka, shalom,* the congregation responds with "Amen."

ટ≈ The melody used by the kohanim for the chanting of the blessing should be uniform and specifically reserved for this rite.

ટ≈ The words of the blessing must be said loudly enough for the congregation to hear. One should not, however, shout nor raise his voice above the others. A pleasant and moderate voice level should be maintained by all the kohanim.

---

* Since the blessing requires Israel to be blessed *with love,* if a kohen despises or hates people in the congregation or the congregation despises, dislikes, or hates him, he should not ascend for the Priestly Benediction, but should step out of the synagogue.

ε⊷ While the kohanim recite the blessing, the congregation faces in the direction of the kohanim. However, their eyes should be cast down as a sign of respect and humility. According to some sources, the reason for not looking at the kohen is to avoid being distracted in concentrating on the words of the blessing.

The custom in some places of turning one's back to the kohanim in order to avoid gazing at them, though well intentioned, is in fact a crude insult which nullifies the merit of the blessing.

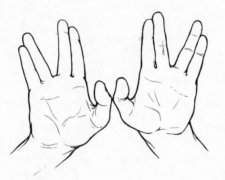

FIGURE 4   *Correct Position for Fingers of Kohen's Hands during Priestly Benediction*

ε⊷ The Priestly Benediction must take place "face to face." The Talmud rules that the people standing behind the kohanim are not included in the blessing, for it indicates that the blessing was not so important to them to make them leave their places and stand before the kohanim to be blessed "face to face" as required.

ε⊷ A kohen who ascends to perform his duty should first have received some instruction and guidance from another kohen or from a rabbi, or he should have consulted the codes for additional details of the ceremony that he needs to know.

ε⊷ If there is no kohen in the congregation, the Reader substitutes the petitionary prayer, which begins with the words, "O God and God of our fathers." This includes the entire Priestly Benediction in the form of a quotation from the Biblical text.

ε⊷ The kohen is given priority in the distribution of religious honors. Thus, it is the kohen who is given the first Aliyah whenever the Torah is read. Unless he agrees to waive his privilege, no one else may be called up first. Similarly, it is the kohen who has priority in leading the grace after meals (*birkat hamazon*), if all the assembled are of equal status.

Part Three

THE SPECIAL OCCASIONS OF THE YEAR

In addition to the daily way of life with its recurring spiritual highpoint—the Sabbath—every seventh day, there are festivals and appointed sacred seasons, special occasions which add extra spice and additional color to Jewish life. These special days constitute additional avenues by which the Jew takes cognizance of God's role in nature and history, and by which the Jew identifies with the land of Israel and Jerusalem, the Holy City. They embody the deepest yearnings and values of the Jewish people. The holidays provide opportunities for the Jew to celebrate and rejoice in the historical-spiritual events which made them a nation and a faith. They provide opportunities to celebrate the victories and successes of the people, as well as to mourn and grieve over the tragedies that have been suffered. The special days provide the Jew with the opportunity to identify with the historical occasions that are religiously significant and need to be commemorated.

The festivals designated by the Torah as "sacred seasons" when "no manner of servile work" may be performed are Sabbath-like in spirit and sanctity. Added are the extra features distinctive to each particular festival. Though the Intermediate days of the festivals and the post-Biblical holidays do not possess the same level of Sabbath-like sanctity, the observances that are unique to each festival respectively contribute immeasurably to making even those days distinctive and "something special" in the life of the Jew.

CHAPTER

10

The Major Festivals

> On the first day you shall hold a
> sacred convocation, and on the sev-
> enth day a sacred convocation; no
> work at all shall be done on them,
> only what every person is to eat,
> that only may be done by you.
> (Exodus 12:16)

THIS Biblical precept—in relation to Pesach—is typical of the
commandments concerning all of the festivals mentioned in the
Torah. Those festivals are Pesach, Shavuot, Succot, Shmini Atzeret,
and Rosh Hashana.

According to the Torah, the first and seventh day of Pesach, the first
day of Succot, the one day of Shavuot, Shmini Atzeret, and Rosh
Hashana are sacred days in which no manner of work is to be done,
much like on the Sabbath. Except for Rosh Hashana, which by
ancient rabbinic edict was extended into a two-day observance and
is so observed even in Israel, this is the pattern traditionally followed
in the land of Israel.

In all the lands of the Diaspora, however, one extra day of observance was added to each of the festivals, with the sacred days
observed being:

· The first and last two days of Pesach.
· The two days of Shavuot.
· The first two days of Succot.
· The two days of Shmini Atzeret (the second day is called Simhat Torah).
· The two days of Rosh Hashana.

The fast day of Yom Kippur, observed only one day in the Diaspora as well as Israel, will be dealt with separately as its observance is unique.

THE SECOND FESTIVAL DAY OF THE DIASPORA

Why these differences in the religious calendar between the religious community of Israel and that of the Diaspora? Why is an extra day added to Rosh Hashana but not to the other festivals in Israel? In what way does Rosh Hashana differ? And why according to the halakha or Jewish religious law, does a Diaspora Jew who is only briefly visiting Israel have to observe the two days of the festivals even while in Israel; while the most pious Israeli Jew on a brief journey to the Diaspora need only observe the one day as he would at home, although he should not publicly do anything that might be regarded as a desecration of the holy day observed by the Diaspora community?

Originally, as far back as the fifth century B.C.E. (and long before then, according to some authorities)—the additional day was observed beyond the borders of Israel because of the doubt as to which of the two days was the correct day. The correct date for the observance of the holy day depended on which day had been proclaimed Rosh Hodesh (the first of the month) by the Sanhedrin, which in turn was determined on the basis of when the new moon was first sighted. The first day of each month could fall out only on one of two possible dates: either on the thirtieth or the thirty-first day following the previous Rosh Hodesh, since the Hebrew month consists of either twenty-nine or thirty days. The people were first notified of the proclamation by the lighting of bonfires atop the hills, which signal was then relayed to the most distant areas where Jews lived, to Babylon and other adjacent countries.

When hostile Samaritans began to interfere deliberately by lighting decoy bonfires, the Sanhedrin was forced to rely on messengers. These messengers could not always get to distant communities in time to inform the people of the correct day, and when this happened, a second day was added to each of the festivals so that the correct Biblical date would not be desecrated. In the Diaspora, this practice gradually became the norm.

After Hillel II, in the fourth century (360 c.e.), established a fixed Jewish calendar upon precise mathematical and astronomical formulations (this system is still in use) so that the precise day of the festival was known to all in advance, the Sages of the Talmud (Betzah 4b) themselves raised the question as to whether or not to continue the observance of the second day of the festival in the countries beyond the land of Israel. After all, the uncertainty was now gone; the permanent calendar had removed all doubt.

The decision of the Talmudic Sages (the Sages in Israel, in fact) was that in view of the many century-long tradition of a two-day festival among Jewish communities in the Diaspora, it had become a practice hallowed through long usage. They cautioned: "be careful to keep the practice your ancestors entrusted to you" (*"hizaharu b'minghag avoteikhem b'yadeikhem"*). This response was embodied in the halakha, and so the second day observance was established on a permanent basis. What had till then been observed because of doubt became fixed as rabbinical enactment (*takanah*).

The full name of this day is *Yom Tov Sheni Shel Galuyot*, which means "The Second Festival Day of the Diaspora." It became binding on all the Diaspora, and only in the Diaspora.

Although the second day of the festival is rooted in rabbinic ordinance and is not prescribed in the Torah, it has nevertheless been preserved with equal sanctity (a few emergency exceptions exist) throughout the centuries, long after the original doubt had been resolved. The Codes, from Maimonides to the Shulhan Arukh, are unanimous in declaring the "second days" an integral part of Judaism in the Diaspora.

The question of Rosh Hashana differs somewhat from the other festivals, if only because it falls on the first of the month. Even in Eretz Yisrael, outside of Jerusalem, most of the people observed Rosh Hashana for two days as early as the days of the Prophets, out of doubt as to which of the two days would be proclaimed the holy day, since messengers were not dispatched on the holy day itself, even to nearby communities. But since testimony for the sighting of the new moon was not received till the morning and only then would the first of the month be proclaimed, even the people in Jerusalem would already have ushered in the holy day on the eve of the first of the two possible dates. It thus happened even in Biblical times when the new moon was not proclaimed till the second of the two possible days that the people observed Rosh Hashana for two days even in Jerusalem proper. There it was the first day that was doubtful and the second day that was certain. After a number of confusing mix-ups this caused in the Temple service, and to avoid the possibility that people would begin to observe the first day as a sacred day only to discover that the next day was the holy day, the Sages legislated that both days of Rosh Hashana were to be observed annually. This enactment obviously was to apply to Eretz Yisrael.

In contrast to the second days of the festivals, the second day of Rosh Hashana is not regarded as "The Second Festival Day of the Diaspora." Its statutory designation in the halakha is that of an extended day (*yom arikhta*), equivalent to the first day in every respect. This religious decree (*gezerah*), though ignored for awhile in Eretz Yisrael after the fourth century, when all doubts regarding the correct days for the observance of the holy days were eliminated, was nevertheless reaffirmed by the Gaonim and Early Authorities as the proper practice for Eretz Yisrael.

Those who today call for a return to the one-day observance on the basis that we now have scientific calendars and can be sure of the precise date of the new month beg the real issue, because we've had scientific calendars ever since the middle of the fourth century, and our people were already sure of the precise dates of all the holidays back in the days of the Talmud.

Furthermore, the more frequent contact world Jewry now has with Israeli Jewry has only served to emphasize the full official name given by the Talmud to the second day, i.e., *of those who live in the Diaspora (shel galuyot)*. If its observance only adds to the Jewish awareness that one is living in the *galut* and does not claim permanent residence in the Holy Land, this too is a very important awareness to preserve.

৪৯ The festivals fall on the following dates (according to the Hebrew calendar):

Rosh Hashana: Tishrai 1 and 2
Yom Kippur: Tishrai 10
Succot: Tishrai 15–21
Shmini Atzeret and Simhat Torah: Tishrai 22–23
Pesach: Nisan 15–22
Shavuot: Sivan 6 and 7

&ed; Just as it is a religious duty to sanctify the Sabbath day, so is it a religious duty to sanctify all the festivals and to derive joy from their observance. All the Biblically ordained festivals are called "sacred assemblies" (*mikra-ey kodesh*) and must be sanctified accordingly.

&ed; The same personal preparations required for the Sabbath are also required for the festivals.

&ed; At least two meals (one in the evening and one in the day) are required to be eaten on a festival, in contrast to the Sabbath when three meals (*shalosh seudot*) are required.

&ed; The candles are lighted. The blessing differs only slightly from the one said for the Sabbath candles. The word *yom tov* (festival) is substituted for the word *shabbat*. In addition, the *sheheheyanu* blessing is also said, except on the seventh and eighth day of Pesach (see page 169).

&ed; The Kiddush is also recited on the festivals.

Kiddush for Festivals

On Friday evenings, begin here:

(וַיְהִי עֶרֶב וַיְהִי בֹקֶר)

יוֹם הַשִּׁשִּׁי. וַיְכֻלּוּ הַשָּׁמַיִם וְהָאָרֶץ וְכָל צְבָאָם. וַיְכַל אֱלֹהִים
בַּיּוֹם הַשְּׁבִיעִי מְלַאכְתּוֹ אֲשֶׁר עָשָׂה, וַיִּשְׁבֹּת בַּיּוֹם הַשְּׁבִיעִי מִכָּל
מְלַאכְתּוֹ אֲשֶׁר עָשָׂה. וַיְבָרֶךְ אֱלֹהִים אֶת יוֹם הַשְּׁבִיעִי וַיְקַדֵּשׁ
אֹתוֹ, כִּי בוֹ שָׁבַת מִכָּל מְלַאכְתּוֹ אֲשֶׁר בָּרָא אֱלֹהִים לַעֲשׂוֹת.)

On other evenings, begin here:

סָבְרִי מָרָנָן וְרַבּוֹתַי.

בָּרוּךְ אַתָּה יְיָ אֱלֹהֵינוּ מֶלֶךְ הָעוֹלָם, בּוֹרֵא פְּרִי הַגָּפֶן.

בָּרוּךְ אַתָּה יְיָ אֱלֹהֵינוּ מֶלֶךְ הָעוֹלָם, אֲשֶׁר בָּחַר בָּנוּ מִכָּל
עָם, וְרוֹמְמָנוּ מִכָּל לָשׁוֹן, וְקִדְּשָׁנוּ בְּמִצְוֹתָיו. וַתִּתֶּן־לָנוּ, יְיָ
אֱלֹהֵינוּ, בְּאַהֲבָה (שַׁבָּתוֹת לִמְנוּחָה וּ)מוֹעֲדִים לְשִׂמְחָה, חַגִּים
וּזְמַנִּים לְשָׂשׂוֹן, אֶת יוֹם (הַשַּׁבָּת הַזֶּה, וְאֶת יוֹם)

Shmini Atzeret and Simhat Torah	Succot	Shavuot	Pesach
הַשְּׁמִינִי, חַג	חַג הַסֻּכּוֹת	חַג הַשָּׁבֻעוֹת	חַג הַמַּצּוֹת
הָעֲצֶרֶת הַזֶּה,	הַזֶּה, זְמַן	הַזֶּה, זְמַן	הַזֶּה, זְמַן
זְמַן שִׂמְחָתֵנוּ,	מַתַּן תּוֹרָתֵנוּ,	שִׂמְחָתֵנוּ,	חֵרוּתֵנוּ,

(בְּאַהֲבָה) מִקְרָא קֹדֶשׁ, זֵכֶר לִיצִיאַת מִצְרָיִם. כִּי בָנוּ בָחַרְתָּ,
וְאוֹתָנוּ קִדַּשְׁתָּ מִכָּל הָעַמִּים, (וְשַׁבָּת) וּמוֹעֲדֵי קָדְשֶׁךָ (בְּאַהֲבָה
וּבְרָצוֹן) בְּשִׂמְחָה וּבְשָׂשׂוֹן הִנְחַלְתָּנוּ. בָּרוּךְ אַתָּה יְיָ, מְקַדֵּשׁ
(הַשַּׁבָּת וְ)יִשְׂרָאֵל וְהַזְּמַנִּים.

It was evening and it was morning.

On the sixth day the heavens and the earth and all their
hosts were completed. For by the seventh day God had completed
his work which he had made, and he rested on the seventh
day from all his work which he had made. Then God blessed the
seventh day and hallowed it, because on it he rested from all
his work which God had created to function thenceforth.

Blessed art Thou, Lord our God, King of the universe who
creates the fruit of the vine.

(On Sabbath add the words in parentheses.)

Blessed art Thou, Lord our God, King of the universe, who
hast chosen us from all peoples, and exalted us above all nations,
and hallowed us by Thy commandments. Thou hast given us
in love, O Lord our God, (Sabbaths for rest,) holy festivals for
gladness, and sacred seasons for joy: (this Sabbath day and)
this day of—

214

On Pesach—the Feast of Unleavened Bread, the season of our Freedom

On Shavuot—the Feast of Weeks, the season of the Giving of our Torah

On Succot—the Feast of Tabernacles, the season of our Gladness

On Shmini Atzeret and *Simhat Torah*—the Eighth-day Feast of Solemn Assembly, the season of our Gladness (in love); a holy convocation, as a memorial of the departure from Egypt; for Thou hast chosen us, and hallowed us above all peoples, and Thy holy (Sabbath and) festivals thou hast caused us to inherit (in love and favour) in joy and gladness. Blessed art Thou, O Lord, who hallowest (the Sabbath), Israel and the festive seasons.

On Saturday night add:

בָּרוּךְ אַתָּה יְיָ אֱלֹהֵינוּ מֶלֶךְ הָעוֹלָם, בּוֹרֵא מְאוֹרֵי הָאֵשׁ.

בָּרוּךְ אַתָּה יְיָ אֱלֹהֵינוּ מֶלֶךְ הָעוֹלָם, הַמַּבְדִּיל בֵּין קֹדֶשׁ

לְחֹל, בֵּין אוֹר לְחשֶׁךְ, בֵּין יִשְׂרָאֵל לָעַמִּים, בֵּין יוֹם הַשְּׁבִיעִי

לְשֵׁשֶׁת יְמֵי הַמַּעֲשֶׂה. בֵּין קְדֻשַּׁת שַׁבָּת לִקְדֻשַּׁת יוֹם טוֹב

הִבְדַּלְתָּ, וְאֶת יוֹם הַשְּׁבִיעִי מִשֵּׁשֶׁת יְמֵי הַמַּעֲשֶׂה קִדַּשְׁתָּ;

הִבְדַּלְתָּ וְקִדַּשְׁתָּ אֶת עַמְּךָ יִשְׂרָאֵל בִּקְדֻשָּׁתֶךָ. בָּרוּךְ אַתָּה יְיָ,

הַמַּבְדִּיל בֵּין קֹדֶשׁ לְקֹדֶשׁ.

Blessed art Thou, Lord our God, King of the universe who creates the lights of the fire.

Blessed art Thou, Lord our God, King of the universe who makes a distinction between sacred and secular, light and darkness, Israel and other peoples, the seventh day and the six days of labor. As Thou hast made a distinction between Sabbath sanctity and festival sanctity, and hast hallowed the seventh day above the six days of work, so hast Thou set apart and sanctified Thy people Israel through Thy holiness. Blessed art Thou Lord, who makes a distinction between degrees of holiness.

Omit only on the last two nights of Pesach:

בָּרוּךְ אַתָּה יְיָ אֱלֹהֵינוּ מֶלֶךְ הָעוֹלָם, שֶׁהֶחֱיָנוּ וְקִיְּמָנוּ

וְהִגִּיעָנוּ לַזְּמַן הַזֶּה.

Blessed art Thou, Lord our God, King of the universe who has given us life and sustenance, and brought us to this season.

In the succah, add:

בָּרוּךְ אַתָּה יְיָ אֱלֹהֵינוּ מֶלֶךְ הָעוֹלָם, אֲשֶׁר קִדְּשָׁנוּ בְּמִצְוֹתָיו וְצִוָּנוּ לֵישֵׁב בַּסֻּכָּה.

Blessed art Thou, Lord our God, King of the universe who has sanctified us with His commandments and commanded us to dwell in the succah.

8❧ The presence of the two "Sabbath loaves" (lehem mishne) on the table is also enjoined for the festival.

8❧ At the conclusion of the festival, Havdalah is also said, except that the Havdalah does not include either the blessing for the light or the blessing for the spices.

8❧ The basic pattern to be followed in the observance of these sacred days is the same as outlined for the observance of the Sabbath, with the following exceptions:

> · It is permissible to transfer fire and to cook and bake on the festival days (unless, of course, they fall on the Sabbath), provided that some of the food is intended for that day and that it is not being cooked solely in preparation for the next day.
> · It is also permissible to carry objects in the public domain on the festival.

8❧ The festivals of Pesach and Succot have special observances and rules which distinguish them from the Sabbath day. These unique features will be covered in the sections dealing with those festivals.

8❧ When a festival day coincides with Friday, the question of preparing on that day for the Sabbath may arise. For while one may cook on a festival day, one may not do so if *all* of the food is intended solely for the next day. By setting up an *eruv tavshilin*, Jewish law ruled it permissible to prepare on the festival day for the next (Sabbath) day. This is done as follows: on the eve of the festival, the head of the household sets aside any two foods, one cooked and one baked (a small hallah, matzah, fish, meat, or an egg, etc.) and recites the following blessing:

בָּרוּךְ אַתָּה, יְיָ אֱלֹהֵינוּ, מֶלֶךְ הָעוֹלָם, אֲשֶׁר קִדְּשָׁנוּ בְּמִצְוֹתָיו
וְצִוָּנוּ עַל מִצְוַת עֵרוּב.

Baruch ata adonai elohainu melech ha-olam asher kidshanu
b'mitzvotav v'tzivanu al mitzvat eruv.

Blessed art Thou, Lord our God, King of the universe who
has sanctified us with His commandments and commanded us
concerning the mitzvah of eruv.

After the blessing, the following declaration is added: "With
this *eruv*, it shall be permitted for us to bake, cook, warm,
kindle light and take care of all our needs on Yom Tov for
the Sabbath."

The foods set aside as the eruv tavshilin may not be eaten until
all the preparations for the Sabbath have been completed.

᠍ If one had forgotten to prepare an eruv tavshilin, or through
no fault of his own could not do so, one may depend upon the eruv
prepared by the religious head of the community of which one is a
part. Or one should see to it that some of the food prepared on the
festival day is also eaten on that day.

11

Passover

Passover, or *Pesach*, as the festival is called in Hebrew, commemorates the deliverance of the children of Israel from over two centuries of Egyptian bondage, and recalls their mass exodus from Egypt about 3300 years ago. The story of Israel's increasingly oppressive servitude and suffering, the Divine mission entrusted to Moses and his brother Aaron, their untiring efforts to secure the release of their people, the stubborn resistance of the Egyptian Pharaoh, the series of Divinely-ordained catastrophes that eventually caused Pharaoh's temporary change of heart, and of the Israelites' escape—are all recounted in Exodus, chapters 1-15. This event became the focal point of Jewish history because it crystallized the Jewish national identity and marked the birth of the Jews as a free people, and also because the lessons gained from the experience of Egyptian slavery and redemption provided a powerful basis for many important concepts of the Jewish faith and ethic.

The Torah calls Pesach by the name of "the Festival of the Unleavened Bread" (*hag hamatzot*), the observance with which it is most distinctly identified. In the prayer book, it is also referred to as "the season of our freedom" (*zman heirutenu*), which is its dominant theme.

The name *Hag ha-Pesach*, meaning the "Festival of Passover," is, however, the most commonly used. Pesach is a reference to the *Paschal offering* brought on the eve of the festival, and commemorative of

God's promise to "pass over you, and there shall be no plague upon you to destroy you" (Exodus 12:13). The name Pesach (Passover) is the one also commonly used in the Mishna and all rabbinic literature.

The agricultural significance of Pesach is that it also marks the early harvest period in the land of Israel. The harvesting of the barley grain was marked by the special offering of the *Omer* on the second day of the Passover.

LAWS OF HAMETZ AND MATZAH

Seven days shall you eat unleavened bread.

(Exodus 12:15)

You shall eat nothing leavened; in all your settlements shall you eat *matzot* (unleavened bread).

(Exodus 12:20)

ξ❧ Unique to Passover is the eating of unleavened bread (*matzah*) and the stringent prohibitions forbidding the *possession* as well as the *eating* of all leavened bread or any food containing leaven (*hametz*). "For whoever eateth leavened (food) from the first day until the seventh day, that person shall be cut off from Israel" (Exodus 12:15). And again: "Seven days shall there be no leaven found in your houses; for whoever eats what is leavened, that person shall be cut off from the congregation, whether he be a stranger or a citizen of the land" (Exodus 12:19).

These precepts were among those conveyed to the children of Israel by Moses prior to their departure from Egypt and their release from bondage. "And you shall observe the (feast of) unleavened bread . . . you shall observe this day throughout your generations as an eternal statute" (Exodus 12:17).

ξ❧ It is also forbidden to possess hametz during the Passover, even if one does not eat it. "No leavened bread shall be *seen* with you and no leaven shall be *seen* with you in all your territory" (Exodus 13:7), and "No leaven shall be *found* in your houses . . ." (Exodus 12:19).

ξ❧ These prohibitions (there shall not be seen nor found) do not apply to hametz which does not belong to a Jew. Where a non-Jew is visiting, working at, or renting quarters on premises belonging to a Jew, it is not forbidden for him to bring hametz onto the premises. The hametz of the non-Jew should, however, be restricted to his own quarters or set apart where it may not inadvertently be taken by a Jew.

ૐ It is also forbidden to derive any benefit, profit, or advantage from hametz during this week, even if the hametz belongs to a non-Jew.

ૐ The prohibitions against leavened food and the prohibitions against leavening agents (such as yeast) are one and the same in all respects.

ૐ The Torah prohibition against hametz goes into effect at noon of the fourteenth day of Nisan. (The festival itself does not actually begin until that evening.) To prevent the inadvertent infringement upon the Biblically proscribed period, the Sages extended the forbidden period by two hours, allowing hametz to be eaten only up to one-third of the day (usually between 9:15 and 9:30 A.M.). The length of the day is reckoned from dawn to nightfall.

ૐ In the Diaspora—all countries outside Israel—the laws pertaining to hametz are extended for an extra day, as Passover must there be observed for eight days.

ૐ What is hametz?

· Hametz is any one of the five major grains, *wheat, rye, barley, oats* and *spelt,* that has come in resting contact with water for at least eighteen minutes. Such grain or flour is considered to have begun the leavening process.
· Hametz is any food or drink made from any of these grains or in which they may be an ingredient, even if only in minute amounts. The only exception is matzah, which is the prescribed unleavened bread in the baking of which special precautions are taken. Matzah in which the necessary precautions are not taken to avoid the onset of the leavening process becomes hametz. That is why matzah produced for year-round consumption will state *Not For Passover Use* on the boxes.
· The use of dishes and utensils in which even minute traces of hametz have been absorbed is forbidden during the Passover, unless it is possible to kasher them and that is first done.
· Ovens and ranges used throughout the year may not be used

on Passover unless first properly cleansed and kashered in accordance with the prescribed procedure.

· Although not classified as hametz by Biblical definition, Ashkenazic Jewry followed the custom of not eating on Passover rice, corn, peanuts, and other vegetables in the pea family, treating them as though they were hametz. The reason was that violations had resulted from the confusion between these products, which were sometimes ground into flour and baked into "bread," and the "true" breads made from the five grains which are hametz.

෫ What is not hametz? Everything else is permitted, unless prepared in hametz utensils or mixed with hametz ingredients which would prohibit the entire preparation. The following categories of food are not hametz in and of themselves:

· Meat, fowl, fish.
· All fruits.
· All vegetables (except corn, rice, and peas among Ashkenazic Jewry).
· All spices.
· Dairy products.

෫ To guarantee that industrially processed foods contain no ingredients that would render them prohibited for the Passover, it is proper to purchase only such canned, bottled or packaged foods as have been certified by competent rabbinic authorities called in to supervise the company's production. Fresh or raw foods in the first four categories above need no special endorsement.

෫ Products made from hametz which are not edible, unfit for *both* human and animal consumption, need not be treated as hametz with respect to possessing, using, or deriving benefit from them. The Biblical prohibitions regarding hametz apply only to items which are edible either for humans or animals.

෫ What is matzah? Matzah is an *unleavened* wafer made from water and the flour of any of the five grains—wheat, rye, barley, oats, or spelt. These grains and the flour thereof must have been carefully watched to avoid premature contact with water or any leavening agent. The entire baking process from the time that the flour and the water are mixed into a dough does not exceed eighteen minutes.

ε❧ Most matzah today is baked by machine, although there are some people who still prefer to use matzah baked by hand. The development of modern machinery to mix the dough, etc. has not only made possible matzah of even quality and standards, but has guaranteed greater speed in the process, thereby reducing the danger of leavening.

ε❧ It does not matter if matzah is round or square; there is no special significance to shape.

ε❧ Once a matzah is baked, it is no longer subject to leavening. Various matzah products are therefore made from the finished matzah which may then be broken or ground up into matzah farfel, matzah cereal, or matzah meal (a fine flour-like product which can be used for baking cakes, etc.).

ε❧ What is matzah *shmurah*? *Shmurah* means *watched* or *guarded*. It derives from the verse: "And you should *keep* the [festival of the] matzot" (Exodus 12:17), which also connotes "and you should *watch* the matzot" [from becoming hametz]. In the opinion of the majority of the Sages—and this is the halakha—such watching is required only from the time when the grain is ground into flour. As all matzah baked for Passover use is thus watched (*misha'at tehinah*), all matzah kosher for Passover is technically matzah shmurah.

In view of the fact, however, that a few Sages were of the opinion that it is necessary to watch the matzah to see that it does not come into contact with water from the time of reaping (*misha'at ketzirah*), those who are especially scrupulous in such matters make a special effort to eat only matzah that has had this extra measure of guarding (*shmirah*). Some do so throughout the week of Passover; others only for the seder night. It is to this matzah which is watched from the time of reaping that the term matzah shmurah is now commonly applied.

ε❧ While hametz is forbidden throughout the week of Passover, beginning with the morning before the festival starts, the commandment to eat matzah applies only to the night(s) of the seder (and then the precept is fulfilled by eating a piece no smaller than the size of a large olive). After the first night(s), eating matzah is entirely optional. No precept is violated, as long as one does not eat hametz.

ε❧ Since it is not permitted to derive any benefit from hametz, one may not feed hametz (food containing any of the five grains) even to one's animals or pets. If it is not possible to change the food of an animal or pet so as to exclude hametz from its diet during this one week, the sale of the animal to a non-Jew should be arranged, and the animal or pet actually turned over to the buyer. The non-Jew may be given to understand that after the Passover, one might be interested in buying it back, even at a higher price.

PREPARING FOR THE PASSOVER

ટે A thorough housecleaning is usually undertaken in preparation for the Passover festival.

ટે Shopping for the week is a special undertaking as it involves scrupulous care in avoiding any food that may contain hametz. When purchasing any processed food, one must make certain that it has been duly supervised and certified by competent rabbinic authority. The general rule to follow is: If in doubt, don't.

ટે Ovens, burners on cooking ranges must be kashered for Passover use. (Many types of cooking vessels or eating utensils may also be kashered, if needed.) This can be done any time before Passover but no later than the morning before the holiday begins. One hour beyond the eating deadline for hametz is the deadline for kashering utensils by the method of boiling (see page 120).

ટે *Ceremony of Bedikat Hametz:* A formal search for hametz must take place on the night before Passover (the eve of the fourteenth of Nisan). It should take place as soon after nightfall as possible.

The Mishna established the requirement of conducting a careful and intensive search for hametz on the night before Passover as a means of finding and cleansing the house of all hametz (even that stored in the crevices of ancient stone walls). Although it has long since become customary to do a thorough cleaning of a home well in advance of the holiday, the formal search required by the Mishna has remained an established observance in preparing for the Passover.

ટે The traditional procedure for the ceremonial search is as follows:

· Before beginning the search, the following blessing is recited:

223

בָּרוּךְ אַתָּה יְיָ אֱלֹהֵינוּ מֶלֶךְ הָעוֹלָם, אֲשֶׁר קִדְּשָׁנוּ בְּמִצְוֹתָיו,
וְצִוָּנוּ עַל בִּעוּר חָמֵץ.

Baruch ata adonai elohainu melech ha-olam asher kidshanu b'mitzvotav v'tzivanu al biur hametz.

Blessed art Thou, Lord our God, King of the universe who has commanded us concerning the destruction of the hametz.

· In darkened rooms, and with a *single* lighted candle in his hand, the head of the household moves from room to room, wherever food may have been brought in at any time, including basements and attics.

· Since it is unlikely that crumbs or other hametz will be found in a household which has already been well-cleaned (creating a situation where a blessing is recited in vain), it became customary to place, prior to the beginning of the formal search, small pieces of bread in various places throughout the house so as to make certain that some hametz is found. (One should not, however, do so indiscriminately, but should know exactly how many pieces were thus placed so as to be sure that they have all been found.)

· A large wooden spoon is traditionally used as a receptacle in which to gather the bread crumbs, and a feather is used to brush the crumbs into the spoon. However, any receptacle such as a paper plate or paper bag, and any other cleaning instrument may be used.

· Hametz food still needed for the next morning should be set aside in one place before the search begins. It need not be gathered up in the search.

· Upon concluding the search and after having gathered up whatever other hametz may have been found, the following Statement of Nullification (*bitul*) must be said:

All leaven and all hametz that is in my possession that I did not see and did not destroy, let it be null and ownerless as the dust of the earth.

This statement should be said in a language that one understands. The purpose of the statement is to legally declare null and void any hametz that may still be around but of which one is unaware. By this declaration, one formally renounces ownership of any such hametz and removes it from his legal possession.

· The hametz found during the search, together with the receptacle used to collect it, should then be wrapped up and put safely away so that it may be burned the next morning.

· Once the blessing has been said, the one making the search should not engage in any conversation (unless it has to do with the search itself) until after it has been completed and the Statement of Nullification has been said.

· In a household where there are children, the ceremonial search for the hametz can be a very impressive and awesome ceremony. They may be encouraged to participate. They may be given the task of distributing the pieces of bread about, though it must not become a game of "hide and seek" with the crumbs, lest some actually not be found. They may follow the one conducting the search as he goes about from room to room and corner to corner.

ક્ક *The Burning of the Hametz** takes place the following morning no later than one hour after the deadline for eating hametz. The hametz that had been gathered the night before in the ceremonial search plus whatever is left from breakfast is thrown into a furnace or incinerator to be burned. A small fire may be lit outdoors in which to burn it. After the hametz is thrown into the flames, the Statement of Nullification is repeated, but with a somewhat more inclusive statement:

All leaven and all hametz that is in my possession that I have seen or have not seen, that I have destroyed or have not destroyed, let it be null and ownerless as the dust of the earth.

ક્ક Should the first night of Passover fall on a Saturday night, the search for the hametz is held two nights before, on Thursday night, and the hametz is burned on Friday morning. The Statement of Nullification is, however, said Saturday morning.

ક્ક In earlier times, the Jew totally divested himself before Passover of all hametz in his possession by either destroying it, giving it away to a non-Jew, or (if it had some marketable value) by selling it to a non-Jew.

As life became more complex and individuals kept larger quantities of hametz, either for business or personal use, liquidating all of

---

* The practice of actually burning some hametz developed in literal conformity to the precept "You shall *destroy* (put an end to) leaven from your houses" (Exodus 12:15).

it just before Passover became difficult and destroying it all would have meant suffering tremendous losses. If there was no other alternative, suffering the losses would have proved no barrier to the faithful in fulfilling the commandments. But a legal alternative was available: *mekhirat hametz*, selling the hametz by having a bonafide bill of sale drawn up with a non-Jew, stating terms of delivery, assessment of value, etc., and involving a down payment by the non-Jewish buyer. Although it is possible to accuse the seller of being interested only in a "sale on paper," the legality of any sale is never dependent upon the sincerity or feelings of the buyer and seller. And since it is a legitimate transaction, it is sufficient to divest oneself of legal ownership of the hametz.

The non-Jewish buyer is usually aware that he can sell it back to the seller after Passover at a slightly higher price, thus making for himself a small profit in the transaction, a profit to which the seller gladly accedes. Although the Jew may assure the non-Jew that he will be prepared to buy it back and offer him a profit in the transaction, under no circumstances may the condition of sale include either an obligation on the part of the non-Jew to sell it back or an obligation on the part of the Jew to buy it back.

It is commonplace for some who do not fully understand it to refer to this sale of the hametz as a token sale. This is precisely what it must not be. As a token sale, it is meaningless and has no legal significance at all. If those Jews who engage in it think of it only as such and no valid sale is arranged, then according to the Torah, they must indeed destroy or otherwise dispose of all the hametz in their possession prior to Passover if they are not to be in violation of the Biblical statutes.

Those who deal in stocks, who sell short or buy futures, who buy and sell quantities of merchandise without ever having laid eyes upon it (and sometimes with but small down payments, if any) should understand better than most that even short term ownership or "sales on paper" represent very real ownership and that during this period, all risks are assumed. This so-called "legal fiction" of selling hametz on Passover is more legal than fiction, and is in fact a common bonafide method of doing business, for the bill of sale involves very real responsibilities and commitments. Should the non-Jew wish to fulfill all the conditions of the sale after Passover and refuse any offer to buy it back, the Jew would have no alternative but to live up to all the conditions in the bill of sale or be sued for breach of contract.

The bill of sale contract would be upheld as valid not only by any Jewish religious court (Beth Din) but by any civil court as well.

The mekhirat hametz transaction is mutually advantageous, in that it enables the Jewish seller to abide by the requirements of his faith and it enables the non-Jewish buyer to reap a profit. This does not detract from its legitimacy. On the contrary, it provides another example of how a living law is applied to changing conditions. Mekhirat hametz is an example of the very flexibility in Jewish law that is usually thought desirable by those who criticize legal rigidity. It is not sufficiently appreciated that mekhirat hametz is a business transaction and not intended to be a religious service of the heart.

&ᴗ Although it is preferable if the hametz sold is actually turned over to the non-Jew, if this is not feasible the Jew may rent the room or the space where the hametz is stored to the non-Jew.* The terms for the space rental are also included in the purchase agreement and bill of sale.

&ᴗ At one time, sale of the hametz was handled separately by each Jewish family. This can still be done but when it became a problem for individual families to arrange this transaction on their own, there developed the practice of assigning power of attorney to one person in the community to act on behalf of all the families when drawing up a proper bill of sale with a non-Jew. The power of attorney to sell the hametz may be signed anytime during the weeks before Passover, but no later than the hour which is the deadline for eating hametz. It is during the hour following that the actual sale of the hametz is consummated.

&ᴗ The question of why the Statement of Nullification does not suffice in lieu of selling the undestroyed hametz was asked and answered by Talmudic scholars. A Statement of Nullification, to be legally effective, must be said with sincerity. One must really mean what one says, so that if a stranger were to walk off with that which was nullified, one would have no objection. In dealing with valuable stocks of food, liquor, merchandise, etc. such sincerity is not assumed.

---

* It is only hametz belonging to a Jew that may not be *found* on the premises of a Jewish place; that belonging to a non-Jew may be found on the premises of a Jewish place, as long as it is not visible or easily handy to the Jew. Thus, a non-Jewish boarder or tenant or guest who rents, leases or has exclusive use of quarters on the premises of a Jewish home is not prohibited from bringing hametz into his own room or quarters.

A legal sale may, however, be fully consummated even where a man's heart is not entirely in it; even if one has reservations about selling it.

కఠ Where hametz is neither sold to a non-Jew nor destroyed by any other means, and remains the property of the Jew on Passover (*she'avar alav ha-Pesach*), not only is the owner in violation of the Biblical laws of Passover, but such hametz, by rabbinic decree, is also forbidden *even after Passover*. This decree is a form of fine (*knas*) to discourage people from keeping hametz in their possession over the Passover with the idea or intent of enjoying it after Passover.

కఠ The search for the hametz (*bedikat hametz*), the nullification of the hametz (*bitul hametz*), the burning and destruction of the hametz (*biur hametz*), and the sale of the hametz (*mekhirat hametz*) are all performed to leave no loophole in the observance of every facet of the commandments:

> You shall *put an end to* leaven from your houses . . .
>
> (Exodus 12:15)

> No leaven shall be *found* in your houses . . .
>
> (Exodus 12:19)

> No leavened bread shall be *seen* with you . . .
>
> (Exodus 13:7)

FAST OF THE FIRST BORN AND PRE-SEDER PRACTICES

కఠ As an expression of gratefulness to God for having spared the first-born sons among the children of Israel when the tenth plague struck Egypt, first-born sons are required to fast on the day before Passover. The fast begins at dawn. However, since it is permissible to break this particular fast for the purpose of partaking of a *seudat mitzvah*, a religious feast in celebration of a wedding, a circumcision, or the completion of a Talmudic tractate, it has become customary for synagogues to arrange for a *siyum*, the completion of a Talmudic tractate, and for a light seudat mitzvah to follow so as to provide first-born sons with an opportunity to participate and thus be relieved of fasting that day.

&» Where the day before Passover falls on a Saturday, the fast of the first born is observed on the Thursday before.

&» It is a special mitzvah to provide Passover necessities to all the poor. The tradition of funds for matzah (*maos hitim* or *kimha d'Pisha*) is very strong in Jewish communities. Special Passover or matzah funds are set up in all Jewish communities to provide for the needy locally as well as in distant Jewish communities. No Jew should sit down to the seder without having made such a contribution in accordance with his means.

&» On the day prior to the seder, it is not permissible to eat matzah, as this would detract from the significance and novelty of the mitzvah when the proper time came for eating the matzah.

&» The seder table should always be set in advance so that everything is in readiness for the beginning of the festival. Preparations in honor of the holiday are basically no different than for the weekly Sabbath (see pages 70–71).

CONDUCTING THE SEDER

&» The seder is the religious service which includes a festive meal on the first night of Passover. (On the first two nights of Passover in the Diaspora.)

&» The word *seder* means *order** (of service). It is so called because it is a ritual meal accompanied by a specific order of service unlike any other festive meal of the year.

&» Aside from the food served for dinner itself, the following items are necessary to fulfill the ritual part of the meal:

   · Wine.
   · Matzah.
   · A vegetable—some use celery; others use parsley or boiled potatoes for *karpas*.

---

* A similar word is *Siddur*—the name for the Hebrew prayer book—which connotes the *order of the prayers*.

· Bitter herbs—some use freshly-grated horseradish, others use romaine lettuce.
· Haroset—a thick mixture of ground apples and walnuts with wine, spiced with cinnamon.
· A dish of salt water.
· One roasted shankbone.
· One egg, either roasted or boiled.
· One large wine glass or cup (for the Cup of Elijah).

৵ Quantities needed: Of the vegetable, the bitter herbs, and the haroset, there should be at least a portion for everyone at the table; there should be three matzot for the head of the table, and at least one-half for everyone else present; there should be enough wine to fill each person's cup four times and the Cup of Elijah once. A cup for an adult should be at least 3.3 oz.

৵ A ceremonial plate on the table should be arranged as follows:

egg   shankbone
bitter herbs
vegetable   haroset
salt water

The plate may be shaped in any way: round or square. Any plate will do if no special ceremonial plate is available.

৵ Three matzot, covered with a napkin, or a special ceremonial matzah cover, are placed at the head of the table before the one conducting the seder.

৵ A *Haggadah* (literally: the *telling*)—the booklet containing the order of the seder service, the blessings, and the prayers to be recited, which recount the Israelite servitude and the exodus from Egypt— should be placed before each setting around the table.

৵ As the ceremonial plate may not be large enough to hold the vegetable and the bitter herbs, etc. for everyone at the table, additional platters or bowls for these items should be utilized.

৵ The symbolic significance of the special ritual food is as follows:

· Matzah—(1) recalls the haste with which our fathers had to leave Egypt as the dough "did not have sufficient time to leaven,"

(2) symbolizes "the poor bread which they ate in the land of Egypt," and (3) commemorates the Paschal offering which the matzah has come to represent after the destruction of the Jerusalem Temple.

· Wine—is the symbol of joy and gladness. The four cups represent a sort of "toast" to the four expressions used in the Torah (Exodus 6:6–7) in relation to Israel's redemption. These are: "I will *bring you out* (*hotzaiti*) from under the burdens of the Egyptians," and "I will *deliver you* (*hitzalti*) from their bondage," and "I will *redeem you* (*ga-alti*) with an outstretched arm and with great judgments," and "I will *take you* (*lakahti*) to me for a people, I will be to you God . . ." The very next verse continues with "And I will *bring you* (*hai-vaitee*) into the land concerning which I vowed to Abraham, to Isaac, and to Jacob." This fifth expression is symbolized by a Fifth Cup which is not drunk because during Israel's long centuries of exile, the people looked upon it as a promise that still needed fulfillment. However, it was set on the table and called the Cup of Elijah. The Prophet Elijah, according to the tradition, is the forerunner of the Messiah whose coming symbolizes the ingathering of the exiles and the reestablishment of Jewish sovereignty over Israel; hence the promise of being brought back into the land of the forefathers is associated with Elijah. Many Jews in Israel have been inclined toward adopting the view of many Early and Later Authorities that calls for drinking, not four, but five cups of wine. Instead of just one more cup following the grace after the meal (which is said over the third cup), an extra cup is introduced in the middle of the latter part of the seder service.

· The bitter herbs—to symbolize the bitterness endured by the Israelites during their bondage.

· Haroset—to represent the mortar used by the Israelites in building the Egyptian cities.

· Salt water—to represent the tears shed by the people in their misery.

· Karpas—a sign of spring, of fruitfulness, and of ever-renewed hope in the future even as it is being dipped into the salt water.

· Shankbone and egg—both recall the destruction of the Temple by symbolizing, respectively, the Paschal offering and the festival offering which were brought when the Temple was in existence. A shankbone is used, rather than any other part because it symbolizes that Israel's redemption was with "an outstretched arm." An egg is used because it is the traditional symbol of mourning.

ક⁀ The egg and shankbone should be prepared in advance, before evening. Neither are eaten on the night of the seder, but may be eaten the next day.

ક⁀ The reason why *three* matzot (three unleavened breads) are set on the seder table is that two whole loaves are required as on every Sabbath and festival upon which to make the blessing on bread. The third matzah is needed to break in half, one part being put aside as the *afikomen* with which to conclude the seder meal.

Once the need for three matzot was halakhically established, however, other symbolic meanings were read into it:

· Representing the forefathers Abraham, Isaac and Jacob.
· Representing the three remaining tribal units: Kohen, Levi, Israel.

ક⁀ The reason for the two "dippings" (the *karpas* in salt water, and the bitter herbs in *haroset*) that form part of the ritual procedure: It was a deliberate departure from customary eating habits so as to arouse the curiosity of the children and encourage them to ask why it was done. Their questioning would open the door to telling and impressing upon them the events of the exodus.

In ancient times, to "dip" once as a sort of appetizer before each meal was routine and customary, so the Sages instructed that it be done twice on this night so as to invite questioning by the children. One version in the Talmud of the Four Questions asks: "Why on all other nights do we dip once, and on this night of Passover, we dip twice?"

There was a deliberate attempt to involve the children in the seder ritual. The Four Questions (*Mah Nishtanah*) were devised especially for the children. The symbolism of Four Sons was used to convey moral instruction, and the childishly worded (but religiously and historically meaningful) songs, such as *Had Gadya* and *Ehad Mi Yodea*, were added. Such playful games as having a child "steal" or "find" the afikomen became customary.

ક⁀ It is also customary to set up a couch-like chair for the one who is leading the seder, in a way that allows him to recline. Reclining at a meal was an ancient practice and the mark of the free man, and thus became specifically associated with the ritual of the seder.

❧ Although it is not obligatory, it is customary in many homes for the one conducting the seder to wear a white robe (*kitel*) symbolizing ritual purity.

❧ The family should be ready to begin the seder immediately upon returning from the Passover evening services at the synagogue.

❧ Unlike on the Sabbath, when it is permissible and proper to recite Kiddush and eat even before nightfall (thus adding from the secular to the sacred), on Passover this may not be done. The mitzvah of eating matzah and drinking the wine (Kiddush counts as one of the four cups) must await nightfall. The Biblical precept states, "In the evening, shall you eat the matzot."

❧ The ritual may be clearly followed in any Haggadah. Various editions in different sizes, with various translations and typography, art, and design are available. Choose one that suits you best.

Briefly, this is the order that is followed:

· The cups of wine are first filled.

· *Kadesh*—The leader of the seder recites the Kiddush. Different customs prevail as to whether he and those about the table sit or stand during its recitation. Either way is correct. Everyone then answers "Amen" and all drink the first cup. (More than half of each cup should be drunk.)

· *Urhatz*—Water and a bowl are brought to the table, and the hands are ritually washed. No blessing is recited.

· *Karpas*—Each one takes a portion of the vegetable and dips it into salt water and recites the blessing:

בָּרוּךְ אַתָּה יְיָ אֱלֹהֵינוּ מֶלֶךְ הָעוֹלָם, בּוֹרֵא פְּרִי הָאֲדָמָה.

Baruch ata adonai elohainu melech ha-olam borai pri ha-adamah.

Blessed art Thou, Lord our God, King of the universe, who creates the fruit of the earth.

· *Yahatz*—The leader of the seder takes the middle matzah, breaks it in two, replaces one part from where it was taken and wraps the other part in a napkin, putting it away for the afikomen.

· The wine cups are then filled again.

· *Maggid*—The story of Passover is recounted. It begins with a statement on the meaning of the matzah followed by the Four Questions. Verses from the Torah, aggadic interpretations, scholars' experiences, and psalms in praise of God—all enrich this section. "It is praiseworthy," the Sages teach us, to elaborate on the events of the exodus, and in telling of the miracles that occurred to our forefathers. Participants in the seder may during this part of the service interrupt the reading of the actual text to offer whatever additional explanations, interpretations or insights they may have studied, heard, or read relevant to the Passover celebration.

· At the conclusion of this part of the service, the second cup of wine is drunk after reciting the blessing for wine.

· *Rahtzah*—The ritual washing of the hands with the blessing now takes place. (See pages 78–79 for detailed procedure.) This may either be done by having all the participants leave the table and go over to a washbasin, or by having water and a basin passed around the table, so that the washing takes place at the table itself. The blessing for washing is recited. After washing, one should not speak until after having eaten of the matzah.

· *Motzi-Matzah*—The two and a half matzot are now taken by the leader of the seder, lifted up, and the following two blessings are said:

בָּרוּךְ אַתָּה יְיָ אֱלֹהֵינוּ מֶלֶךְ הָעוֹלָם, הַמּוֹצִיא לֶחֶם מִן הָאָרֶץ.

Baruch ata adonai elohainu melech ha-olam hamotzi lehem min ha-aretz.

Blessed art Thou, Lord our God, who brings forth bread from the earth.

בָּרוּךְ אַתָּה יְיָ אֱלֹהֵינוּ מֶלֶךְ הָעוֹלָם, אֲשֶׁר קִדְּשָׁנוּ בְּמִצְוֹתָיו וְצִוָּנוּ עַל אֲכִילַת מַצָּה.

Baruch ata adonai elohainu melech ha-olam asher kidshanu b'mitzvotav v'tzivanu al akhilat matzah.

Blessed art Thou, Lord our God, King of the universe who has sanctified us with His commandments and commanded us regarding the eating of matzah.

Pieces of the unleavened bread (matzah) are broken off and distributed to all to be eaten.

· *Maror*—An olive-sized amount of bitter herbs is now taken, and dipped into some haroset, and eaten after the recitation of the following blessing:

בָּרוּךְ אַתָּה יְיָ אֱלֹהֵינוּ מֶלֶךְ הָעוֹלָם, אֲשֶׁר קִדְּשָׁנוּ בְּמִצְוֹתָיו וְצִוָּנוּ עַל אֲכִילַת מָרוֹר.

Baruch ata adonai elohainu melech ha-olam asher kidshanu b'mitzvotav v'tzivanu al akhilat maror.

Blessed art Thou, Lord our God, King of the universe who has sanctified us with His commandments and commanded us regarding the eating of bitter herbs.

· *Korekh*—A small sandwich of matzah with bitter herbs and haroset is made and eaten, as a reminder that during the existence of the Holy Temple in Jerusalem the great sage Hillel would eat bitter herbs *together with matzah* and not separately as it is written "With unleavened bread *and* bitter herbs shall they eat it" (Numbers 9:11), and ". . . unleavened bread *with* bitter herbs they shall eat it" (Exodus 12:18).

· *Shulhan Orekh*—The regular dinner meal is now served. (In many homes of East European origin, it is customary to begin the dinner meal with an entree consisting of hard-boiled eggs in salt water.)

· *Afikomen*—After dinner is completed, the afikomen (the half a matzah that was put away) is taken out and everyone is given a piece as the final "dessert" of the meal. This is because the afikomen is symbolic of the Paschal offering, which was the last thing to be eaten at the seder. (Should the afikomen be misplaced during the course of the evening and not be found, it is permissible to use any other matzah for this purpose.)

· *Barekh*—The wine cups are filled for the third time and the leader of the seder and all the participants proceed to recite or chant the grace after meals. The grace concludes with the blessing for and the drinking of the third cup of wine.

· The cups are now filled for the fourth time. The Cup of Elijah should also be filled to overflowing.

· *Hallel*—Psalms and a number of additional prayers with the theme of praise of God are now recited. This section of prayers concludes with the blessing for and the drinking of the fourth cup of wine.

· *Nirtzah*—Formally concluding the seder is a declaration containing the hope that the service was acceptable to the Lord.

A number of concluding songs have been incorporated into the finale of the seder. Their lively melodies and their childish poetic forms were specifically designed to motivate the children to stay awake to the very end. The content of these songs is far from childish, however, as it is based on the basic principles of Jewish faith (*Ehad Mi Yodea*—Who Knows One) and represents a bird's-eye review of the history of Israel among the nations (*Had Gadya*).

Next Year in Jerusalem Rebuilt—L'shanah haba-ah b'Yerushalayim habnuyah—is the final chant of the evening.

COUNTING THE OMER

From the day after the day of rest,* the day that you bring the sheaf (Omer) of wave offering, you shall keep count for seven full weeks; you shall count fifty days, until the day after the seventh week (Lev. 23:5–16); (then) there shall be a holy convocation to you;† you shall do no manner of servile work; it is a law for all time . . . throughout the generations.

(Lev. 23:21)

ప Beginning with the second night of Passover and every night thereafter, it is a religious duty to count the days for a period of seven full weeks (forty-nine days). The fiftieth day is the major festival of Shavuot (literally, weeks—so called on account of the seven-week period of counting that precedes it. The festival is sometimes referred to as Pentecost, which means fiftieth day).

ప The purpose of the counting appears to be to connect the festival of Pesach with the festival of Shavuot, to impress upon us that the release from physical bondage and the political freedom that is represented by Pesach does not constitute complete freedom unless it culminates in the spiritual restraints, disciplines and duties represented

---

* Referring to the first day of Passover.
† The festival of Shavuot.

by Shavuot, which celebrates the giving of the Ten Commandments, God's revelation to Israel, and Israel's acceptance of the Torah.

驿 Since the start of the counting coincides with the day on which a certain measurement (*omer*) of barley was cut down and brought to the Temple as an offering (on the second day of Passover), the entire period of the counting became known as the *Sefirat HaOmer*, The Counting of the Omer. It is briefly referred to as the period of Sefira (the Counting).

驿 The counting itself is performed simply. Each evening the following blessing is first recited:

בָּרוּךְ אַתָּה יְיָ אֱלֹהֵינוּ מֶלֶךְ הָעוֹלָם, אֲשֶׁר קִדְּשָׁנוּ בְּמִצְוֹתָיו וְצִוָּנוּ עַל סְפִירַת הָעֹמֶר.

Baruch ata adonai elohainu melech ha-olam asher kidshanu b'mitzvotav v'tzivanu al sefirat ha-omer.

Blessed art Thou, Lord our God, King of the universe who has sanctified us with His commandments, and commanded us regarding the counting of the Omer.

Then mention is made of the number of the day that it is, and the equivalent number of weeks and days that it represents. For example:

· Today is five days of the Omer.
· Today is fourteen days, which is two weeks of the Omer.
· Today is thirty days, which is four weeks and two days of the Omer, and so on.

驿 If one forgets to count at night one may count the next day, but without reciting the blessing. On the following nights, one may resume counting with the blessing.

驿 If, however, one has skipped an entire day or more in the counting, the counting may be resumed till the end of the required period, but without reciting the blessing. (If in the synagogue, such a person only answers "Amen" to the blessing recited by the reader.)

驿 If one has not yet formally counted the Omer and it is past sundown, one should not mention the number of the day that is about to be counted if asked, "What day of the Omer do we count tonight?" For by answering the question, one in effect declares his count, and can no longer recite the blessing (as all blessings are recited before performing the act) on that night. In response to all such inquiries, one should instead mention the number counted yesterday and thus answer the question indirectly.

ঙ In the synagogue on Friday evenings, the Omer is counted following the Kiddush; on Saturday evenings, the Omer is counted before the Havdalah. The reasoning behind the order of priorities is the eagerness to sanctify the Sabbath as early as possible and to postpone the departure of the Sabbath (symbolized by the Havdalah) as late as possible, even if it is only a matter of another few minutes.

ঙ It was during a thirty-three day period of the Sefira that many thousands of the disciples of Rabbi Akiva in the second century are said to have perished in a plague.

Since then, thirty-three days of the Sefira period are observed in partial mourning. Weddings are not conducted, haircuts are not taken, and dances and dinners with music are forbidden. These restrictions are waived on the special festive days of Lag b'Omer and Yom Yerushalayim. Except for weddings, the restrictions are also waived on Yom Atzmaut.

ঙ As there are differences of opinion among the Sages as to exactly which thirty-three days out of the total forty-nine-day period of Sefira are to be observed in partial mourning, different communities have developed varying practices in this regard. In each city, however, a single uniform practice ought to prevail based upon the judgment of the local religious leadership.

12

Shavuot

Shavuot commemorates the awesome event experienced by the children of Israel seven weeks after their exodus from Egypt when they camped at the foot of Mt. Sinai somewhere in the Sinai Peninsula. This event was the Revelation, when God's will was revealed to Israel. It marked the declaration of the Ten Commandments. Though these commandments do not constitute the entire Torah, which consists of 613 commandments (*taryag mitzvot*), they were its foundation. These Ten Commandments also became the moral bedrock for much of Western civilization.

While the exact *manner* of this communication between God and man is not known and was always subject to various opinions by the great thinkers and Sages of Israel, it was an event of awesome proportions and a *unique* spiritual experience that indelibly stamped the Israelites with their unique character, their faith, and their destiny.

In the prayer book, this festival is referred to as *zman matan Torateinu*, "the season of the giving of our Torah," for this is the dominant theme of the festival. The everlasting significance of this theme is emphasized by the answer to the question of why this festival is not called "the season of the receiving of our Torah" instead. The answer is that while the *giving* may have taken place at one time and the occasion can be commemorated, the *receiving* of the Torah by Jews must continue to take place every day and everywhere.

While the Jews who were present at Sinai affirmed their Covenant with God, declaring, "We will do and we will listen" (*naaseh v'nishma*), the Torah emphasizes that "Neither with you only [do I make this Covenant], but with him that standeth here with us, and *also with him that is not here with us this day*" (Deut. 29:13–14). The Talmud interprets the latter part of the verse as a clear reference also to *future generations of Jews*, and *to the future proselytes who would later accept the faith* (Shevuot 39a).

The festival of Shavuot emphasizes the spiritually significant lesson that the release from bondage and the winning of political freedom does not constitute complete freedom unless it culminates in the spiritual restraints, disciplines, and duties inherent in the Revelation to Israel and in Israel's acceptance of the Torah.

The name *Shavuot*, by which name the Torah refers to the festival, means simply "weeks" and is derived from the fact that it is observed after *seven full weeks of counting* from the second day of the Passover. The Talmud used the name *Atzeret* (which implies a concluding festival) by which to refer to it, an indication that the Sages regarded it as tied to and concluding the festival of Passover.

Its significance as an agricultural festival in the land of Israel is also reflected by two other names by which this festival is known: *Hag Hakatzir*, "the Festival of the Harvest," for it marks the harvesting of the wheat, the last grain harvest of the season, and *Yom HaBikkurim*, the "Day of the First Fruits," for it also marks the beginning of the fruit harvest and was the occasion for the bringing of the first ripe fruits to the Temple as an offering of thanksgiving.

THE CUSTOM OF EATING DAIRY FOOD ON SHAVUOT

Special foods or dishes characteristic of certain festivals are often a result of some religious symbolism. Thus it has become customary on Shavuot to eat at least one dairy meal during the holiday. Some see this as symbolizing "a land flowing with *milk* and honey." Others see it as emphasizing, on this festival which marks the giving of the Torah, the interdependence and unity of the Written and Oral Torah. For the very same verses that speak of bringing "the choicest first fruits of the land unto the house of the Lord your God" in celebration of

Shavuot also stress that "You must not boil a kid in its mother's milk" (Exodus 23:19, 34:26). On the basis of the latter part of these verses, the Oral Torah based its prohibition of eating meat and milk together. Hence, a separate dairy meal is deliberately eaten to emphasize the total unity of the verse and the authenticity of the Oral Torah.

CHAPTER

13

The Days of Awe

HOW THE YEARS ARE COUNTED

The point of reference for the counting of years differed in antiquity from people to people and from nation to nation, based as it was on some significant historical event. Usually the reign of a new king marked year One in the reign of so and so, and thus the count continued until a new king arose and the clock was turned back to the beginning. These years were used to date official documents and record historical events. The Bible offers many examples of such usage.

Early Christians also based the counting of their years on the reign of the one they regarded as their "spiritual king," considering the year of his birth to have been year One. The dominance of Christian civilization in world affairs has resulted in the Christian count's becoming the world's most widely used dating system. While Christians use the intrinsically religious postscript B.C. and A.D., Jewish texts generally substitute the notation B.C.E. and C.E., meaning *Before the Common Era* and *Common Era*.

The Jews for many centuries used as their point of reference in counting the years the exodus from Egypt, in addition to using the reign of the current ruler. Thus by the beginning of the Christian era the Jews were already into their fourteenth century of counting years. Had they continued on that basis, we would today be in the midst of our thirty-fourth century, or at approximately the year 3350.

However, after the destruction of the Jerusalem Temple in the seventieth year of the common era and the dispersion of the Jews, we find the use of the exodus as a point of reference for counting years being displaced by other focal points. The destruction of the Temple served as one such basis and dates based upon that event are found in documents well into the early medieval period. However, the system that gained the widest popularity among Jews and which is still in use today is one based not on an event or symbol whose significance is limited to our own faith or people, but on a theme of universal significance and applicability, namely the Creation of the world.

The number of years since Creation was arrived at by the Sages by going back over all the records then in existence, reviewing the Biblical record in terms of personal life spans, equating the years mentioned in early chapters of Genesis as equivalent to our own, and regarding the seven days of Creation as days like our own. That those seven "days" of Creation may in fact have been time periods of extremely long duration, that they correspond to "stages" rather than days similar to our own twenty-four-hour day,* does not detract from the spiritual or ethical significance of the Creation as the conceptual basis of the Jewish year. It is what the number 5733 stands for and what it implies—God's sovereignty over the universe—that is important, not the technical or scientific accuracy of the count, for no exact figure is possible.

WHY THE FIRST OF TISHRAI IS CELEBRATED AS THE NEW YEAR

The Torah refers to the month of Nisan (when Passover occurs) as the *first month* of the year in the Jewish calendar, and makes no reference to a day to be known as Rosh Hashana, the New Year. The first day of Tishrai (the seventh month, according to the Bible) is

---

* Even according to the Torah (Genesis), the sun by whose "rising and setting" we figure our days, was not created until the fourth day and yet reference is made to "day one" and "day two."

mentioned in the Torah as the holy day of the Day of Remembrance (*Yom Hazikaron*) and the Day of Sounding the Shofar (*Yom Teruah*).

Based on a tradition of hoary antiquity which assigned the event of Creation to the first of Tishrai, this holy day also became known as Rosh Hashana, the New Year, especially after Creation was made the point of reference for counting the years. It is the Mishna (Rosh Hashana 1:1) which first refers to Rosh Hashana, but to four different New Year days: (a) the first of Nisan, as the New Year day for Kings, according to which date Israel's kings calculated the years of their reign. (No matter when they assumed the throne, the first of Nisan was the cut-off point when the second year of the reign began.) This was also the New Year day for figuring the festivals, so that Passover counted as the year's first festival; (b) the first of Tishrai, as the New Year for Years, by which the years were counted, and from which day the Sabbatical and Jubilee years were calculated. This is the day we observe as Rosh Hashana; (c) the first of Elul as the New Year for the tithing of animals; and (d) the fifteenth of Shevat as the New Year for Trees.

Those of us who are used to working with fiscal years that differ from calendar years can understand the distinctions.

In the prayer book, the holy day that we call Rosh Hashana is still referred to by its Biblical names, although the tradition of this day's being the anniversary of the world's Creation and the concomitant idea of God's sovereignty over the universe are dominant themes of the prayers. Among the masses, however, the name *Rosh Hashana* (New Year) is the most popular and best known. The term *High Holydays* developed in English usage as a reference to Rosh Hashana and Yom Kippur. There is no equivalent Hebrew term. In Hebrew, these days have traditionally been called *Yamim Noraim* which means *Days of Awe.*

ROSH HASHANA

In the seventh month, on the first day of the month, you shall observe a day of rest, a memorial proclaimed with the blast of the horn, a holy convocation. You shall not do any servile work . . .

(Lev. 23:24-25)

&⤸ In the Torah and in the prayer book this sacred day is called the Day of Remembrance (*Yom Hazikaron*) and the Day of Sounding the Shofar (*Yom Teruah*). It marks the start of a ten-day period of spiritual self-examination and repentance which culminates with Yom Kippur, the Day of Atonement. Inasmuch as the years are reckoned from the first of Tishrai, however, this day became known throughout the Jewish world as Rosh Hashana, the New Year.

&⤸ Intensive prayer is the central mood of this day. Acknowledgment of God's sovereignty over the world and His rulership over mankind are the major themes of the prayers.

&⤸ The special Biblical precept that is most identified with Rosh Hashana is the blowing of the shofar. It is a religious duty on this day to listen to the shofar sounds.

The one who blows the shofar recites the blessing: "Blessed art Thou, Lord our God, King of the universe who has sanctified us with His commandments and commanded us to hear the sound of the shofar." The congregation responds with *Amen*. During the course of the Rosh Hashana service, a total of 100 notes are sounded.

Ancient tradition has handed down three distinct shofar-notes: a long drawn-out sound (*tekiah*), a broken, plaintive sound (*shevarim*), a series of sharp, staccato sounds (*teruah*).

&⤸ People confined to their homes who cannot be in the synagogue to listen to the shofar should try to obtain the services of someone who can stop by to blow the shofar for them.

&⤸ The sound of the shofar has been regarded from time immemorial as a call to penitence and as a reminder of the shofar sound at Sinai. According to Maimonides, the Scriptural precept to blow the shofar on this day has profound meaning. It tells us, he says:

Awake, ye sleepers from your sleep . . . and ponder over your deeds; remember your Creator and go back to Him in penitence. Be not of those who miss realities in their pursuit of shadows and waste their years in seeking after vain things which cannot profit or deliver. Look well to your souls and consider your acts; forsake each of you his wrong ways and improper thoughts and return to God so that He may have mercy upon you (Hil. Teshuvah 3:4).

&⤸ If Rosh Hashana falls out on the Sabbath, the shofar is not blown on that day.

245

&ampe; At the conclusion of the evening service, the proper greeting to extend to one another is:

To a male: *L'shana tovah tikatev v'taihatem.*
To a female: *L'shana tovah tikatevi v'taihatemi.*

May you be inscribed and sealed for a good year.

&ampe; A number of symbolic customs have evolved concerning the holy day's dinner meals. The most widespread is that of dipping a piece of hallah or a slice of apple into honey and saying before eating it:

יְהִי רָצוֹן שֶׁתְּחַדֵּשׁ עָלֵינוּ שָׁנָה טוֹבָה וּמְתוּקָה.

Yehi ratzon she-t'hadesh alenu shanah tovah um'tukah.

May it be the Lord's will to renew for us a year that will be good and sweet.

&ampe; The entire period from Rosh Hashana through Yom Kippur is known as the Ten Days of Repentance, or *aseret y'mai teshuvah.* It is marked by special penitential prayers that are recited each day in the synagogue.

The Sabbath which falls during this ten-day period is known as Shabbat Teshuvah, the Sabbath of Repentance, or as Shabbat Shuvah, the Sabbath of Return.* The latter word is taken from the opening of the chapter from the Prophets read on this Sabbath: *Shuvah Yisrael,* "Return O Israel unto the Lord, your God" (Hosea 14:2).

&ampe; The proper greeting to extend during the period following Rosh Hashana is *gmar hatimah tovah,* "May the final seal be for good." The greeting reflects the belief that Rosh Hashana and Yom Kippur are Days of Judgment (*Yom Hadin*) for all people.

YOM KIPPUR

The Lord spoke to Moses saying: ". . . the tenth day of this seventh month is the Day of Atonement: It shall be a holy convocation to you, and *you shall afflict your souls*; . . .

---

* Repentance (*Teshuvah*) and Return (*Shuvah*) are words that have a common root, and whose meaning in this instance is equivalent.

The Days of Awe

You shall do no work throughout that day; for it is a day
of atonement . . . For whoever does not afflict his soul
throughout this day, shall be cut off from his people. And
whoever does any work on that day, that person will I
cause to perish from among his people. Do no work whatever; it is a law for all time throughout the generations in
all your settlements. It shall be a Sabbath of complete rest
for you and *you shall afflict your souls*; on the *ninth day
of the month at evening, from evening until evening,* shall
you rest on your Sabbath."

(Lev. 23:26-32)

ࠇ The day before Yom Kippur is a day of preparation for the fast:

· Charity money should be set aside and brought to the synagogue prior to the evening services for distribution to various
religious and social welfare institutions.
· Since Yom Kippur does not atone for sins committed against
one's fellow man unless the grieved party has been pacified and
has agreed to forgive the wrongdoer, this day should be regarded
as a deadline date for reconciliation, for expressing regrets and
asking forgiveness. It matters not whether the wrong committed
was in material things or by verbal insult. God does not forgive
unless the grieved party has first forgiven.

Where attempts to pacify take place, the grieved party must
feel it incumbent upon himself to extend forgiveness with a full
heart. If he stubbornly persists in refusing to be pacified, he is
regarded as cruel, as himself behaving evilly and not as a worthy
son of the Israelite people.
· The meal in the late afternoon prior to the fast should be a
festive meal. One should not, however, overeat, or eat anything
that might cause thirst as it will make the fasting more difficult.
· Before leaving for the synagogue it is customary for the father
to bless his sons and daughters. (See page 76.)

ࠇ The Torah specifies that the fast is to begin on the *ninth* day,
so that the fasting on Yom Kippur actually begins *before sundown*
while it is still light. It does not conclude till the *evening* of the
next day. By "the evening" is not meant sundown, but rather nightfall when the stars appear, which is somewhat later. How much later
depends on the geographical latitude. (In northern parts of the
United States it generally occurs about forty minutes after sundown.)

১৯ The Biblical commandment to "afflict your souls" is observed by a complete and total fast, by abstaining from all *eating* and *drinking* for the entire period (approximately twenty-five hours).

১৯ With regard to work, the Day of Atonement follows the same rules as the weekly Sabbath, with similar exceptions where life is endangered. Whatever is forbidden on the Sabbath is forbidden on Yom Kippur.

১৯ It is forbidden to fast on a Sabbath day because it would detract from the delight which the day should provide, and all other fasts which coincide with the Sabbath are either postponed to Sunday or moved back to Thursday. But if Yom Kippur falls on a Sabbath day, it is still required to fast and "afflict the soul." Some offer the explanation that fasting *for the purpose of atonement* does not clash with the Sabbath requirement of *oneg* or delight. Others simply regard the Yom Kippur requirement as taking precedence and base their view on the fact that Yom Kippur is called *Shabbat Shabbaton*, implying a Sabbath of Sabbaths.

১৯ The Oral Torah teaches us that in addition to prohibiting eating and drinking, "to afflict your souls" also involves, though with less severe sanctions, prohibitions against washing and bathing, anointing one's body, wearing of shoes (applies only to shoes made of leather), and sexual relations.

১৯ The washing that is forbidden is that which is done for pleasure, or to help one feel more comfortable and pleasant (*shel ta'anug*). But that which is done to wash away dirt, or upon rising in the morning, or after taking care of one's needs is permitted (*k'darko tamid*).

১৯ A person who is ill or whose feet pain him is permitted to wear shoes normally.

১৯ Children under the age of nine should not be permitted to fast at all, as it may be injurious to their health. From the age of nine, they should be gradually trained to fast for longer and longer periods. Girls from the age of twelve and boys from thirteen years must fast as any adult.

১৯ The Yom Kippur fast may be broken only for reasons of critical illness. The sick person's expressed wish or the opinion of physicians may be the determining factor in granting the dispensation. A rabbi's decision in any such case should be sought.

&ᴠ A woman in childbirth (from the moment she begins to feel birthpains) and for the first three days following birth is not permitted to fast at all, even if she insists upon it. From the third through the seventh day she may fast if she wants to, but is permitted to break the fast if she feels the need.

&ᴠ The service which introduces Yom Kippur is called *Kol Nidre* (All Vows) from the name of the historically meaningful and moving prayer that is then recited. The concluding service of Yom Kippur on the next day is called *Neilah* which means "the Closing" (of the Gates). Except for the time when one goes home to sleep or rest, the entire period is spent in prayer.

&ᴠ The wearing of white on Yom Kippur—white clothes, white robe (*kitel*), white skullcap—is a time-honored custom intended to recall the white robes (*takhrikhim*) in which the dead are buried, and thus to mellow the heart of the worshipper. White also represents purity and symbolizes the Prophetic promise: "Though your sins be as scarlet, they shall be as *white* as snow" (Isaiah 1:18).

&ᴠ The conclusion of Yom Kippur is marked by a single long blast of the shofar. It is symbolic of "when the ram's horn sounded long . . ." which marked the conclusion of the Revelation at Sinai (Exodus 19:13). It also commemorates the blowing of the shofar on Yom Kippur in ancient times to signify the start of the Jubilee Year.

&ᴠ Following Yom Kippur, one should begin to prepare for the festival of Succot, four days later, by building a succah and acquiring a lulav and etrog.

CHAPTER

14

Succot

Succot means "tabernacles," "booths," or "temporary huts," and refers to the temporary dwelling places used by the children of Israel in the desert during the forty-year period of their wandering following the exodus from Egypt. "For in booths did I make the children of Israel dwell when I brought them out of the land of Egypt" (Lev. 23:42). The festival commemorates that period of Israel's history.

Its significance, however, is not exhausted by or limited to the historical commemoration. For the underlying spiritual motif of remembering (and reenacting) the dwelling in the "temporary huts" emphasizes the notion of trust in God's Divine protection, or *bitahon*. With the desert experiences (the manna, the water, etc.) highlighting the motif, this festival emphasizes the faith that somehow God provides for man's needs, and that man in turn must be grateful. It is symbolized by the *succah*, the hut with its exposed and insecure roof into which the Jew is bidden to move for the week.

This spiritual motif was given additional emphasis by the Torah in that the date of its observance (which could have been any time during the year, as it was not tied to a specific historical event) was fixed to coincide with the final harvest of the year "after the ingathering from your threshing floor and your wine press" (Deut. 16:13), when the spirit of thankfulness and gratefulness to the Lord for providing for people's needs is more naturally forthcoming.

Reflecting its agricultural significance, the Torah also calls the festival *Hag Ha-Asif*, "the Festival of the Ingathering" (Exodus 23:16; 34:22) observed "at the end of the year when you gather in the results of your work from the field." In the prayer book, the festival is also referred to as "the season of our rejoicing," *zman simhatainu*, based on the thrice-repeated Biblical injunction in connection with this festival: "and you shall rejoice in your festival" (*v'samahta b'hagekha*).

Gay religious celebrations, highlighted by much singing and dancing, are particularly associated with this holiday.

DWELLING IN THE SUCCAH

The Lord spoke to Moses, saying: "Say to the children of Israel: On the fifteenth day of this seventh month there shall be the Feast of Tabernacles (*Hag HaSuccot*) to the Lord for seven days. The first day shall be a holy convocation; you shall not do any servile work . . . on the eighth day shall you observe a holy convocation . . . it is a day of assembly (*atzeret*); you shall not do any servile work.

(Lev. 23:33-36)

. . . the first day shall be a day of rest (*shabbaton*) and the eighth day shall be a day of rest (*shabbaton*). On the first day, you shall take for yourselves the fruit of the *hadar* tree (citron), the branches of *tmarim* (palm trees); and boughs of *avot* trees (thick leaved trees; myrtle), and the *arvei-nahal* (willows of the brook), and *you shall rejoice* before your Lord your God seven days.

And you shall observe it as a festival of the Lord for seven days in the year; an eternal law throughout the generations. . . .

You shall dwell in succot seven days . . . that your generations may know that I made the children of Israel to dwell in succot when I brought them out of the land of Egypt. . . ."

(Lev. 23:39-42)

৪৯ The unique feature of the festival of Succot is the observance of the precept to dwell in the succah. The succah must be a temporary

251

hut (see pages 253–254 for laws governing its construction) in which one lives as much as possible during the week in lieu of one's permanent home. In colder climates, at least all of one's meals are taken in the succah.

  The blessing one recites whenever fulfilling this precept is:

בָּרוּךְ אַתָּה יְיָ אֱלֹהֵינוּ מֶלֶךְ הָעוֹלָם, אֲשֶׁר קִדְּשָׁנוּ בְּמִצְוֹתָיו
וְצִוָּנוּ לֵשֵׁב בַּסֻּכָּה.

Baruch ata adonai elohainu melech ha-olam asher kidshanu b'mitzvotav v'tzivanu lay-shev ba-succah.

Blessed art Thou, Lord our God, King of the universe who has sanctified us with His commandments and commanded us to dwell in the succah.

This blessing is said immediately following the blessing over the bread whenever one sits down to eat a meal in the succah. Where this is said as part of the Kiddush on the festival days, it need not be repeated again following the blessing over the bread.

  If one forgets to recite the above mentioned benediction at the proper time, one may recite it anytime during the meal, as long as he is not about to leave the succah.

  One is not required to eat in a succah that which might be classified as refreshments or a light snack (*akhilat ara-ey*) and not as a regular meal (*akhilat keva*). Eating bread always classifies a meal as regular.

  In case of rain or extreme cold, one is excused from the succah. One is also excused from sitting in the succah if he is ill, or if he is concerned and anxious (*mitztaer*) about getting chilled, or is otherwise grieved by uncomfortable weather or other conditions. The latter leniency does not apply the first night of Succot or the first two nights in the Diaspora when the obligation of eating in the succah takes precedence.

  A traveler on the road is excused from eating in the succah if there is none available.

  Women are excused from the obligation of eating in the succah. Although not required to observe it, they may recite the appropriate benediction if and when they do.

CONSTRUCTION OF THE SUCCAH

∾ A succah must have at least three walls. The fourth side may be left open.

∾ The walls of the succah may be of any material (metal, wood, canvas, brick, stone). They should be firmly fixed so as not to be easily blown down or flap in the wind.

∾ A succah constructed adjacent to a permanent house may count one or more walls of the house as its own walls.

∾ A succah may be small, suitable for only one person to sit in, or it may be large enough to accommodate hundreds of people.

∾ The "temporary" quality of a succah is in the roof or the ceiling. That which may be used to construct the ceiling of the succah is called *sekhakh*. Anything which *grows from the ground* and has been *cut off* from the ground qualifies, as long as it is not subject to ritual impurity, which excludes fruits. Otherwise, branches cut from trees or bushes, cornstalks, two-by-fours, bamboo reeds, and sticks all qualify as kosher sekhakh. When put on the succah, these must be loose and not tied in bundles.

∾ Poles, sticks, branches, etc. not only qualify as sekhakh but may also serve as appropriate supports on which to place smaller, more decorative types of sekhakh such as tree branches or boughs of evergreen leaves.

∾ Sufficient sekhakh must be put on the roof so that more shade than sunlight is provided.

Some air space in the sekhakh is desirable so that the stars may be visible through it on a clear night, although the succah is kosher and not disqualified if the sekhakh is too thick for that. One should, however, be careful that no opening between the sekhakh provides an empty space wider than ten inches (three *tefahim*).

On the other hand, the sekhakh must not be so thick that in case of rain it serves as a protective covering and prevents the rain from dripping in. This would disqualify the succah.

∾ The sekhakh must always be put on after the walls are completed and never before, so that the succah is completed with the putting on of the sekhakh.

&~ A succah built under a tree or under some permanent roof such as a porch is invalid and disqualified.

&~ A permanent overhang that extends over a succah for more than seventy-two inches or six feet also disqualifies the entire succah. However, the entire succah is not disqualified if the overhang is less than seventy-two inches or six feet (*arba amot*). Even so, the area under the overhang itself is not considered part of the succah and one should not sit there.

&~ It is proper and even praiseworthy to decorate a succah to make it inviting and cheerful, pretty and pleasant. It is customary to hang different fruits from the sekhakh, to hang pictures and decorations on the walls, to put up decorative tapestries.

&~ The involvement of the whole family in the building and decorating of the succah can make it one of the more exciting and eagerly-awaited occasions of the year.

THE FOUR SPECIES

&~ Another distinctive observance related to Succot is the precept to take the four species—a citron (*etrog*), a palm branch (*lulav*), a myrtle branch (*hadas*), and a willow branch (*arava*)—and with them to rejoice before the Lord.

&~ Whereas the lulav, the hadas and the arava are bound together as a unit, the etrog is separate. Each man should acquire a set of the *four species* for himself, in fulfillment of the Biblical precept.

&~ The lulav (to which are bound also the myrtle and the willow twigs) is held in the right hand and the etrog is held in the left, with the stem (where it had been cut off from the tree) on top. Holding the two together, the following blessing is said on every day of Succot:

בָּרוּךְ אַתָּה יְיָ אֱלֹהֵינוּ מֶלֶךְ הָעוֹלָם, אֲשֶׁר קִדְּשָׁנוּ בְּמִצְוֹתָיו וְצִוָּנוּ עַל נְטִילַת לוּלָב.

Baruch ata adonai elohainu melech ha-olam asher kidshanu b'mitzvotav v'tzivanu al netilat lulav.

254

Blessed art Thou, Lord our God, King of the universe who has sanctified us with His commandments and commanded us concerning the taking of the lulav.

(Since the lulav is the largest of the four species, the entire unit is called by its name).

On the first day of Succot, the benediction of *sheheheyanu* is added (see page 169).

* Upon completing the benediction, the etrog is turned over so that the stem is below and the *pitom* on top. Holding the etrog next to the lulav, the lulav is then waved in all four directions—east, south, west, north,—upwards and then downwards.

(Many symbolic interpretations have been assigned to the four species and to the significance of their being waved in all directions. The simplest is that "in rejoicing before the Lord" with the four species, they are waved in all directions to indicate the presence of God everywhere.)

* The lulav and etrog are also held during the recitation of the *Hallel*, the psalms in praise of God, said every day of the festival during the morning service and waved in the same fashion at several points during that prayer at the verses: "Give thanks unto the Lord, for He is good, for His kindness endures forever," and "We beseech Thee, O Lord, save us!"

* During that special portion of the festival service known as *Hoshanot*, everyone in the synagogue with a lulav and etrog joins in a procession around the bimah. Every day of Succot there is one such procession, while on the seventh day of Succot (also known as Hoshana Rabbah), there are seven such processions. These processions around the bimah commemorate similar processions around the altar of the ancient Temple in Jerusalem during the festival of Succot.

* The lulav and etrog are not taken and blessed on that day of Succot which falls out on the Sabbath, be it the first day or any of the other days.

SHMINI ATZERET AND SIMHAT TORAH

... On the eighth day you shall observe a holy convocation
... it is a day of solemn assembly; you shall not do any
servile work. . . .

(Lev. 23:36)

৪৯ The concluding eighth day (in the Diaspora, it is the eighth and ninth days) of the Succot festival is not technically called Succot, but rather *Shmini Atzeret* (the Eighth Day of Solemn Assembly). It is independent of Succot.

Although its purpose is to conclude the festival of Succot, and it *is* commonly regarded as simply the final day(s) of the Succot festival, Shmini Atzeret reflects none of the special observances related to Succot. The Sages described the reason for the eighth day in terms of the following parable, which is based on the other meaning of the term *atzeret*. (Note: while *atzeret* is translated as *assembly*, it also has the meaning of *holding back*, of *stopping and waiting*.)

God is like a king who invites all his children to a feast to last for just so many days; when the time comes for them to depart, he says to them: "My children, I have a request to make of you. Stay yet another day; your departure is difficult for me."

Like Succot, Shmini Atzeret is also referred to in the prayer book as *zman simhatainu*, the "season of our rejoicing."

৪৯ The Kiddush, the grace after meals, and those portions of the services that refer to the holiday by name no longer refer to Succot, but to Shmini Atzeret or Hag haAtzeret.

৪৯ On Shmini Atzeret, one takes leave of the succah and returns to his permanent dwelling, there to complete the festive week. The four species are not used on Shmini Atzeret.

৪৯ Since it is on Shmini Atzeret that the annual cycle of the weekly Torah reading is completed, it has also become known as *Simhat Torah*, Rejoicing of the Torah. (In the Diaspora only the second day of Shmini Atzeret is so called since the Torah completion ceremonies and festivities are reserved for that day.)

256

&⤳ Simhat Torah is probably the most joyously celebrated festival day of the year. It is marked by seven processions around the synagogue with all the scrolls of the Torah. As many worshippers as possible are given an opportunity to carry a Torah scroll.

&⤳ It is customary for the children to be provided with special flags or banners, sometimes with miniature scrolls, and for them to join in the processions. During the processions, spirited singing of religious and liturgical songs as well as spirited group dancing with the Torah scrolls is customary. The kind of decorum that is associated with solemn services is completely waived in the face of the celebration.

&⤳ To see a Simhat Torah celebration in Jerusalem is to witness the heights to which religious ecstasy can rise.

CHAPTER

15

The Post-Biblical Holidays and Fast Days

THESE days are not sanctified with a Sabbath-like atmosphere. However, various religious observances have been instituted to reflect their special historical significance. The most important of these post-Biblical occasions are Hanukah, Purim and Tisha b'Av.

HANUKAH

Hanukah is observed for eight days, beginning with the twenty-fifth day of Kislev. It commemorates the historic victory of the Maccabeans following a three-year long uprising against the ruling Assyrian-Greek regime and their Jewish Hellenist supporters who conspired to impose restrictions against Jewish religious practices and values. The struggle culminated with the recapture of the Temple of Jerusalem in 165 B.C.E. and the restoration of its traditional Jewish service. The victory also restored Jewish political sovereignty over the land. Hanukah means *dedication* and refers to the rededication of the Temple to the service of God after it had been defiled with pagan images and practices.

The Post-Biblical Holidays and Fast Days

ह It is permissible to perform regular work on Hanukah.

ह The major religious observance consists of lighting the lights of a Hanukah menorah each night of the holiday.

ह The Hanukah menorah is an eight-branched candelabrum, with an additional place for the "service" light. It is designed either for candles or oil wicks. The lights are lighted with the "service" candle or light (called the *shamash* candle). The "service candle" is then placed in its designated spot on the menorah.

ह The Hanukah lights are lighted as soon after nightfall as possible.

ह While one is holding a lighted "service candle," but before lighting the menorah, the following two blessings are recited:

בָּרוּךְ אַתָּה יְיָ אֱלֹהֵינוּ מֶלֶךְ הָעוֹלָם, אֲשֶׁר קִדְּשָׁנוּ בְּמִצְוֹתָיו וְצִוָּנוּ לְהַדְלִיק נֵר שֶׁל חֲנֻכָּה.

Baruch ata adonai elohainu melech ha-olam asher kidshanu b'mitzvotav v'tzivanu l'hadlik ner shel Hanukah.

Blessed art Thou, Lord our God, King of the universe who has sanctified us with His commandments and commanded us to kindle the Hanukah light.

בָּרוּךְ אַתָּה יְיָ אֱלֹהֵינוּ מֶלֶךְ הָעוֹלָם, שֶׁעָשָׂה נִסִּים לַאֲבוֹתֵינוּ בַּיָּמִים הָהֵם בַּזְּמַן הַזֶּה.

Baruch ata adonai elohainu melech ha-olam she-asah nisim la-avotainu ba-yamim ha-hem bazman hazeh.

Blessed art Thou, Lord our God, King of the universe who has performed miracles for our forefathers in those days, at this time.

On the first night only, a third benediction is added, that of *sheheheyanu* (see page 169).

ह On the first night, only one light is lighted. Facing the menorah, it is the one on the far right. On the second night, two lights are lighted, and so on through the eighth night, when the entire menorah is lighted.

Although the additional lights each night are added toward the left, *the lighting itself takes place from left to right.*

ટ્ After lighting the menorah, additional prayers and songs found in the prayer book brighten the festive spirit of the occasion if chanted or sung by the entire household.

ટ્ The light of the Hanukah menorah may not be used for any utilitarian purpose—to read by, to light a room, to light a cigarette, etc. It is for this reason that the "service" or "shamash" candle is placed near the others, so that if it becomes necessary to use the flame, this candle will be available.

ટ્ The lighted menorah should preferably be placed near a window so that it may be seen from without, thus publicly testifying to the miracle of Hanukah.

ટ્ It is praiseworthy if every member of the household has a separate menorah enabling each one to light the Hanukah candles. However, this is not required as long as each household has one menorah and one lights for all.

ટ્ A woman may light the menorah on behalf of all the members of her household.

ટ્ On Friday evening during the week of Hanukah, the menorah is lighted before the Sabbath candles even though it is not yet nightfall. On Saturday night, the menorah is lighted at home after the recitation of Havdalah.

ટ્ It is now a custom to present the children with Hanukah coins (*gelt*) or other appropriate gifts on Hanukah.

ટ્ The *Hallel*, the special prayers of praise, and passages of gratitude to God for the victories and the miracles are added to the prayer services and to the recitation of grace after meals throughout the week of Hanukah.

PURIM

Purim is a one-day celebration observed on the fourteenth day of Adar (one month before Passover). It commemorates the saving of the Jewish communities living under Persian rule from Haman's evil designs to exterminate them. Although there is some uncertainty about the date, the events described in the book of Esther, took place about 450 B.C.E. The name *Purim* derives from the word *pur* which means a lottery, the method used by Haman to select the date on which he intended to release his hordes for a general massacre of the Jews.

The designs of Haman have had their unfortunate parallel in the evil designs of many other rulers throughout the centuries in whose lands Jews lived. The precarious nature of Jewish survival in countless countries of the Diaspora where the fate of the Jew was often subject to the whim and caprice of the local ruler is epitomized by the story of Purim. The sudden turn of events in the story of Purim which turned the tables on the oppressor and enabled the Jewish community to defend itself against assault has provided a spark of hope and encouragement to oppressed and victimized Jewish communities throughout the centuries.

ะ๛ The most prominent ritual feature in the observance of the holiday is to attend the synagogue on Purim eve to listen to the reading of the Scroll of Esther, more popularly called the *Megillah*. The Megillah is also read at the shachrit service the following morning—Purim day.

ะ๛ Both men and women are required to listen to the reading of the Megillah. Children should also be trained to attend the synagogue to fulfill this duty, although very small children who are likely to disturb the congregation should not be brought to the synagogue.*

ะ๛ The religious observances related to Purim are based on the following quotation from the book of Esther:

> And Mordechai wrote these things and sent letters to all
> the Jews . . . to enjoin them that they should keep the four-

---

* The tendency to bring very small children to the Purim Megillah reading who are otherwise never taken to the synagogue is misguided. If the customary "noisemaking upon hearing the name of Haman" is experienced by the child after having been at many regular worship services where the child has been trained to have reverence and respect for the synagogue and to behave quietly and with decorum, it marks a pleasant distinction. But when a child is only brought to the synagogue on Purim (and perhaps on Simhat Torah) the experience can only give him a distorted impression of a synagogue as being more of a circus or "fun place" than a "holy place" for worship.

teenth day of the month of Adar . . . that they should make
them days of feasting and gladness, and of sending portions
one to another, and gifts to the poor. And the Jews took
upon themselves to do . . . and upon their descendants,
and upon all such as joined themselves unto them . . .
that they would keep these two* days according to the writing thereof and according to the appointed time, every
year.

(Esther 9:20-23, 27)

ఏ A second requirement of Purim observance is to "eat, drink
and be merry." A festive family dinner† should be held on Purim
day. This is called a *seudah,* and is in fulfillment of the directive in
the book of Esther that these be days of feasting (*y'mai mishteh*).

ఏ A third and fourth observance are the requirements that:

· Each person "send portions" to a friend. The "portions"
referred to consist of gifts of food or drink. The minimum should
be two items of baked *or* cooked food *or* fruit *or* candy *or* drink.
Although the minimum obligation is fulfilled by sending such
a gift to only one person, it is customary to "send out portions"
to several friends. This "sending out of portions" is called in
Hebrew *shalach manos* or *mishloach manot.* It is customary
for the children to serve as the messengers in delivering the
portions.

· Each person give gifts (charity) to at least *two* poor people or
worthy needy causes. Even a poor person who is himself a recipient of charity must give to others. If one is in a place where
there are no poor people or is otherwise unable to distribute it
that day, the money should be set aside for later distribution.

ఏ Since Talmudic times, Purim has been the day when the usual
restraints against excessive drinking of intoxicating beverages were
relaxed. "A person is required to drink on Purim until he does not
know the difference between 'cursed be Haman' and 'blessed be

---

* Because the capital city of Shushan celebrated on the fifteenth, cities like Shushan
which have been walled since "the days of Joshua" were to observe Purim a day later,
on the fifteenth of Adar. That day is now called Shushan Purim. In Jerusalem, Purim
is observed on the fifteenth of the month instead of the fourteenth.

† In the grace after meals and in the regular prayer service, the special prayer, *Al
Hanisim,* expressing gratefulness and thankfulness to God for the miracles that occurred
are included.

Mordechai' " (Megillah 75), said the Sages. Nevertheless, if a person knows that if he drinks more than usual he may unwittingly disregard or violate some religious precepts or that it will vulgarize his behavior, it is better that he should not permit himself to become intoxicated, even on Purim.

৯৯ Although there is no prohibition of work on Purim as there is on the Sabbath or on the major festival days, it is nonetheless proper to abstain from one's regular job on Purim day and celebrate the holiday in the appropriate manner.

৯৯ The custom has spread in many Jewish communities to hold parades, carnival-type celebrations, and parties on Purim. The wearing of costumes and similar merrymaking, especially by the children, is a particularly popular form of Purim festivity.

TISHA B'AV

The saddest and most tragic day in the year is the Fast of the Ninth of Av (Tisha b'Av). It is a day of fasting and mourning which commemorates the destruction of the First Temple in Jerusalem in 586 B.C.E. and by historical coincidence also the destruction of the Second Temple in 70 C.E. (The first Temple was ransacked and burned to the ground by the Babylonians, the second by the Romans.) The destruction of the Temple, the religious center of the people, was not only a religious disaster but also marked the end of the First and Second Jewish Commonwealths, respectively, and the exile of most of the Jewish people from their land.

In subsequent centuries, Tisha b'Av became identified with still other tragic events in the life of the Jewish people. It was on Tisha b'Av, 1492, that the decree ordering the expulsion of all Jews from Spain was issued, the only alternative being either death or conversion to Christianity.

Though the Jewish State was reestablished in 1948, and Jerusalem was reunited in 1967 under Jewish sovereignty for the first time since 70 C.E., the significance of Tisha b'Av has nevertheless been reaffirmed by contemporary thinkers and scholars.

In the first place, the Temple itself—the destruction of which is the basic reason for the mourning of Tisha b'Av—is still not restored. The Temple Mount in fact was appropriated by Islamic leaders, who in the year 691 C.E. built on Judaism's holiest site a major Islamic shrine. This only highlights the Temple's loss to the faith of Israel.

Secondly, there is no more appropriate occasion in the year to remember, mourn and grieve over all those occasions in Israel's history which were steeped in sorrow and suffering, in death and torture, in cruelty and oppression, all of which reached their climax in the European holocaust (1940–1945) when over a third of all the Jewish people, more than six million men, women, and children, were systematically and barbarically put to death after the most unbelievable suffering.

ᢒᴗ Tisha b'Av is a day of total fasting. As on Yom Kippur, eating or drinking anything from before sundown on the eighth of Av till nightfall on the following day is forbidden.

ᢒᴗ The mourning practices in force on Tisha b'Av are the following:

· Not wearing regular leather shoes. (There are no prohibitions against footwear made from rubber, cloth, or non-leather materials.)
· Abstaining from washing or bathing. (This applies only to washing for personal comfort or pleasure. It does not apply to washing to wash off dirt, or to washing upon arising, or after taking care of one's needs.)
· Abstaining from shaving (and women from their cosmetics.)
· Abstaining from sexual relations.
· Abstaining from studying Torah, for such study gladdens the heart, as it is written: "The precepts of the Lord are right, rejoicing the heart" (Psalms 19:9). It is, however, permissible to read or study such books as Lamentations, Job, selections of Jeremiah, and parts of the Talmud that deal with the destruction of the Temple or with the laws of mourning.
· Abstaining from doing any work (in the usual sense of the word, not in the Sabbath definition of work), at least all evening and until noon of the fast day. After noon on Tisha b'Av, it is permissible to engage in all work, if necessary, although the fasting and mourning may make it difficult to do so.
· Wherever possible, at least until noon, it is customary to sit only on lower stools after the fashion of those who sit in mourning during the week of shiva.

ટ્ર A lenient attitude is adopted toward sick persons, even those who are not dangerously or critically ill. Such persons are permitted to fast for only part of the day and are not required to complete the entire fast.

ટ્ર In the synagogue following the evening services, the *Book of Lamentations* (*Megillat Aichah*), is read in the mournful chant traditionally associated with it. In the evening as well as in the morning, dirge or *kinot* prayers are recited following the services with the worshippers sitting on the ground or low stools. A person who prays by himself, without a minyan, should also read the Book of Lamentations and recite the kinot.

ટ્ર To emphasize the mournful character of the day, it is customary to remove the *parokhet*, the curtain from the Holy Ark, and the decorative cover from the Reader's Table, providing a stark appearance. (In some communities, the Ark is draped in black.) It is customary in some communities to extinguish most of the lights, reciting the kinot by the dim light of candles held by the worshippers.

ટ્ર Because a tallit and tefillin are called religious adornments, symbols of beauty, neither is worn at the morning services of Tisha b'Av. They are instead put on for the afternoon minha service.

ટ્ર Although the fast of Tisha b'Av ends at nightfall, one should not eat meat or drink wine or celebrate in any way until noon of the next day. This is done because according to historical tradition, the Temple burned all through the night and most of the day of the tenth of Av. Because of this, weddings on the night immediately following Tisha b'Av are still forbidden.

ટ્ર Tisha b'Av marks the culmination of a period of three weeks that is observed in semi-mourning, beginning with the minor Fast of the Seventeenth of Tammuz (three weeks earlier), which marks the first breach in the walls of Jerusalem made by the attacking Babylonian forces.

During this three week period, weddings are not permitted; or are any other celebrations and festive gatherings, particularly if accompanied by music. It is customary not to cut one's hair during this period.

ટ્ર The semi-mourning becomes somewhat more intensified on the first of Av, during the period referred to as the Nine Days. A widespread custom is to abstain from meat and wine during this period, except for the Sabbath day and except for a religious feast (seudat mitzvah). It is also the practice not to purchase or put on new clothing during this time, until after Tisha b'Av.

OTHER SPECIAL DAYS

Tu b'Shevat

ह⋟ *Hamisha Asar* or *Tu b'Shevat*, the fifteenth of Shevat, is mentioned in the Mishna as the New Year for Trees. The year is reckoned from this date in matters relating to tithing of the fruit of the tree and to such other laws. The only custom associated with this day is that of making a point of eating of a fruit that is prevalent in Israel. The fruit of the carob tree (*bokser*, or St. John's Bread) is an unusual fruit that is often eaten on Tu b'Shevat.

ह⋟ In Israel, it is customary for the school children to go out on field trips on Tu b'Shevat and take part in planting young saplings.

Lag b'Omer

Lag b'Omer, the thirty-third day of the Counting of the Omer corresponding to the eighteenth of Iyar, marks the culmination of a plague that was killing the disciples of Rabbi Akiva, and which made the Omer period a time of semi-mourning. This day is therefore observed as a semi-holiday, when weddings are permitted. Other forms of semi-mourning practiced during this period are suspended. Because of its identification with Rabbi Akiva and his disciples, the day has become known as the Scholars Festival. There are no special ritual observances connected with it.

Yom Atzmaut

Yom Atzmaut, the Day of Independence on the fifth of Iyar, marks the reestablishment of the State of Israel in 1948. Other than communal celebrations, this day is marked in the synagogue by the recitation of special prayers of praise to God. The full religious meaning of this day and the religious forms of its observance are still in the process of being evolved.

Yom Yerushalayim

The twenty-eighth day of Iyar commemorates the reunification of Jerusalem and the return of the ancient parts of the city with its Western Wall and the Temple Mount to Jewish sovereignty for the first time since 70 C.E. These events, reflecting unexpected miraculous elements, are felt to be of great religious significance. The nature of its religious observance is yet to evolve.

Minor Fast Days

The minor Public Fast Days are observed only from dawn to nightfall.

They are:

* The Tenth of Tevet, which marks the beginning of the Babylonian siege of Jerusalem.
* The Fast of Esther, observed the day before Purim on the thirteenth of Adar, in commemoration of the days of fasting and prayer requested by Esther.
* The Seventeenth of Tammuz, which marks the first breach in the walls of Jerusalem during the Babylonian siege.
* The Fast of Gedaliah, observed on the third of Tishrai, the day following Rosh Hashana. It commemorates the assassination of Gedaliah, who was appointed Governor of the Jews by Nebuchadnezzar. This marked the final blow in the destruction of the First Commonwealth.

Halakha is lenient for those who find fasting particularly difficult on these days.

Part Four

THE SPECIAL OCCASIONS OF LIFE

I N the life of every individual and of every family, there are special occasions that call for celebration as well as occasions that call forth grief and mourning. Every people from time immemorial and every religious faith has seen fit to mark these occasions by special ceremonies and special observances.

Judaism too has developed rites and ceremonies, rules and procedures for these occasions of life. While there are relatively few Torah laws that bear directly on these occasions, the guidelines set down by the rabbis for their observances are derived from the whole framework of spiritual values inherent in the Jewish faith. The examples shown by the Patriarchs, the attitudes derived from numerous Biblical passages, including the Prophets and the Writings, and the influence of Jewish mystical sources have all contributed to the halakhik framework that is applied to and that governs birth, puberty, marriage, and death. These are also replete with customs that have developed and emerged among Jews during the centuries. It is precisely these areas which have been most susceptible to environmental influences and where local custom has often prevailed. As long as these local customs do not violate basic Jewish values or contradict Jewish laws they add to the variety and color of local Jewish life.

This section dealing with these occasions has been deliberately kept to a minimum in this volume because we sought to limit ourselves to those rules that are halakhikally binding upon all Jews, omitting the customs that may differ from community to community and from country to country.

A Jew whose identification with Judaism is only in his adherence to these rites has assured himself only of Jewish legal status. While this too is most important, neither the nobility of Jewish belief nor the entire Jewish way of life is thereby reflected. Indeed, for one to whom the Jewish rites of passage constitute the sum total of his religious identification, the "Jewish religion" is spiritually non-existent.

CHAPTER

16

Birth

T HOSE who bring a child into the world must recognize the basic obligation they have toward providing for the infant the loving care it craves and physical attention it needs. And they must recognize the obligation they have for providing the moral guidance the child should have. There is no more important role in life than raising a child to responsible adulthood.

At birth, man is pure, free of all sin. The daily morning prayer taken from the Talmud (Berakhot 60b) says it succinctly: "O my God, the soul which you gave me is pure, you created it, you fashioned it, you breathed it into me." "Blessed shall you be in your coming in" (Deut. 28:6) is interpreted as meaning also "in your coming into this world" (Baba Mezia 107a). It is only in the course of life that acts contrary to God's will accumulate, weighing down the soul. The course set for a child by its parents during his first days and early years is worth the most serious reflection and attention.

NAMING OF CHILDREN

&ᴥ A male child is named during the ceremony of the Covenant of the Circumcision (brit milah); a female child is named in the synagogue the week following her birth when the father is called up

271

to the Torah and a prayer (*mi she-beirakh*) is made for the health of the mother and the newborn infant.

The full Hebrew name as used for all religious purposes and Hebrew legal documents is: *name* ben (son of) *father's name*, or *name* bat (daughter of) *father's name*. If the father is of Priestly or Levitical descent, the title Ha-Kohen or Ha-Levi is appended to the name. (Aside from those who are identified as descendants of the tribe of Levi and of the Kohen class, all other Jews are classified simply as *Yisrael*, Israel.)

ß❧ There are no other religious or halakhic guidelines pertaining to the naming of Jewish children, although in the United States, the rabbis are probably asked more questions about what is and is not permissible in this area than about any other single area of ritual, moral, or ethical conduct.

ß❧ In the Diaspora, where children are generally given gentile names in the civil birth records, the giving of an additional Yiddish or Hebrew name provides an important identification with the Jewish people and the Hebrew faith. It is this Hebrew or Yiddish name that is given at the brit or in the synagogue, as the case may be, which is thereafter used for all religious purposes, religious documents and prayers. It is by this name that a person is called up to the Torah and that one uses in offering prayers for one's health, in drawing up a wedding contract, etc.

ß❧ If the Hebrew name given at birth is never referred to by a family and is never used in the synagogue, it obviously loses all significance, and the so-called "naming" was, in retrospect, a futile and meaningless exercise. In this instance, the *real* name of the person— even for religious documents—is the name by which he is actually called, be it an Anglo-Saxon, Spanish, French or German name.

ß❧ There is a widespread custom among Jews, particularly those of Ashkenazic background, to name a child after a closely deceased relative whose memory they wish to honor and perpetuate.

Although there is no religious obligation to do so, most seem anxious to follow this time-honored custom. It is a noble and worthy custom, but young parents should not deceive themselves. The custom loses all meaning and no one's memory is really honored if the name that the child is given is never used, is forgotten by all, and the child is actually called by another name. Similarly, the custom has little significance if the only relationship between the child's name and the name of the deceased is a common first letter.

&❧ The formal naming of a child is *not* a mystical rite through which the child is introduced into Judaism. In other words, "giving a Jewish name" does not by itself provide status as a Jew if the other requisites of Jewishness are absent. Are there not many gentiles whose names are thoroughly Hebraic or Biblical?

&❧ On the other hand, the absence of a "formal naming" either at the brit or at the synagogue, or the absence of a distinctively Hebraic name, does not detract from one's Jewish status, *if* all other requisites are present. (There have been occasions in Jewish history when at the "formal naming," the child was given a distinctively non-Jewish or non-Hebraic name. Alexander, taken from Alexander the Great, is one such example of a name that has come down in Jewish families as a "Jewish" name.)

&❧ The revival of Hebrew language and culture, the reestablishment of the State of Israel, and the desire to identify as Jews on the part of Diaspora Jewry should encourage young parents to use Biblical and Hebraic names, both classical and contemporary, not only for the "formal naming" and for religious purposes, but also as the *legal* name of the child to be recorded in the civil birth records, the name by which he or she will *really* be known to all.

BRIS: THE COVENANT OF CIRCUMCISION

> This is My Covenant which you shall keep . . . every male among you shall be circumcised . . . that shall be the sign of the Covenant between Me and you. At the age of eight days every male among you shall be circumcised throughout the generations . . . And the uncircumcised male . . . shall be cut off from his people; he has broken My Covenant.
>
> (Genesis 17:10-14)

&❧ It is incumbent upon every father to fulfill the Biblical precept to circumcise his son on the eighth day, or to designate a qualified representative to do so on his behalf.

୫ This ritual is known as the *bris* or *brit* (in Sephardic pronunciation). The word itself means *covenant*. The word for circumcision is *milah*. *Brit milah* is, therefore, the full name, meaning "the Covenant of Circumcision."

୫ The person qualified to perform the brit milah is known as a *mohel*. He should be a pious, observant Jew who has been carefully trained to perform the circumcision. He should be thoroughly conversant with the laws of circumcision as spelled out in the Shulhan Arukh (Yoreh Deah 260–266), and should be trained in the most advanced techniques of surgical hygiene.

୫ There is no religious justification whatsoever for the practice among some Jews of having a physician or surgeon perform the circumcision with a rabbi standing by to recite the blessings and prayers that accompany the rite. A physician may be qualified to do the surgery of circumcision, but he is not necessarily qualified to perform *the Covenant of Circumcision*. It is the adherence to the terms of that Covenant and not the recitation of prayers that determines the religious validity of the circumcision. Rabbinic prayers do not validate a religiously improper circumcision.

୫ The brit milah has been adhered to by Jews throughout the centuries, sometimes under the most trying circumstances and often in the face of prohibitive anti-Semitic legislation, not because it was considered of hygienic value or of medical importance (which we now know it also is) but because it marked for us the eternal Covenant between God and Israel. Only a milah performed by a qualified mohel can continue to reflect the significance of that brit or Covenant.

୫ The brit must take place on the eighth day even if it is the Sabbath or Yom Kippur. Thus, if a child is born on a Monday, the brit is the following Monday; if he is born on a Saturday, the brit is on the following Saturday. Since a day is counted from the onset of night and not from midnight, a child born on a Wednesday night after nightfall, for example, would have his brit the following Thursday.

୫ A brit is always held during the day, preferably in the morning.

୫ Only when an infant is sick, weak, or premature and medical opinion indicates that a circumcision would be dangerous may the brit be postponed. In case of doubt as to the condition of the infant, Jewish law prescribes caution and delay.

&❧ During the circumcision ritual, the father of the infant recites the following benediction:

בָּרוּךְ אַתָּה יְיָ אֱלֹהֵינוּ מֶלֶךְ הָעוֹלָם, אֲשֶׁר קִדְּשָׁנוּ בְּמִצְוֹתָיו וְצִוָּנוּ לְהַכְנִיסוֹ בִּבְרִיתוֹ שֶׁל אַבְרָהָם אָבִינוּ.

Baruch ata adonai elohainu melech ha-olam asher kidshanu b'mitzvotav v'tzivanu l'hakhniso bivrito shel Avraham avinu.

Blessed art Thou, Lord our God, King of the universe who has sanctified us with His commandments and commanded us to bring him (the child) into the Covenant of our father Abraham.

&❧ The attending guests answer "Amen" to this blessing and respond aloud with their own prayer:

כְּשֵׁם שֶׁנִּכְנַס לַבְּרִית, כֵּן יִכָּנֵס לְתוֹרָה וּלְחֻפָּה וּלְמַעֲשִׂים טוֹבִים.

K'shem she-nikhnas labrit, ken yikanes l'Torah, u-l'hupah u-l'maasim tovim.

Just as he entered the Covenant, so may he enter into a study of Torah, into marriage and into the performance of good deeds.

&❧ It is during the brit milah that the child is formally named. For a male child, naming does not take place at synagogue services.

&❧ The person holding the infant during the circumcision is known as the *sandek*. Since ancient times, it has been deemed an honor to act in this capacity. Other roles of honor have arisen in Europe and America, and constitute legitimate customs.

&❧ Although it is preferable to have a minyan (ten men, including the father and mohel) at the brit since it enhances the observance of this mitzvah and adds to the joy of the occasion, it is not absolutely necessary. Where circumstances are such that a minyan cannot be obtained or is not advisable, the brit milah may be performed by the mohel in the presence of the father alone.

&❧ As with all religious ceremonies that are performed with joy and gladness, it is proper to celebrate a brit with a festive meal. The meal served in conjunction with a brit is classified as a religious feast (seudat mitzvah).

&❧ If a child is born as if circumcised or was circumcised before the eighth day, it is required to have a symbolic circumcision which involves a pin-prick, letting a spot of blood taken from the skin just underneath the corona. This rite is called *hatafat dam brit* when the Covenant of Abraham is affirmed.

PIDYON HABEN: REDEMPTION OF THE FIRST BORN

&❧ It is incumbent upon every Israelite father to fulfill the positive Biblical precept to redeem from a kohen the first-born son of his mother.

&❧ It was originally intended that the first-born sons constitute the priesthood and be consecrated to the service of the Lord: "For every first born among the children of Israel is Mine . . . I consecrated them to Myself on the day that I smote every first born in the land of Egypt" (Numbers 8:17). This was part of the concept that the first of everything belongs to God, be it man, beast, or first fruits.

In the wake of Israel's backsliding in the incident of the Golden Calf, when the first born showed themselves unworthy of the priestly office, when only the tribe of Levi was not guilty of this sin, the Levites were chosen to replace the first born in the service of the Sanctuary, with Aaron and his descendants (all Levites) becoming the kohanim.

> Thus shall you set the Levites apart from among the children of Israel; and the Levites shall be Mine . . . in place of all the first issue of the womb, of all the first born of all the children of Israel . . .
>
> (Numbers 8:14, 16)
>
> Now I take the Levites instead of every first born among the children of Israel.
>
> (Numbers 8:18)

&❧ Since initially the first born had been the ones whose lives were to be consecrated to the lifelong service of the Lord, they now had to be formally redeemed from that role, and the redemption money turned over to the kohen.

> The first born of man you shall redeem . . .—from a month old shall you redeem them—and their redemption money shall be according to your valuation, five shekels of silver . . .
>
> (Numbers 18:15-16)

The ceremony at which this redemption takes place is called a *Pidyon HaBen.*

&> The beautiful idea upon which the redemption of the first born is based is that the first and the best of everything we earn or possess is due the Lord as an offering, and not the leftovers or the mediocre that we possess.

&> A Pidyon HaBen is required if:

· the child is the first born of his mother, "that opens the womb," and
· the child is male, and
· the father is not a kohen or a Levi, nor is the mother a daughter of a kohen or a Levi.

If any of the above conditions is absent, a Pidyon HaBen ceremony is not performed.

&> A first-born male child delivered by Caesarean section is *not* required to have a Pidyon HaBen.
A male child born normally following a previous Caesarean birth is also *not* required to have a Pidyon HaBen. (Y.D. 305:24)

&> A first-born male child who is born following a previous miscarriage by the mother does not require a Pidyon HaBen, if the miscarriage took place after the third month of pregnancy. If the miscarriage took place during the first forty days of pregnancy, a Pidyon HaBen for a son born afterwards is required. After forty days and until such time as the fetus develops definite characteristics, a Pidyon HaBen is still required, but the blessing recited by the father is omitted. In all such questions, the guidance of a rabbi should be sought.

ʘ• The Pidyon HaBen ceremony should be held on the thirty-first day following the birth. (The day of the birth is counted as the first day.) If the redemption is held before then, it is not valid and must be done again.

ʘ• A Pidyon HaBen is not held on the Sabbath or a festival or a fast day. If the thirty-first day should fall on any one of these days, the redemption takes place immediately upon the termination of these days.

ʘ• The duty of redeeming the child rests upon the father of the child. If the redemption is neglected at the proper time, the father remains under continuous obligation to arrange for it until after the child becomes thirteen, when the child assumes the responsibility for redeeming himself.

ʘ• If the father is not at the same place as the child, he may arrange to redeem the child from a kohen wherever he is. Instead of using the formula: "This is my son . . . ," he says, "I have a first-born son to redeem . . ." and the kohen responds with the usual formula.

ʘ• A kohen is needed to perform the ceremony. The greatest rabbinic scholar, if he is not a kohen, does not qualify. One should, however, try to secure the services of a kohen who is a pious person and who is familiar with the procedure of the redemption ceremony.

ʘ• It is customary to use five silver coins of the basic money of the realm, i.e., five silver dollars, five Israeli lirot, etc., symbolizing the five silver shekels (sic) that was prescribed in the Torah as the redemption amount.

ʘ• The ceremony itself is a simple one. The father brings the first born before the kohen and informs him that he is the first born of his mother. The kohen then asks the father, "Which do you prefer, to give me your son or to redeem him?" The father answers, "To redeem him." Then, while holding the five silver coins (or its equivalent) in his hand, the father says the following benediction:

בָּרוּךְ אַתָּה יְיָ אֱלֹהֵינוּ מֶלֶךְ הָעוֹלָם, אֲשֶׁר קִדְּשָׁנוּ בְּמִצְוֹתָיו וְצִוָּנוּ עַל פִּדְיוֹן הַבֵּן.

Baruch ata adonai elohainu melech ha-olam asher kidshanu b'mitzvotav v'tzivanu al pidyon haben.

Blessed art Thou, Lord our God, King of the universe who has sanctified us with His commandments and commanded us concerning the redemption of the first-born son.

He follows this with the benediction of *sheheheyanu* (see page 169). The father then turns the money over to the kohen. The kohen takes the money in his hand and passes it over the child's head, saying: "This is in place of this . . . ." The kohen then puts the money down, and raising his hands over the head of the child says the Priestly Benediction. He concludes the ceremony with a blessing over a cup of wine.*

---

* The full text of the ceremony can be found in any comprehensive daily prayer book.

CHAPTER

17

Adoption and Conversion

ADOPTION OF A JEWISH CHILD

ও Since Jewish law does not regard children as the property of parents, the notion of transferring title to the children to someone else through adoption simply does not exist. Jewish law regards the relationship between natural parents and their offspring to be irrevocable.

Nevertheless, the idea of spiritual parenthood is acknowledged. "He who raises someone else's child is regarded as if he had actually brought him into the world physically" (Megillah 13a, Sanhedrin 19b). It is one of the noblest acts of charity to extend care and love to children whose natural parents were either unwilling or unable to discharge their obligations to their children.

ও The adoption of a Jewish child does not change the religious status of the child as Kohen, Levite, or Israelite, nor does it change the criteria that determine whether or not a Pidyon HaBen must take place.

If the child's natural father is known to have been a kohen or a Levite, the child maintains that designation even if the adoptive father is not of that classification.

If the adopted child is the first born to its natural mother and would have required a Pidyon HaBen, then the adopting parents must arrange for it.

ç In view of the close spiritual ties, however, the adopted child may be named as the son or daughter of the adoptive parent. If a girl, she should be named in the synagogue. If a boy, it should be done at the circumcision. If the child had already been circumcised before it was adopted, but did not have a proper *brit*, an *hatafat dam brit* should be arranged and the child named then.

ç If the adoptive father is a kohen or a Levite, that designation is not transferred to the adopted child.

ç Therefore, whenever adopting a child whose natural mother is known to be Jewish, it is most important to ascertain the status of both natural parents on several points in order to determine the religious obligations of the parent to the child:

· If a boy, is this the first born to its mother?
· Is the mother the daughter of a kohen or Levite?
· Is the natural father Jewish? If so, is he a kohen or a Levite?
· Were any other children given away for adoption? If so, it would be important to ascertain with whom there might exist a brother-sister relationship.

ç Adopted children are expected to show reverence and loyalty to deceased adoptive parents through the recital of Kaddish. It is appropriate for them to observe all the laws of mourning as they would for natural parents.

ADOPTION AND CONVERSION OF A NON-JEWISH CHILD

ç Increasing instances of Jewish families adopting children born to non-Jewish mothers make it imperative that the basic principles of this hitherto rarely utilized area of Jewish law become better known.

ç A child born to a non-Jewish mother, regardless of who the father is, has the status of a non-Jew according to Jewish law.

ชิ๊ The legal or civil adoption by a Jewish couple of such a child does not automatically confer the religious status of Jew upon the child.

ชิ๊ For a non-Jewish adopted child to be regarded as Jewish in the view of the religion, he or she must go through a formal conversion. Even if the child is raised as a Jew, and grows up to be an ultra-devout, ultra-orthodox person whose Jewish faith is unquestioned, whose religious commitments are without reservations, and whose devotion and loyalty to the Jewish people are beyond question, his legal status as a Jew is denied him unless he has also gone through the rite of conversion.

ชิ๊ Merely giving a Yiddish or Hebrew name to an adopted non-Jewish child, even if the prayer is made in the synagogue, is of no religious consequence at all and does not affect or alter the non-Jewish status of the child.

ชิ๊ The conversion of a child must be done with the approval of and in the presence of a rabbinic court (Beth Din) consisting of three qualified persons. A Beth Din will not act in any such case unless the request for the conversion is made by the adopting parents.

ชิ๊ The conversion rites for a male child consist of the following:

· The child must be circumcised *with the intent of conversion*. Such intent must be made known to the mohel, so that he may arrange for the presence of a qualified Beth Din, and recite the proper benedictions.
· If the child has already been circumcised by a doctor for reasons of health, a mohel must still be called in to perform a symbolic circumcision. This consists of the rite of *hatafat dam brit* which involves a pin-prick, letting a spot of blood. The required prayers relating to the conversion and affirming the Covenant (brit) are said.
· When the child is about a year old (it may not be safe to do it much earlier), or older, it must be immersed in a ritual bath (mikvah). The Beth Din recites the appropriate benedictions relative to "the immersion of proselytes."

ชิ๊ The conversion rite for a female child consists only of immersing her in the ritual bath. The appropriate benedictions relative to "the immersion of proselytes" are recited by the Beth Din.

&❧ In either case, it is customary for a Hebrew name to be given to the child by the officiating Beth Din following the ritual of immersion.

&❧ The absence of immersion in a *kosher mikvah** for either a male or a female, or the absence of a proper circumcision (or of the *hatafat dam brit* substitute) in the case of a male renders the conversion invalid, no matter how spiritually sincere and faithfully observant the proselyte is or may turn out to be. Such individuals should seek to correct the legal religious deficiency, if such deficiencies are later discovered.

&❧ The formal rite of conversion for a child must be followed up by education and training that will instill in him a profound love for the faith that will encourage him to observe the commandments of the Lord and become a loyal and devoted Jew.

&❧ Once the proper rite of conversion has been fulfilled, the adopted child is regarded as being as Jewish as any other born Jew, subject to all the requirements and disciplines as well as the privileges of the Jewish faith.

CONVERSION

&❧ Adult conversions to Judaism have the same basic requirements as those for the conversion of children described above, except that in the case of an adult the rite of conversion must be preceded by study of Judaism, by an affirmation of its basic principles of faith and by a sincere resolution of heart and mind to observe its precepts and practices in everyday life.

"To accept the yoke of the Kingdom of God" and "to accept the yoke of the commandments" are the pivotal requirements upon which the validity of the conversion ritual hinges for an adult. The lack of such an acceptance makes the conversion a farce and a meaningless exercise. Acceptance, on the other hand, not only gives meaning to but validates the required ritual. It is the acceptance of the *yoke of the commandments* which determines whether or not a proselyte is a righteous proselyte (*ger tzedek*).

---

* An ordinary swimming pool does *not* qualify as a mikvah.

ৡ The length of time it takes for an adult to be converted to Judaism depends entirely upon the circumstances: the background that the prospective proselyte brings, the amount of study he requires and the time he is prepared to give to his preparation. It rarely takes less than six months, usually a year, and sometimes longer.

ৡ In accepting the faith, the convert is also adopted into the greater Jewish family. He or she joins the Jewish people. In taking a Hebrew name, the convert is designated not as the son or daughter of his natural parents but as the son or daughter of Abraham, our Father.

CHAPTER

18

Bar=Mitzvah and Bat=Mitzvah

A BOY reaches his religious majority upon reaching the anniversary of his thirteenth birthday according to the Hebrew calendar. A girl reaches her religious majority upon reaching the anniversary of her twelfth birthday according to the Hebrew calendar.

&❧ A boy who reaches this age is known as a Bar-Mitzvah; a girl is called a Bat-Mitzvah. These words mean "subject to the commandments" and imply that the person reaching this age is no longer treated as a minor by Jewish law, but as an adult. If new religious privileges and religious rights are now extended to him, it is because he assumes full responsibility for the observance of all precepts and commandments.

&❧ To mark this religious turning point in the life of a Jewish boy, it is customary to provide him with an opportunity to fulfill publicly a mitzvah not heretofore extended him. This usually takes the form of being called up to the reading of the Torah, there to recite the appropriate benedictions.* (See pp. 165–166.)

The custom has become widespread for the celebrant to be called up for the final Aliyah (*maftir*) which also calls for the reading of

---

* The same form of honor in the synagogue is extended upon every significant occasion in life: When a man is about to be married; when a child is born; after one has been through a difficult or dangerous illness; upon the observance of a yahrzeit, etc.

a section from the Prophets (*haftorah*), thus providing him with a greater role in the service.

৯০ Different communities have different customs as to what the young man is called upon to do. They range from the honor of an Aliyah to the conducting of a part or even of the whole religious service. Among Yeshiva students, it is a practice also to deliver a learned address on some Biblical or Talmudic theme. Much depends upon the educational background of the child as well as upon the standards followed in the community.

৯০ Bar-Mitzvah is not a mystical ritual confirmation which somehow confers "Jewishness" upon the child. As indicated above, it is a religious-legal term which implies a coming of age. This the child becomes whether or not he marks the occasion in any formal way. The synagogue honors extended to a Bar-Mitzvah form part of the regular service and are no different than those which may be extended to any adult Jew on any other occasion. Marking one's Bar-Mitzvah in the synagogue testifies at least to having had some basic religious instruction.

৯০ Because women do not participate in the conduct of synagogue services, no formal traditional ceremony has ever developed to mark the time when a girl becomes Bat-Mitzvah. In our own times, however, some families, religious schools, and synagogues do try to mark this religious turning point in the life of a young lady in some way. As long as the forms that are developed are not in violation of the halakha, there is no objection to such innovations.

৯০ The nature and extent of the festivities which accompany the Bar-Mitzvah are a matter of local custom, and a reflection of the personal taste and/or the means of the family. These may range from simple refreshments following the synagogue services to the most elaborate of feasts on the following day. Where the festivities are held in such a way as to violate not only the spirit of Judaism but also its specific precepts and values, the celebration only tends to secularize the event, cheapening the religious significance in the eyes of the guests but especially so in the eyes of the young man himself. As the years go by, a serious and intelligent young man will rightly look back upon such a celebration as a religious mockery. It also behooves parents to resist the temptations to turn a Bar-Mitzvah into a gala, ostentatious *birthday party* for a thirteen-year-old.

CHAPTER

19

~~~~~~

Marriage

"No man without a wife, neither a woman without a husband, nor both of them without God" (Genesis Rabbah 8:9). This relationship is reflected in the Jewish wedding ceremony. By law and tradition, the ceremony establishes a new family.

Although the preparations for a wedding ceremony often involve some anxiety, it is in truth far simpler to prepare for a wedding ceremony than it is to prepare for marriage. How much easier it is to recognize the onset of physical maturity and economic sufficiency than it is to know whether one has reached emotional maturity and psychological readiness. The proper preparation for a wedding should begin with a thorough consideration of the nature of the Family Life (pp. 121–141) and of the nature of the Relationship of Husband and Wife (pp. 133–135).

THE WEDDING CEREMONY

ક્રે Jewish wedding ceremonies are made up of two parts:

· Betrothal or Sanctification (*Kiddushin*), during which the bride is betrothed to the groom as he places a ring upon her finger and says to her:

הֲרֵי אַתְּ מְקֻדֶּשֶׁת לִי בְּטַבַּעַת זוֹ כְּדַת מֹשֶׁה וְיִשְׂרָאֵל.

Harai at mekudeshet lee, b'ta-ba-at zu, k'dat Mosheh v'Yisrael.

Be sanctified (betrothed) to me with this ring in accordance with the law of Moses and Israel.

    With this statement, and the bride's consent, she becomes his wife. This part requires the presence of two qualified witnesses.

· Marriage (*Nisuin*), is the consummation of the betrothal. It is symbolized by the bride and groom standing beneath the covering (*hupah*), while the Seven Benedictions (*Sheva Brakhot*) are recited. The recitation of these benedictions requires the presence of a minyan.

❦ The blessings appropriate for these two parts of the ceremony are said over a cup of wine by those officiating. The bride and groom drink from the wine.

❦ Since a wedding contract (*ketuba*), which obligates the husband to support his wife must be drawn up prior to the ceremony, it is customary for this ketuba to be read during the wedding ceremony between the Kiddushin and the Nisuin.

❦ The custom is not to use rings with diamonds or other precious stones for the ceremony. This is related to the age-old desire to avoid any possibility of fraud which would legally invalidate the marriage. (If the bride's consent to the marriage was motivated by the value of the gift that she was getting and the "precious" stones turned out to be fake, or of far less value than she assumed, grounds for invalidating the marriage would exist.) If a ring with precious stones is used and the bride is aware of its value, there is no question as to the validity of the marriage ceremony.

❦ The ring that is given to the bride at the ceremony may not be borrowed, but *must* belong to the groom. The ring is regarded as a gift to the bride and not just as an object used in a symbolic act. One cannot give away something that one has only borrowed and does not himself own.

    If there is a family heirloom which possesses a sentimental value and the couple wants to use it for the ceremony, it may be done if the groom acquires it from its legal owner as a gift or through purchase. Then he is free to give it to his bride. The ring becomes hers to do with as she wishes.

ટ≥ It is customary to break a small glass at the conclusion of the wedding ceremony to recall the destruction of the ancient Temple in Jerusalem in 70 c.e. by the Romans (see Tisha b'Av, page 263). "Breaking a glass" and similar practices on other occasions is called for by the Mishna to recall the destruction.

Though the Jewish State was reestablished in 1948 and Jewish sovereignty over the Temple Mount returned in 1967, the Temple itself has not yet been restored. Thus, the broken glass continues to symbolize the incompleteness of the religious restoration of Israel.

ટ≥ The *hupah* covering symbolizes the consummation of the marriage. This is also indicated by having the bride and groom retire to a room by themselves for a short period of privacy immediately following the ceremony.

ટ≥ The festive meal that follows the ceremony is classified as a seudat mitzvah, a religious feast. The *Sheva Brakhot* that were said at the wedding ceremony are repeated at the conclusion of the wedding dinner as well.

ટ≥ It is a great mitzvah to "make the groom and bride merry." Music, dancing and expressions of great joy traditionally accompany all Jewish wedding ceremonies.

ટ≥ Wedding ceremonies may not take place on the Sabbath nor on the festivals (even the Intermediate days of Pesach and Succot), nor during the three weeks from the seventeenth of Tammuz through Tisha b'Av, nor during a thirty-three day period during Sefira, nor on a regular fast day.

PROHIBITED MARRIAGES

ટ≥ All unions, whether temporary or permanent, of a single occasion, or of an ongoing nature, of a man with a woman in any of the following categories are classified as incestuous and are sternly prohibited:

- Blood relations: mother, daughter, sister, granddaughter, aunt (the sister of one's father or mother).
- Cases of affinity: the wives of blood relations, i.e., son's wife,

father's wife, uncle's wife (aunt by marriage), brother's wife, etc.* The blood relations of one's wife are also included in this category, i.e., wife's mother, wife's sister, wife's children (by a previous marriage).

· The wife of another man, who has not been divorced by a valid Jewish divorce (*get*) from her husband.

· Whichever is the second relationship in the union of a man with a woman and her daughter or granddaughter, whether both are living or after the death of one.

· A wife's sister, during the wife's lifetime even if the wife had been divorced from him. After the death of a wife or ex-wife, it is permitted to marry her sister.

ક• All the foregoing unions are forbidden by the Torah. Under no circumstances can any of these unions be deemed a marriage even if contracted under and approved by civil law or blessed by a "Jewish spiritual leader." Such relationships have no binding force whatsoever under Jewish religious law and no *get* is ever required for their dissolution. Children born from such unions are illegitimate (*mamzerim*). "Do not defile yourselves in any of those ways . . . for all those abhorrent things were done by the people who were in the land before you . . . all who do any of those abhorrent things, such persons shall be cut off from their people . . ." (Lev. 18:24, 27, 29). "You shall keep My charge, not to engage in any of the abhorrent practices that were carried on before you, lest you defile yourselves through them. I am the Lord, your God" (Lev. 18:30).

ક• A child born "out of wedlock," however repugnant to Jewish morality it is, is not classified as illegitimate under Jewish law. Such a child bears no special stigma. The Hebrew term for bastard, *mamzer* (as used in the Torah), refers only to issue of the forbidden relationships enumerated above.

ક• The "marriage" of a Jew with a non-Jew has no binding force under Jewish religious law and is not recognized as religiously valid even if performed and blessed by a hundred rabbis. The basis for a

---

* *Brother's wife:* for the exception see Deut. 25:5 where an obligation is placed upon a man to marry his brother's widow, should his brother have died without children. Under rabbinic law, however, such a man must exercise his "right of refusal" to enter into such a levirate marriage and by participating in the ceremony of *halitzah*, to release the brother's widow to marry someone else.

sanctified relationship in accordance with the Law of Moses and Israel is the creation of an atmosphere in which the precepts of the Lord will be fulfilled, and where children will be raised in an atmosphere of religious faith. Judaism does not conceive of the marriage bond purely as a legal device designed to lend approval to the gratification of the physical or emotional desires of a couple. In a mixed marriage where one partner is of another faith, the very foundation of the Jewish marriage and its purposes are absent. The children of such a "marriage" are, however, not regarded as illegitimate. Their status as Jews depends upon whether or not the mother is Jewish.

* By Torah law (Lev. 21: 6–7), a kohen is forbidden to marry a woman in any of the following categories: (1) a divorcee, (2) one who has been released through *halitzah*, (3) a proselyte, (4) one who is known to be promiscuous or to have been involved in forbidden sexual relations, or (5) one who is herself an offspring of a forbidden marriage entered into by a kohen with a woman in any of the preceding categories.*

* Although the Torah forbids a kohen from entering into any of the above marriages, and the halakha prohibits a rabbi from officiating at such a marriage, should the kohen nevertheless contract and consummate the relationship, the marriage as a marriage is valid. This differs from the prohibited relations where no legal marriage takes hold and where the offspring are illegitimate.

* Such a marriage disqualifies the kohen from his duties and privileges and affects the status of the children born. Male children (*halal*) are also disqualified from the privileges and duties of a kohen, and female children (*halala*) are forbidden to marry a kohen.

---

* The High Priest (*Kohen Gadol*) was also forbidden to take a *widow* as a wife (Lev. 21:14), although this is permitted to the ordinary kohen.

CHAPTER

20

Divorce Proceedings

"WHEN one divorces his first wife, even the Altar sheds tears" (Gittin 90b). In Jewish life, divorce is regarded as a tragic last resort, to be turned to only after all other possibilities for reestablishing marital harmony and for rekindling the love and affection that once existed between the couple have been exhausted. But when every hope of healing the breach has been lost, then "the law of divorce is given for the sake of peace. . . . And those who divorce when they must, bring good upon themselves, not evil" (Eliyahu Kitov).

It is suggested that the discussion of divorce in Family Life (pp. 135–136) be read as an introduction to the actual divorce proceedings which follow.

&> A marriage consecrated "according to the Law of Moses and Israel" is not dissolved except "according to the Law of Moses and Israel." Its procedure, based upon Biblical precept, is strictly governed by the halakha. (Divorces granted under secular or civil law by civil authorities have no validity under Jewish law. Civil divorces possess no moral or spiritual significance in severing the consecrated bonds of religious marriage.)

&> The Jewish divorce proceedings must be supervised by a Beth Din, a rabbinic court consisting of three rabbis competent in the laws of marriage and divorce.

ৰু In addition to the Beth Din, a scribe (*sofer*) and two witnesses comprise the personnel needed in the issuance of a Jewish divorce (*get*). Members of the Beth Din may serve as the witnesses if other persons are unavailable.

ৰু Although a Beth Din will not authorize a *get* to be written unless it has made every effort to reconcile a couple and unless the grounds are sufficiently compelling, where a civil divorce has been granted and a mutually agreed property settlement has been reached in connection with the civil divorce, it is unnecessary for the Beth Din to involve itself in the grounds for divorce or the financial settlement. Under Jewish law the desire of both parties to dissolve the marriage constitutes, in the final analysis, sufficient grounds.

ৰু The entire procedure may take one and a half to two hours. The bulk of the time is taken up by the writing of the get by the scribe. The document is lettered like and is similar in appearance to a column of a Torah scroll. The get is written individually on behalf of the husband and wife. It contains their names, the date, and the name of city where it is written. The document itself mentions no grounds for divorce and no charge by either husband or wife.

ৰু Both husband and wife are asked a number of routine questions to ascertain their free will and consent in the divorce action. While the formal ceremony—based upon Biblical verses—provides for the husband to "give" the get and for the wife to "receive" it, this is basically procedural. In actual practice, one does not give nor does the other receive without the respective consent and approval of each. This is especially so in countries outside of Israel where Jewish religious courts do not possess the power to compel a husband to consent to give the get, or to compel a wife to consent to receive the get. Only moral pressure can be exercised.

Adherence to the tenets of Jewish law in the Diaspora in matters of personal family status—marriage and divorce—is entirely voluntary. While the voluntary aspect may seem desirable, it has its drawbacks in the powerlessness of religious courts to correct flagrant injustices against one or the other partner.

ৰু Bills of Divorce may not be form-printed. They must be written in entirety specifically for the particular man and the particular woman for the specific purpose of effecting the particular divorce.

&ᴥ The scribe and the two witnesses must be pious, observant people, none of whom is related to the other, nor to the husband or the wife.

&ᴥ While the proceedings are simplest when both husband and wife are present at the same time, should this be difficult or should it be undesirable for them to meet, it is possible to arrange for the proceedings to be finalized through the appointment of a messenger. In that case, the husband places the document into the hands of the messenger who acts on behalf of the husband. One member of the Beth Din, one of the witnesses, or the scribe himself may serve as the messenger.

&ᴥ After the proceedings are completed, a tear is made in the divorce document to indicate that it has been used and cannot be used again. The document itself is retained by the Beth Din and kept in a permanent file. Official letters, called a release (*ptur*) are given to the man and the woman testifying that the get has taken place and affirming their right to remarry. (If a ptur is lost, another copy can be obtained. If the original Bill of Divorce is lost, it is impossible to replace.)

&ᴥ The woman may not remarry following the get for a period of ninety-two days. The reason for the waiting period is to remove all doubt as to paternity which might be raised should she marry and conceive right away.

&ᴥ The laws relating to the writing of a document valid according to halakha and to the proceedings themselves are numerous and complex. None but the most learned in the law of divorce may preside over it, lest an error result in the invalidation of the get.

HALITZAH—THE CEREMONY OF RELEASE

Based on the passage in Deuteronomy 25:7–10, this ceremony is the prescribed alternative to *yibum* and releases the widow of a man who died childless to marry someone other than the deceased husband's brother.

Although a union with a brother's wife is among the incestuous relationships forbidden in the Torah, and applies even when the wife becomes widowed or divorced, the one exception provided for in the Torah is when the brother died without children (Deut. 25: 5–6). "To avert the calamity of the family line becoming extinct and of a man's name perishing, the surviving brother of such a childless man was required to marry the widow so as to raise up an heir to that man's name" (Hertz Pentateuch). The name for such a marriage is *yibum* or levirate marriage (in Latin, *levir* is a husband's brother). The brother could, however, refuse to enter into marriage with his deceased brother's wife. In this case, the Torah provides for the ceremony of *halitzah*, which releases one from the other.

Rabbinic law, however, *requires* the surviving brother to exercise his "right of refusal" and to release his brother's widow to marry someone else. On moral grounds, the rabbis felt constrained to prevent a levirate marriage from being consummated. They felt that it would be extremely difficult for a man to cohabit with his sister-in-law with only the intent of fulfilling the religious duty. Without such singular intent, the relationship would be incestuous.

Just as a get serves to release a husband and wife from each other according to the Law of Moses and Israel, halitzah serves to release the childless widow and the surviving brother from the Jewish legal bond to one another. The ceremony of halitzah must be presided over by a competent Beth Din.

CHAPTER

21

Death and Mourning

THE Jewish tradition cherishes life. The Torah was given to Israel so that "you shall live" by the teachings and "not die through them." Death has no virtue since "The dead cannot praise the Lord . . ." (Psalms 115:17).

Nevertheless, the Jewish tradition has been realistic about death. "For dust you are and to dust shall you return" (Genesis 3:19), "but the spirit returns to God who gave it" (Ecclesiastes 12:7). "The end of man is death," said Rabbi Johanan (Berakhot 17a). Simply put, we shall all die.

In itself, death is not a tragedy. What we call a "tragic death" is determined by the untimely nature of the death or the unfortunate circumstances surrounding it. When a peaceful death follows a long life which was blessed with good health and vitality of mind and body, a life rich in good deeds, then death cannot be regarded as tragic—no matter how great the loss and the sorrow. "Blessed is he that has been reared in the Torah and whose toil is in the Torah, and acts so as to please his Creator, and has grown up with a good name and departed with a good name. Concerning him, Solomon said, 'A good name is better than precious oil; and the day of death than the day of one's birth' (Ecclesiastes 7:1)" (Berakhot 17a).

The world we live in is viewed as a corridor that leads to still another world. The belief in an afterlife, in a world to come (*Olam Haba*) where man is judged and where his soul continues to flourish is imbedded in Jewish thought. "All Israel have a share in the world to come" (Mishna Sanhedrin 11:1).

But the worthier the individual, the greater is his loss to the living. The more he meant to those about him—family, friends, community, the deeper the grief and sharper the anguish. The traditional Jewish observances surrounding death and mourning address themselves to maintaining the dignity of the deceased and to comforting the pain of the mourners.

BURIAL AND AUTOPSIES

ৰ্ত্ত The religious laws and practices relating to death and mourning are based upon two fundamental principles:

· The honor and respect due even to a lifeless human being (*kibud ha-met*).
· The concern for the mental, emotional, and spiritual well being of the living mourners, and the requirement of extending comfort to them (*nihum avelim*).

ৰ্ত্ত The dead must be clothed in white robes (*takhrikhim*) after having been carefully washed and cleansed. (The simple white garment was instituted in the Talmudic period when burials became terribly burdensome and expensive for the masses, to emphasize the equality in death of the rich and poor alike. Until then the more affluent had usually been buried in richer clothing. The Sages were sensitive to the honor of the deceased poor.)

ৰ্ত্ত The male dead are also wrapped in a tallit whose fringes (tzitzit) are made invalid, symbolically indicating that the earthly requirements are no longer incumbent upon him.

ৰ্ত্ত Embalming is forbidden. The blood of a deceased is part of himself which must also be buried and not discarded as waste.

ৰ্ত্ত For the deceased to be put on display in an open casket has traditionally been looked upon as a dishonor to him. The Sages felt that to be placed on display, enabling not only friend but also foe to march by and gaze disparagingly and mockingly at the body is disrespectful to the deceased. Although the intent of this practice in Western culture is an honorable one, Jewish values discourage it.

&~ Cremation is forbidden; burial must take place in the earth. The Biblical observation "For dust you are and to dust you shall return" (Genesis 3:19), is made even more emphatic by the Torah when it says that "you must surely bury him" (Deut. 21:23).

&~ When cremation takes place and the ashes are not buried in the earth but kept in an urn above the ground or scattered over the seas, the family of the deceased is not required to observe the period of shiva.

&~ Autopsies: The consensus of rabbinic rulings during the past several centuries has strongly prohibited post-mortem examinations as a desecration of the dead. However, allowances have been made if there was a reasonable prospect that it would contribute to saving the life of another patient at hand. It was thus permitted in cases of hereditary diseases, to safeguard the life of surviving relations, and where required by the civil law of the land (because of foul play, etc.). Where the general prohibition against autopsies is set aside, it is vital that several safeguards be followed:

 · Only the minimum required tissues needed for the examination should be used.
 · All parts removed from the body should be returned for interment.
 · Unless required by law, the autopsy should never be done without the express permission of the family or the prior consent of the deceased during his lifetime.

Since each case is different and authoritative rabbinic opinion may differ as to what conditions must be met to secure permission, the guidance of one's own rabbi is suggested.

&~ Burial must take place as soon as possible following death. To delay interment beyond the next day is permissible only for the honor of the dead such as awaiting the arrival of close relatives from distant points, or if a Sabbath or festival intervenes.

&~ It is forbidden to bury the dead on the Sabbath. Jews are also forbidden to participate in the burial on the first day of the festivals. While it is permissible to bury on the second day of festivals, it is only the actual interment that is permitted. No other violation of the festival is condoned. Under contemporary conditions, it is preferable not to conduct a funeral on either day of the festival so as not to lead to major desecration of the holiday and thus to the indirect dishonor of the dead.

᷇᷇ Caring for the dead, preparing them for burial, watching over them, and handling the burial itself is a sacred religious task which only the most pious and worthy members of a Jewish community were called upon to do. The organized communal society that concerns itself with this is called the Sacred Society (*Hevra Kadisha*).

᷇᷇ Tearing a garment that one is wearing is the religiously proper way to express grief for the dead. It is a time-honored and ancient sign of grief and mourning among Jews extending back to Biblical times. The garment that is torn is worn throughout the week of mourning (*shiva*) except for the Sabbath day. (Cutting a small black ribbon is not a religiously authorized substitute for rending the garment, or *kriah*.)

᷇᷇ When rending the garment, the following blessing is said by the mourners: *Baruch ata adonai elohainu melech ha-olam dayan ha-emet.* Blessed art Thou, Lord our God, the true Judge.

MOURNING PERIODS

᷇᷇ Jewish law provides for three successive periods of mourning following the burial, each observed with increasingly less intensity. The first period is known as *shiva*, which means *seven* and refers to the seven-day period of mourning following the burial.

᷇᷇ Shiva is observed for the following relations: father, mother, wife (husband), son, daughter, brother, or sister.

᷇᷇ It is most proper for a family to observe the shiva together in the home where the deceased lived. However, this is not mandatory and the members of a family may observe the shiva at any other convenient place, even separately—in their respective homes, if circumstances require it.

 howeredb Practices observed during shiva:

· Mourners do not sit on seats of normal height, but on low stools. Footstools or hassacks may serve the purpose.

Some follow the practice of removing the cushions from couches or armchairs, sitting on the lower frame. This is permissible. (Sephardic families follow the more ancient practice of sitting on the floor.) From this practice derives the expression "sitting" shiva, although it is not necessary that the mourners actually sit all the time.

· Mourners do not wear shoes made of leather. Slippers, canvas or rubber shoes may be worn as an alternative to stockinged feet.

· Male mourners refrain from shaving and hair cutting; female mourners avoid the use of cosmetics.

· Mourners may not go to work. The local rabbi should be consulted for exceptions, as there may be extenuating circumstances in individual cases.

· Avoidance of pleasure:

> One does not bathe or shower for comfort, although it is permissible to wash for cleanliness, unless it is a matter of severe discomfort.
>
> One may not engage in sexual relations.
>
> One may not put on new or freshly-laundered clothing.
>
> One may not engage in Torah study, except for books or chapters dealing with laws of mourning, and books such as Job, Lamentations, and parts of Jeremiah, which speak of grief and anguish.

howeredb The shiva period is concluded on the morning of the seventh day following the morning services. The day of the burial is counted as the first day of shiva.

Should the seventh day be a Sabbath the public aspects of shiva are concluded just prior to the Sabbath allowing only for the time necessary to prepare for the Sabbath. (The widespread notion that shiva concludes at noon on a Friday or a festival eve has no basis in Jewish law.)

howeredb Should the Sabbath come in the midst of the shiva period, the public mourning practices associated with shiva are suspended for the Sabbath, but resume after the Sabbath. The Sabbath is nevertheless counted in reckoning the seven days.

&ᴥ Should one of the Biblical festivals interrupt the shiva, the remainder of the shiva is completely terminated and is not resumed after the festival.

&ᴥ Should a funeral take place during the week of Passover or Succot, shiva is observed but it does not begin until after the entire festival is concluded. In the Diaspora, the last day of the festival is counted as the first day of shiva.

&ᴥ Purim and Hanukah are not among the holidays which terminate mourning, although the mourner is permitted to attend the synagogue for the Megillah reading on Purim.

&ᴥ If there is a delay in learning of a death because one has been away or lives in a distant city, the mourner begins to observe all the mourning practices of shiva from the time he receives the news. If the rest of the family is still in the midst of the shiva period in the city where death or burial occurred, he may join them and rise from shiva at the same time they do. If one cannot join the rest of the mourners, or if the week of shiva has already passed, the day on which the news is received is counted as the first day of shiva.

&ᴥ If news of the death is received after thirty days have passed since the day of death, shiva is not observed. One need only remove one's shoes and sit on a low seat for an hour, indicating a token observance. The mourner's benediction, "Blessed . . . the true Judge" is said. Where the deceased is a parent, the garment is also rended.

&ᴥ The second period is known as *shloshim*, which means *thirty* and refers to the period from the end of shiva through the thirtieth day after burial. Attending parties even where no music is played and getting married is forbidden during this period; so is shaving or cutting one's hair for the entire month. This concludes the mourning for all relatives other than mother or father.

&ᴥ The period of shloshim is concluded on the morning of the thirtieth day. The day of the burial is counted as the first day.

&ᴥ Should one of the major festivals occur during the shloshim period, mourning is treated as having been concluded. Its special restrictions are not resumed after the festival.

&ᴥ The third period observed for a mother or father is known simply as *avelut*, mourning. It terminates at the end of twelve (Hebrew) months from the day of death. It extends from the end of shloshim through the first anniversary of the day of death. During this period, joyous events, dinners with music, theaters, and concerts should be avoided. Kaddish is said daily by sons for eleven months of the year. After the year, it is forbidden to continue practices or restraints that openly indicate the continuation of the grief.

COMFORTING THE MOURNER

୫୬ The requirement to comfort the mourner does not begin till after the burial. Until that time the bereaved should be allowed to give fullest expression to his grief. No formal condolences should be extended during this time. The practice followed in some communities of encouraging condolence visits to the mourning family prior to the burial—whether at their residence or at a funeral home —is not in keeping with Jewish custom and procedure. (Only the closest family or friends whose assistance is required in making arrangements for the funeral or in other matters should visit with the family of the deceased before the funeral.)

୫୬ Following the burial, the mourners' very first meal may not consist of their own food. It should be prepared for them by neighbors, friends, or relatives. The practice is based on a passage from Ezekiel 24:17 which speaks negatively of the then prevailing mourning practices and says ". . . and eat not the bread of men." It is therefore regarded as a mitzvah for neighbors or friends of the mourners to provide the first meal for them. This meal is called the "Meal of Comfort." This meal customarily contains hard-boiled eggs, a food that has become a symbol for mourning and condolences. The egg's roundness in a way symbolizes the continuous nature of life and perhaps also suggests that from despair there may follow renewal and joy. Although there are no special restrictions concerning this meal, care should be taken that it not be given a party-like atmosphere. It should be eaten quietly and in contemplation by the mourners. The meal is not intended for the visitors.

The meal of comfort is not served if the mourners return from a funeral in the late afternoon preceding a Sabbath or festival day. It is served on the Intermediate days of Pesach and Succot (*hol ha-moed*) even though there is no shiva.

&❧ Upon entering a house of mourning one does not extend greetings. Since words cannot adequately express the depth of sympathy a comforter wishes to convey and what is said is often shallow, it is best to say nothing. Tradition dictates that the visitor does not open the conversation with the mourner, but allows the latter to do so.

&❧ It is proper to turn the conversation to the deceased, to reminisce, and to mention the good qualities which endeared him to others. Those who purposely steer clear of mentioning the deceased, believing that in this way they take the mind of the mourner off his grief, do not fully understand the psychology of grief. To spend the visit talking about trivialities is far less comforting and far more painful to the mourner than to talk about the deceased.

&❧ Upon taking leave of mourners in a house of mourning anytime during the week of shiva, the traditional formula of sympathy said to them is:

הַמָּקוֹם יְנַחֵם אֶתְכֶם בְּתוֹךְ שְׁאָר אֲבֵלֵי צִיּוֹן וִירוּשָׁלָיִם.

Hamakom y'nahaim etkhem b'tokh sh'ar availai tziyon vee-yerushalayim.

May the Lord comfort you with all the mourners of Zion and Jerusalem.

Although there is no need to say more than this prayer, additional words of comfort or hope may be said if the comforter feels inclined to do so and can find the proper words.

SPECIAL RULES FOR THE KOHEN

And the Lord said unto Moses: Speak unto the priests, the sons of Aaron, and say unto them: None shall defile himself for the dead among his people, except for his kind that is near unto him, for his mother and for his father, and for his son and for his daughter and for his brother. And for his sister, a virgin . . . that had no husband, for her may he defile himself. . . . He shall not defile himself . . . to profane himself.

(Lev. 21:1-4)

ஃ A kohen, one who is a descendant of the priestly tribe, is forbidden to come in contact with the dead. This prohibition involves not only actual physical contact, but includes being in the same room with a corpse, no matter how large the room. If there are openings or passages leading to other rooms, then the prohibition extends to all such connecting rooms.

ஃ After a corpse is removed from a room or a building, a kohen may enter it, as the "spirit of defilement" is said to depart with the corpse.

ஃ Even under the open skies, a kohen may not approach a grave any closer than four *amot* (approximately 6 feet). However, it is not necessary that the kohen remove himself any further than four *tefahim* (approximately fifteen inches), from a body being carried to burial under the open skies.

ஃ It is permissible, and according to some even a religious duty, for a kohen to ritually defile himself for the following seven categories of relatives: wife, father, mother, son, daughter, brother, and unmarried sister, in order to arrange for, assist in, and attend the burial.

ஃ The restrictions against ritual defilement apply only to the male members of the family. They do not apply to the wife nor the daughters of a kohen.

KADDISH

ஃ A son is duty bound to recite the Kaddish prayer at daily religious services beginning with the day of burial and each day thereafter for an eleven-month period. This devotion is regarded as an act of reverence for a deceased parent.

ஃ The recitation of the Kaddish requires a minyan, a quorum of ten Jewish male adults. It is not said when praying alone.

ஃ The Kaddish is said while standing, feet together, in a respectful stance. In some congregations, only one person at a time is designated to recite the Kaddish. In most congregations, it is customary for all the mourners to recite the Kaddish in unison. The congregants who hear the Kaddish recited are required to respond with the words *Yehai shmai rabba m'vorakh l'olam ul'almai almaya*, "may His great name be blessed forever and ever," and *Amen*.

&❧ The language of Kaddish is not Hebrew but Aramaic, which was the language spoken by the masses. The unlearned were thus better able to comprehend its meaning.

&❧ The Kaddish is not technically a prayer for the dead. There *are* special prayers for the dead such as the *El Molai Rahamim* prayer and the *Yizkor* prayer, but the Kaddish is not one of them. It makes no reference to the dead or to mourning. It is a prayer in praise of God. It is a declaration of deep faith in the exalted greatness of the Almighty and a petition for ultimate redemption and salvation. The word *Kaddish* means *holy*, and is similar to the word *Kiddush*, which is the prayer of sanctification for the Sabbath or the festival. The Kaddish is one of the oldest prayers in Jewish liturgy, extending well back to the days of the Second Temple. It reads as follows:

יִתְגַּדַּל וְיִתְקַדַּשׁ שְׁמֵהּ רַבָּא בְּעָלְמָא דִּי בְרָא כִרְעוּתֵהּ;

וְיַמְלִיךְ מַלְכוּתֵהּ * בְּחַיֵּיכוֹן וּבְיוֹמֵיכוֹן וּבְחַיֵּי דְכָל בֵּית יִשְׂרָאֵל,

בַּעֲגָלָא וּבִזְמַן קָרִיב, וְאִמְרוּ אָמֵן.

יְהֵא שְׁמֵהּ רַבָּא מְבָרַךְ לְעָלַם וּלְעָלְמֵי עָלְמַיָּא.

יִתְבָּרַךְ וְיִשְׁתַּבַּח וְיִתְפָּאַר וְיִתְרוֹמַם וְיִתְנַשֵּׂא וְיִתְהַדָּר

וְיִתְעַלֶּה וְיִתְהַלָּל שְׁמֵהּ דְּקֻדְשָׁא, בְּרִיךְ הוּא, לְעֵלָּא מִן כָּל

בִּרְכָתָא וְשִׁירָתָא, תֻּשְׁבְּחָתָא וְנֶחֱמָתָא, דַּאֲמִירָן בְּעָלְמָא,

וְאִמְרוּ אָמֵן.

יְהֵא שְׁלָמָא רַבָּא מִן שְׁמַיָּא, וְחַיִּים, עָלֵינוּ וְעַל כָּל יִשְׂרָאֵל,

וְאִמְרוּ אָמֵן.

עֹשֶׂה שָׁלוֹם בִּמְרוֹמָיו, הוּא יַעֲשֶׂה שָׁלוֹם עָלֵינוּ וְעַל כָּל

יִשְׂרָאֵל, וְאִמְרוּ אָמֵן.

*In *nusach Sephard* add:

וְיַצְמַח פּוּרְקָנֵהּ וִיקָרֵב מְשִׁיחֵהּ

Magnified and sanctified be His great Name in the world which He created according to His will. May He establish His kingdom during your life and during your days, and during the life of all the house of Israel, speedily and in the near future, and say Amen. May His great Name be blessed forever and ever. Blessed, praised and glorified, exalted, extolled and honored, adored and lauded be the Name of the Holy One, Blessed be He; Who is beyond all blessings and hymns, praises and songs that are uttered in the world; and say Amen. May there be abundant peace from heaven, and life for us and for all Israel; and say Amen. May He who maketh peace in the heavens, make peace for us and for all Israel; and say Amen.

§► Originally, the Kaddish was recited only at the conclusion of a session of Torah study. As the Rabbinical Kaddish, the *Kaddish d'Rabbanan*, it is still said at such times. These are surely appropriate words and sentiments with which to conclude a period devoted to the study of the Divine Word. Sometime during the early Middle Ages, during the post-Talmudic period, it also became identified with mourners.

If, in the midst of grief and personal loss, when the tendency to blame and reject God might arise, a person nevertheless rises *publicly* to express these words of faith and trust in God—this is an act of great merit to the soul of the deceased, for the deceased is credited with having raised a child capable of such an act of faith. In this sense only can the Kaddish be regarded as an indirect "prayer for the dead." Its recitation accrues to the merit of the soul in the judgment that takes place in the world to come.

§► While a daughter is not under religious obligation to recite the Kaddish daily, she may rise to recite the Kaddish at religious services if she feels inclined to do so. Some religious scholars do not share this latter view.

§► It is permissible and proper for one under thirteen years, though he has not reached the age of religious majority, to observe the recitation of the Kaddish for a deceased parent.

§► It has become customary to engage the services of a religious person to say the Kaddish when a deceased leaves no sons. Where there is a son, however, there is no merit to such a practice. The very credit to the deceased that such a commitment on the part of the living is supposed to represent is negated by hiring a substitute. Better for a son to say Kaddish even once a day than for a stranger to say it a hundred times a day.

ફ≫ It is regarded as meritorious to the soul of the deceased if the mourner leads the congregation in the services and participates in the study of the Mishna in addition to reciting the Kaddish.

ફ≫ While there is no obligation to do so, it is permissible for mourners to recite the Kaddish on behalf of deceased relatives other than parents. Where both parents are living, however, it is not proper to recite the mourner's Kaddish on behalf of other relatives.

ફ≫ The most important way by which Divine grace for deceased parents is earned and by which honor is extended to their memory is in the manner of life followed by the children: by their living a life of righteousness, by their doing good deeds, and by their devotion to the ways of the Lord. In evaluating the life of a parent, consideration is given to the influence upon children. The lives of children thus provide the ultimate test of the value of a parent's years on earth.

As the Zohar says, "If the son walks in the crooked path, he brings dishonor and shame on his father. If he walks in the straight path and his deeds are upright, then he confers honor on him both in this world among men and in the next world with God."

SETTING UP A TOMBSTONE

ફ≫ It is an ancient custom among Jews extending back to the Patriarchs to set up a tombstone at the head of the grave as an act of reverence and respect for the deceased, so that they not be forgotten and their final resting place not be desecrated.

ફ≫ It is the custom in some communities not to put up a tombstone until a year after burial. One of the reasons for this delay is that during the first year the dead are remembered daily by the mourners and a tombstone is therefore not required. However, there are no rules regarding this, and it is religiously correct to set up the tombstone at the earliest possible opportunity. In Israel, the practice is widespread for the tombstone to be set soon after the thirty-day period of mourning (shloshim).

ફ≫ It is important to distinguish between the requirement of setting up a tombstone, which is a time-honored custom, and the *unveiling* of a tombstone accompanied by a special service and ritual. The *unveiling service* has no basis in ritual law or halakhic requirement, and is a rather contemporary innovation. While such a service provides an occasion for additional tribute and respect to a worthy individual, no family need feel religiously compelled to arrange for a formal unveiling service. Setting up an appropriate tombstone, and a private visit to the grave site is sufficient.

SELECTED MEMORIAL PRAYERS

The following memorial prayer may be recited when visiting the grave of a deceased.

For a man:

אֵל מָלֵא רַחֲמִים, שׁוֹכֵן בַּמְּרוֹמִים, הַמְצֵא מְנוּחָה נְכוֹנָה
תַּחַת כַּנְפֵי הַשְּׁכִינָה, בְּמַעֲלוֹת קְדוֹשִׁים וּטְהוֹרִים כְּזֹהַר הָרָקִיעַ
מַזְהִירִים, אֶת נִשְׁמַת ____* שֶׁהָלַךְ לְעוֹלָמוֹ. בַּעֲבוּר שֶׁאֲנִי נוֹדֵר
צְדָקָה בְּעַד הַזְכָּרַת נִשְׁמָתוֹ, בְּגַן עֵדֶן תְּהֵא מְנוּחָתוֹ. לָכֵן בַּעַל
הָרַחֲמִים יַסְתִּירֵהוּ בְּסֵתֶר כְּנָפָיו לְעוֹלָמִים, וְיִצְרוֹר בִּצְרוֹר
הַחַיִּים אֶת נִשְׁמָתוֹ. יְיָ הוּא נַחֲלָתוֹ; וְיָנוּחַ עַל מִשְׁכָּבוֹ בְּשָׁלוֹם,
וְנֹאמַר אָמֵן.

For a woman:

אֵל מָלֵא רַחֲמִים, שׁוֹכֵן בַּמְּרוֹמִים, הַמְצֵא מְנוּחָה נְכוֹנָה
תַּחַת כַּנְפֵי הַשְּׁכִינָה, בְּמַעֲלוֹת קְדוֹשִׁים וּטְהוֹרִים כְּזֹהַר הָרָקִיעַ
מַזְהִירִים, אֶת נִשְׁמַת ____* שֶׁהָלְכָה לְעוֹלָמָהּ. בַּעֲבוּר שֶׁאֲנִי
נוֹדֵר צְדָקָה בְּעַד הַזְכָּרַת נִשְׁמָתָהּ, בְּגַן עֵדֶן תְּהֵא מְנוּחָתָהּ.
לָכֵן בַּעַל הָרַחֲמִים יַסְתִּירֶהָ בְּסֵתֶר כְּנָפָיו לְעוֹלָמִים, וְיִצְרוֹר
בִּצְרוֹר הַחַיִּים אֶת נִשְׁמָתָהּ. יְיָ הוּא נַחֲלָתָהּ; וְתָנוּחַ עַל מִשְׁכָּבָהּ
בְּשָׁלוֹם, וְנֹאמַר אָמֵן.

* Insert the name of the deceased.

God, full of compassion who dwells on high, grant perfect rest to the soul of _ _ _ _ _ _ who is recalled this day in blessed memory. May he (she) be under the wings of Thy Divine Presence in the celestial realm of paradise, in the sphere of the holy and pure who shine resplendent as the luminous firmament. In his (her) memory I offer charity. Bind up his (her) soul in the bond of life with Thee as his (her) eternal heritage. God of Mercy, may he (she) rest evermore in the shelter of Thy wings at peace and let us say, Amen.

The Yizkor Memorial prayer is recited in the synagogue on Yom Kippur and on the last day of Pesach, Shavuot, and Succot.

In memory of a father:

יִזְכֹּר אֱלֹהִים נִשְׁמַת אָבִי מוֹרִי——* שֶׁהָלַךְ לְעוֹלָמוֹ. בַּעֲבוּר שֶׁאֲנִי נוֹדֵר צְדָקָה בַּעֲדוֹ, בִּשְׂכַר זֶה, תְּהֵא נַפְשׁוֹ צְרוּרָה בִּצְרוֹר הַחַיִּים עִם נִשְׁמוֹת אַבְרָהָם יִצְחָק וְיַעֲקֹב, שָׂרָה רִבְקָה רָחֵל וְלֵאָה, וְעִם שְׁאָר צַדִּיקִים וְצִדְקָנִיּוֹת שֶׁבְּגַן עֵדֶן. אָמֵן.

In memory of a mother:

יִזְכֹּר אֱלֹהִים נִשְׁמַת אִמִּי מוֹרָתִי ——* שֶׁהָלְכָה לְעוֹלָמָהּ. בַּעֲבוּר שֶׁאֲנִי נוֹדֵר צְדָקָה בַּעֲדָהּ, בִּשְׂכַר זֶה, תְּהֵא נַפְשָׁהּ צְרוּרָה בִּצְרוֹר הַחַיִּים עִם נִשְׁמוֹת אַבְרָהָם יִצְחָק וְיַעֲקֹב, שָׂרָה רִבְקָה רָחֵל וְלֵאָה, וְעִם שְׁאָר צַדִּיקִים וְצִדְקָנִיּוֹת שֶׁבְּגַן עֵדֶן. אָמֵן.

* Insert the name of the deceased.

God, remember the soul of my beloved _ _ _ _ _ who has been called to his (her) eternal home. In his (her) memory I offer charity. May his (her) soul be bound up in the bond of life with the souls of Abraham, Isaac, Jacob, Sarah, Rebeccah, Rachel, Leah, and all the other righteous ones in eternal bliss, Amen.

THE YAHRZEIT

৯৯ The *yahrzeit* refers to the anniversary of the day of death. It is always observed on the day of death according to the Hebrew calendar, even on the first anniversary. However, if burial took place three or more days after the day of death, then the first yahrzeit is observed on the anniversary of the day of burial.

৯৯ Sons are obligated to recite the Kaddish on the yahrzeit day. If one is able, he should also lead the services and arrange to be called to the Torah for an Aliyah.

৯৯ It is customary to kindle a light on the eve of the yahrzeit to be kept burning for the entire twenty-four hour period. This practice is based on the thought expressed in Proverbs 20:27, "The spirit of man is the lamp of the Lord." It is permissible to substitute an electric memorial lamp for the wick and flame of the candle if circumstances recommend it.

৯৯ The yahrzeit day is a particularly suitable day for performing acts of kindness and for the giving of charity.

There are other laws and practices of long tradition associated with burial and mourning. Some customs depend upon the practice of the local Jewish community (*minhag hamakom*). A comprehensive review of the laws and customs related to death, burial, and mourning is *The Jewish Way in Death and Mourning* by Maurice Lamm, New York: Jonathan David Publishers, 1969.

THE MEANING OF RETURN

A RETURN to the faith of Israel is always possible for those who have drifted away or deliberately rebelled. Whether the road along which such a returnee must travel is a long road or a short one, to begin to travel along it is one of the most significant of religious acts. This journey is known as *teshuvah*; the one who takes it is called a *baal-teshuvah*.

The word *teshuvah* is often translated as repentance. The root of the word, however, means simply, *returning*. "Return O Israel unto the Lord your God" (Hosea 14:2) is the essence of teshuvah, the key to atonement. *A return to God* is not just an acknowledgment of His existence, or simply saying "I believe in Him." Nor does merely joining a synagogue constitute a return to Him. These are but first steps in that direction. Teshuvah means nothing less than becoming a servant of the Lord, an *eved hashem*. A servant is one who not only acknowledges that his master exists but one who submits to his rule and jurisdiction, who abides by the commands and requests of the master. Israel's relationship to God is no less. But in yielding to God, we proclaim our freedom from human servitude. "You shall be My servants, said the Lord, and not servants to My servants."

There is still another relationship to God that Israel is called upon to cement: that of loving God. Twice a day in the Shema ("Hear

O Israel" prayer) we are reminded of the commandment, "And you shall love the Lord your God with all your heart. . . ." Israel's relationship with God is described in terms of an eternal marriage between lovers also:

> I will betroth you to Me forever; I will betroth you to Me
> in justice and in righteousness, in kindness and in mercy;
> I will betroth you to Me in faithfulness and you shall
> know the Lord.
>
> (Hosea 2:21-22)

While the behavioral response of a servant is universally recognized, that of a loved betrothed is not as universally appreciated, even by a generation that is exposed to more public lovemaking in any one year than previous generations could witness in a lifetime. For true love is not just the mouthing of expressions, nor does it consist only of declarations of affection. True love involves giving, not taking. Self-gratification at the expense of the loved one is not true love. True love is not expressed by a stubborn refusal to yield one's pleasures and desires, but by a willingness even to sacrifice in order to satisfy the object of one's love.

Marriages—and all relationships based upon love—deteriorate where selfishness predominates. Where one of the parties behaves as though it is only his or her own wants, needs, and pleasures that matter, there, true love evaporates. And religion, which at its highest level is based upon love of God, also deteriorates in the presence of selfishness. When people act as though it is only their own wants and needs, their own likes and conveniences that matter, regardless of what might please the Almighty, love of God also evaporates.

From the pragmatic view, there really is not much difference if a relationship to God is built on a basis of deep love or out of an acceptance of the master-servant relationship. Although from a philosophical and spiritual view there is no doubt about the superiority of the former relationship, in practical terms the results are the same. It is only for reasons that go deep into the personal psyche that some people feel more disposed to emphasize one rather than the other of these two very legitimate relationships.

From either approach, our relationship to God involves more than prayer. It calls for a personal transformation, a self-reconstruction that involves obeying Him where heretofore He had been disobeyed; satisfying Him where heretofore we thought only of satisfying ourselves.

314

To effect such a transformation requires a double effort. One involves the kind of study from which should emerge understanding in breadth and depth of the entire heritage of Israel. "It is not more religion that is needed in higher education but more higher education that is needed in religion."[1] The other involves experiences, the experience of living as a Jew, of behaving as a Jew.

Knowledge requires understanding, and the greatest understanding derives from personal involvement and not merely from textbook learning. To know from within is surely superior to only observing from without. An intellectual acknowledgment of the importance of being a Jew cannot compare to the intuitive appreciation of its value which comes from doing. Although the intellect must be there to reinforce it, particularly in our day and age, the direct sensation of what it really is comes from doing, not just knowing. If an intuitive or emotional appreciation of Jewish values and ideas is by itself no longer strong enough to withstand the light of critical examination in the marketplace of ideas and requires solid intellectual and academic support, the latter by itself will bring no commitment to Jewish living.

> The first article in every creed is the belief . . . . But it is hard to see how a mere idea could have this efficacy . . . . It is not enough that we think of them (the ideas), it is also indispensable that we place ourselves within their sphere of action and that we set ourselves where we may best feel their influence; in a word, it is necessary that we act. . . .[2]

Let us face the issue squarely. Survival of Jewry is not in and of itself sufficient to justify loyalty to Judaism or on which to base the will to remain a Jew. If being a Jew has no meaning, then the survival of Jewry as a distinct people or faith is of no consequence. And if one believes deep down that it is of consequence, then it must also have meaning and implications on the personal level.

"Return O Israel unto the Lord your God" is the cry of the Hebrew Prophets that has rung out throughout the generations whenever our people have drifted away from Him. Central to our faith is the notion that *it is never too late for such a return*. Whether one is six or sixty, ten or a hundred, he is called upon to purify his heart and his thoughts and to direct or redirect himself to the Almighty.

> Let no returnee to God (penitent) imagine that he is too distant from the level of the righteous on account of his

past sins and transgressions. This is not so. Loved and dear is he before the Creator as though he never sinned . . . Not only that, but his reward is even greater, for he tasted of transgression and turned away from it, mastering his evil inclination. Our Sages said, in the place that a *baalteshuvah* stands, even the perfectly righteous cannot stand. In other words, their spiritual level is even greater than those who have never sinned. . . . All the Prophets called for repentance, and the final redemption of Israel will only come about through repentance. . . .

(Hil. Teshuvah 7:4, 5)

We might also note the conclusion of the wise Koheleth, who after all his searching for the meaning of life and after all his seeking for it, from asceticism to hedonism, concluded that: "After all things being heard . . . revere the Lord and keep His commandments. For this is the whole of man" (Ecclesiastes 12:13).

If he who saves a life is credited in our tradition with saving a world, it follows that he who destroys a life is guilty of destroying a world. If he who spiritually suffocates a Jewish life, be it his own or that of his own children, is accountable for the spiritual suffocation of a whole Jewish world, it also follows that he who spiritually revives a Jewish life—be it only his own—is as though he spiritually revived a Jewish world.

NOTES

CHAPTER 1
The Cornerstones of Judaism

1. Eric Hoffer, "Reflections," *Washington Daily News*, May 28, 1968.
2. Dr. J. H. Hertz in commentary on *The Authorized Daily Prayerbook* (London: Soncino Press, 1948).

CHAPTER 2
Halakha: The Jewish Way

1. Samuel Belkin, *In His Image* (New York: Abelard-Schuman, 1960), pp. 15–16.
2. Ernst Simon, "The Halakhik Dimension: Law and Observance in Jewish Experiences," *Dimensions of Jewish Existence Today* (Washington, D.C.: B'nai B'rith Hillel Foundations, 1965), pp. 61–62.
3. Louis Ginzberg, *Students, Scholars and Saints* (New York: Meridian Books, Inc., and Jewish Publication Society, 1958), p. 117.
4. Seymour Siegel, "Jews and Christians: The Next Step," *Conservative Judaism* 19 (1965): 9.
5. Abraham Joshua Heschel, *Between Man and God: An Interpretation of Judaism*, ed. Fritz A. Rothschild (New York: Harper & Bros., 1959), p. 177.

CHAPTER 4
Kindness: A Means and an End

1. Jacob B. Agus, *The Vision and the Way* (New York: Frederick Ungar, 1966), p. 10.
2. Chafetz Chaim, *Ahavath Chesed*, translated by Leonard Oschry (Jerusalem and New York: Feldheim Publishers, 1967).
3. Samuel David Luzzatto, "The Foundations of the Torah," in *Studies in Torah Judaism: Luzzatto's Ethico-Psychological Interpretation of Judaism*, ed. Noah H. Rosenbloom (New York: Yeshiva University, 1965), p. 157.

CHAPTER 5
The Sabbath: An Island in Time

1. Herman Wouk, *This Is My God* (New York: Doubleday, 1959), p. 61.
2. Samson Raphael Hirsch, *Horeb: A Philosophy of Jewish Laws and Observances* (London: Soncino Press, 1962), pp. 63–64. Reprinted with permission of Soncino Press, Ltd.
3. I. Grunfeld, *The Sabbath* (New York: Feldheim, 1959), p. 10.
4. Lewis Mumford, *The Conduct of Life* (New York: Harcourt Brace & Co., 1951), pp. 258–259.
5. Grunfeld, *The Sabbath*, pp. 40–41.

317

NOTES

CHAPTER 6
The Dietary Laws: A Diet for the Soul

1. Moses Mendelssohn, quoted in *The Pentateuch and Haftorahs* (London: Soncino Press, 1960), p. 318.

CHAPTER 7
Family Life: A Key to Happiness

1. Nedarim 20b; Niddah 31a; Maimonides Hil. Ishut 15; Hil. Isurai Biah 21.
2. A. E. Kitov, *The Jew and His Home* (New York: Shengold, 1963), p. 59.
3. Ibid., p. 53.

EPILOGUE
The Meaning of Return

1. Alfred Jospe, *Intermarriage and the Future of the American Jew.* Proceedings of a Conference (New York: Commission on Synagogue Relations, Federation of Jewish Philanthropies, 1964), p. 97.
2. Émile Durkheim, *Elementary Forms of the Religious Life,* translated by Joseph W. Swain (New York: The Free Press, 1954), pp. 416–417.

SUGGESTIONS FOR FURTHER READING AND STUDY: A SELECTED LIST

Primary and Classical Works

The Authorized Daily Prayerbook. With commentary by Joseph H. Hertz. London: Soncino Press, 1948.

The Hirsch Siddur. Translation and commentary by Samson Raphael Hirsch. N.Y.: Feldheim Publishing Co., 1969.

Mishnayoth (The Mishna), 7 Vols. Translation and notes by Philip Blackman. London: Mishna Press, 1951.

The Pentateuch and Haftorahs. With commentary by Joseph H. Hertz. London: Soncino Press, 1960.

The Soncino Books of the Bible. London: Soncino Press.

Jewish Thought and Philosophy

A Maimonides Reader. Edited by Isadore Twersky. N.Y.: Behrman House, 1972.

Book of Kuzari. Judah Halevi. Translation by H. Hirschfeld. N.Y.: Pardes Publishing Co., 1946.

Franz Rosenzweig: His Life and Thought. Nahum N. Glatzer. N.Y.: Schocken, 1961.

God In Search of Man: A Philosophy of Judaism. Abraham J. Heschel. Philadelphia: Jewish Publication Society, 1955.

God, Man, & History. Eliezer Berkovits. N.Y.: Jonathan David, 1959.

Horeb: A Philosophy of Jewish Laws and Observances, 2 Volumes. Samson Raphael Hirsch. Translation by I. Grunfeld. London: Soncino Press, 1962.

In His Image: The Jewish Philosophy of Man as Expressed in Rabbinic Tradition. Samuel Belkin. N.Y.: Abelard-Schuman, 1960.

Judaism, 3 Volumes. George Foot Moore. Cambridge: Harvard University Press, 1954.

Man Is Not Alone: A Philosophy of Religion. Abraham J. Heschel. N.Y.: Farrar, Straus, and Giroux, 1951.

The Faith of Judaism. Isidore Epstein. London: Soncino Press, 1954.

The Modern Jew Faces Eternal Problems. Aron Barth. Jerusalem: Youth and Hechalutz Department, Zionist Organization, 1956.

The Pharisees. R. Travers Herford. Boston: Beacon Press, 1962.

Jewish Law and Observance

Horeb: A Philosophy of Jewish Laws and Observances, 2 Volumes. Samson Raphael Hirsch. Translated by I. Grunfeld. London: Soncino Press, 1962.

Prayer. Abraham Kon. London: Soncino Press, 1972.
The Jewish Way in Death and Mourning. Maurice Lamm. N.Y.: Jonathan David, 1969.
The Sabbath. Isidor Grunfeld. N.Y.: Feldheim, 1959.
The Ways of The Righteous (On Jewish Ethics). Translation by Seymour J. Cohen.
    N.Y.: Feldheim, 1969.

Jewish History

A *History of the Jewish People.* Max L. Margolis and Alexander Marx. Philadelphia:
    Jewish Publication Society, 1944.
A *History of the Jews.* Cecil Roth. N.Y.: Schocken, 1961.
Israel: A History of the Jewish People. Rufus Learsi. N.Y.: World Publishing Company,
    1949.
Jews, God and History. Max I. Dimont. N.Y.: Simon & Shuster, 1962.
My People: The Story of the Jews. Abba Eban. N.Y.: Random House, 1968.
Portrait of a People. Charles Raddock. N.Y.: Judaica Press, 1965.

General Works

A *Book of Jewish Concepts.* Philip Birnbaum. N.Y.: Hebrew Publishing Company, 1964.
Judaism: Religion and Ethics. Meyer Waxman. New Jersey: Thomas Yoseloff, 1958.
The Authentic Jew and His Judaism. Leonard B. Gewirtz. N.Y.: Bloch, 1961.
The Jewish Library: Faith, Volume I; *Folk,* Volume II; *Woman,* Volume III; *Judaism
    in a Changing World,* Volume IV. Edited by Leo Jung. London: Soncino Press,
    1968.
The Jews: Their History, Culture and Religion, 3 Volumes. Louis Finkelstein. New
    York: Schocken, 1970.
The Judaic Tradition. Edited by Nahum N. Glatzer. Boston: Beacon Press, 1969.
This Is My God. Herman Wouk. New York: Doubleday, 1959.

Studies on the Holocaust

The Holocaust: The Destruction of European Jewry. Nora Levin. New York: Crowell,
    1968.
Treblinka. Jean-Francois Steiner. New York: Simon and Schuster, 1967.
The Destruction of the European Jews. Raul Hilberg. Chicago: Quadrangle Books, 1961.
Forged In Fury. Michael Elkins. New York: Ballantine Books, 1971.
The Last of the Just. André-Schwarz-Bart. New York: Atheneum, 1960.

Holocaust in Historical Fiction

Night. Elie Wiesel. New York: Hill & Wang, 1960.
Dawn. Elie Wiesel. New York: Hill & Wang, 1961.

Studies on Anti-Semitism

Europe and the Jews. Malcolm Hay. Boston: Beacon, 1950.
The Anguish of the Jews. Edward H. Flannery. New York: Macmillan, 1965.
The Conflict of the Church and the Synagogue. James Parkes. New York: Meridian, 1961.
The Jewish-Christian Argument: A History of Theologies in Conflict. Hans Joachim Schoeps. New York: Holt, Rinehart and Winston, 1963.
The Teaching of Contempt. Jules Isaac. New York: Holt, Rinehart and Winston, 1964.

Zionism and the State of Israel

A History of Zionism. Rufus Learsi. New York: World Publishing, 1949.
From War To War: The Arab-Israel Confrontation, 1948–1967. Nadav Safran. New York: Pegasus, 1969.
Israel: An Echo of Eternity. Abraham J. Heschel. New York: Farrar, Straus and Giroux, 1967.
The Case for Israel. Frank Gervasi. New York: Viking, 1967.
The Long March of Israel: From Theodor Herzl to the Present Day. Jacques Soustelle. New York: American Heritage, 1969.
The Zionist Idea. Arthur Hertzberg. New York: Doubleday, 1959.

General Reference Works

Encyclopaedia Judaica, 16 Volumes. New York: Keter Inc., 1972.
The Jewish Encyclopedia, 12 Volumes. New York: Funk & Wagnalls, 1912.
The Universal Jewish Encyclopaedia, 10 Volumes. New York: Ktav Publishing House, 1969.

Helpful Guides to Kosher Cooking

Jewish Cookery. Leah W. Leonard. New York: Crown Publishing Company, 1968.
The Complete American Jewish Cookbook. Anne London and Bertha Bishor. Cleveland: World Publishing Company, 1952.
The Israeli Cookbook. Molly Lyons Bar-David. New York: Crown Publishing Company, 1964.

Recordings: Helpful Aids to Traditional Jewish Melodies

New Joyous Hebrew Songs and Zmirot for the Sabbath. Sung by Hass Family Quintet. Gila Records, New York.
Oneg Shabbat with U.S.Y. Produced by Cantor Robert H. Segal, Department of Youth Activities, United Synagogue of America, New York.

Shabbat and Hassidic Songs. Sung by Nira Rabinovitz and Shlomo Nitzan (3 Records). Produced by Hed-Artzi, Ltd., Israel.

Shabbat Shalom: 18 Favorite Sabbath Songs and five other records for all the holidays. Selected and arranged by Harry Coopersmith, Jewish Education Press, New York.

The Joy of the Shabbat in Song and Story. Produced by Talma Alyagon, narrated in English by Chaim Yavin, Israel.

INDEX

Aaron, 198, 199, 200, 218, 276
abortion, 140–141
Abraham, 7, 8, 12, 18, 19, 20, 22, 48, 160, 161, 167, 232
Adam, 123
Adon Olam, 176–177
adoption
    of Jewish child, 280–281
    of non-Jewish child, 281–284
adultery, 124, 139
adults, instruction in Hebrew reading for, 177
afikomen, as symbol, 232, 233, 235
afterlife, *see Olam Haba*
afternoon service, *see minha* service
agada, 31
Ahad Ha' Am, 69
Ahavath Chesed (The Chafetz Chaim), 44
Akiva, Rabbi, 41, 134, 238, 266
Alexander the Great, 273
Al Hanisim prayer, 262
Aliyah
    on being called to Torah, 165
    and Prophets, 285–286
"amen," as affirmation, 174
Amidah prayer, 15, 75, 150n., 151, 159–160, 162–163, 192
    and *minyan*, 167
amud (lectern), 193–194
anger
    in marriage, 134
    and sexual intercourse, 133
animals
    clean and unclean, 98–99, 104
    cruelty to, 56
    and *hametz*, 222–223
    hind quarter of, 116
    kindness to, 56–57
    slaughtering of, 26, 105–107
    see also meat

anti-Semitism, 32
Arab countries, Jewish refugees from, 17
arava, see Four Species
arba kanfat, see tallit katan
Aristotle, 25, 64
arvit, see maariv service
aron kodesh, see Holy Ark
Asara b'Tevet, *see* Tenth of Tevet
ascetic ideal, in Christian tradition, 122
asceticism, 36
Ashkenazic Jews, 146, 192, 193–194, 221, 272–273
assimilation, 32, 102, 103, 177, 189–190
Astarte (pagan deity), 140
atheism, 20
atzeret, meaning of, 256
automobile (driving), and Sabbath, 93–95
autopsies, 298
avelut period, 301–302
Avodah (Divine Service), 203
avodah she'blev, see "service of the heart"

Baal (pagan deity), 20, 140
baal-teshuvah, 313, 316
Babylonians, 13, 192, 263, 265, 267
Barekh, 235
Bar-Mitzvah, 83, 145, 151, 285–286
Bat-Mitzvah, 285, 286
bayn hashmashot period, 85
beard, and Torah law, 181
Bedikat Hametz ceremony (Pesach), 223–225
behavior
    modesty in, 139
    and Torah, 26
Beit Hamikdash, 36, 160n.
Beit Knesset, 36
    see also synagogue
Beit Midrash, 36, 183–184, 191
Beit Sefer (elementary school), 184